POINTS OF VIEW

POINTS OF VIEW

REX MURPHY

M&S

National Library of Canada Cataloguing in Publication

Murphy, Rex
    Points of view / Rex Murphy.

ISBN 0-7710-6527-2

    I. Title.

AC8.M92 2003   081   C2003-902774-0

We acknowledge the financial support of the Government of Canada through the Book Publishing Industry Development Program and that of the Government of Ontario through the Ontario Media Development Corporation's Ontario Book Initiative. We further acknowledge the support of the Canada Council for the Arts and the Ontario Arts Council for our publishing program.

Typeset in Minion by M&S, Toronto
Printed and bound in Canada

This book is printed on acid-free paper that is 100% recycled, ancient-forest friendly (100% post-consumer recycled).

McClelland & Stewart Ltd.
The Canadian Publishers
481 University Avenue
Toronto, Ontario
M5G 2E9
www.mcclelland.com

2 3 4 5   07 06 05 04

DEDICATION: MARIE

Contents

ACKNOWLEDGEMENTS   xi

INTRODUCTION   xiii

POINTS OF VIEW

An Ode to a Leader (Huh? Where?)   3

The Man Who Refused to Strut   6

The Barefoot MP: Splendour in the Crass   9

Tom Wappel: The Veteran and the MP   12

MP Raises   14

The Sublime Ralph Klein   16

Brian Chiding Jean for Sleaze: Sweet!   18

Newfoundland's Cod Fishery   21

Crop Cycle Versus the Spin Cycle   23

The Romanow Report   25

Brrrr-ing on That Global Warming!   27

The Walkerton Ceasefire   29

Canada Must Be Made Safe from Live-in Nannies   31

NEWFOUNDLAND

Between the Rock and a Hard Place   35

Bardot and the Other Cleavage-Scientists Sealed Our Fate   43

My Favourite Place: A Cove of Inner Peace on Newfoundland's
Cape Shore   46

Alas, Joey Smallwood Was Larger Than Fiction   48

Fratricide, St. John's Style   51

Newfoundland Calls to Amend Constitution   54

THE WAY WE LIVE NOW

Why People Get Fat   59

My Rage Against the Machine   61

If You Need a Cop, Just Light Up   64

You're Sick and It's All Your Fault   67

Air Rage? Nope, Just Another Fool   70

Cellphones   73

Time for Closure   75

The Blue Box of Paradise   77

Is There an Expert in the House?   80

IN MEMORIAM: SIX CANADIANS

John Munro Ross   85

Mordecai Richler   87

W.O. Mitchell   90

Pythons, Misfits, and Canadians – Gzowski Talked to Us All   92

Glenn Gould   95

Pierre Trudeau: He Has Gone to His Grace, and That Leaves
    So Much Less of Ours   97

THE POLITICS OF LANGUAGE

That's "Fisherman" to You, Son   101

What Fools These Moralists Be   104

Is There a Gender Doctor in the House?   107

Death Is Too Good for the Word Weasels   110

TO READ OR NOT TO READ

The Author Eater   115

To Read or Not to Read   119

Reading, Writing, and More Writing   126

Enough Said   129

What Likeness ... Through Yonder Window Breaks?   132

The Real Dr. J Gets Stuffed   136

Keen Memory Made Tender: Nabokov the Prodigy   140

The Memoir of a Casanova of the Mind   144

TOWER OF BABEL

See Geri, See Geri Binge, Love Her Now   151

The Answer Is Blowin' in the Wind   155

C-2 Much of C-3PO? I Have ...   158

007: Licensed to Inhale   161

My Garret: The SkyDome   164

The Ruckus Over Uncouth and Occult   167

Céline's Child: At a Church Near You   170

A Fine Moonwalker Whine   173

Even Martha's Cooked   176

Buckingham Versus Bedlam   179

CANADIANA

Gretzky: The Great One   185

The Loonie   187

Woodchuck Checkout: The Death of Wiarton Willie   189

Good Lord! The Barbarians Are Us   191

Anne and the New Criticism   194

Snowstorm   197

FIVE BOOKS AND A THONG

Monica's Story: Andrew Morton Flashes His Thong ...
    but Close Your Eyes and Just Keep Walking   201

His Master's (Surprisingly Clear) Voice   206

Communism's "Useful Idiots" Scorned   213

Nasty, Mean, and Sly: Paul Theroux a Foul "Friend" to V.S. Naipaul   217

Saul Slays His Thousands, but Strictly in Straw   222

Orwell and Hitchens: Enemies of Compromise   227

VAGRANT OPINIONS

Pope John Paul II   233

Clinton: Pinocchio Priapus on the Potomac   235

Sorry, Jean, the Career Is Your Legacy. What's Left Is Footnotes   238

The Only Thing Worse Than Being Irish Is Not Being Irish   241

Babble from Genocide's Bystanders   244

Let's Try Zundel-Denial   247

Tampering with the Tree of Knowledge   250

Selling Something, Dr. Suzuki?   252

SEPTEMBER 11 AND AFTER

No Room on This Planet for Us Both   257

The Prince of Darkness Visible   260

Osama, Try Reading Gibbon   263

The Dogs of War v. the Dogs of Law   266

A Wake-up More Than a Nightmare   269

"The Poetry Is in the Pity"   272

What Joey Could Teach Saddam When It Comes to Elections   275

Saddam Is a Stand-in Osama   278

The Phony War's About to Get Real   281

September 11 Was the Smoking Gun   284

To War or Not to War: Canada Faces a Morality Test   287

In Search of Past Glories   289

The Removal of a Tyrant: George W. Bush Got It Right   292

Acknowledgements

The people who have had most to do with these pieces, besides the wretch who penned them, is Bob Bishop, who guards their submission to *The National*, and Val Ross, an eagle of scrutiny, who pares them of mischiefs of grammar and sense, for the *Globe and Mail*. I'd like to thank them in public.

Patrick Martin, the *Globe*'s "Comment" editor, bears the weightier burden of allowing them into his paper in the first place. I cannot, therefore, fail to salute a judgement so impeccable.

Martin Levin, the editor of the "Books" section of the *Globe and Mail*, played something of John the Baptist to my entry into its pages. I'm not sure if he'll be comfortable with this reference, but I am unwilling to surrender the second half of the analogy.

I would like as well to wave to Peter Simpson and Jenny Jackson of the *Ottawa Citizen* for the hospitality of their persons and pages. Barbara Sears searched out these pieces, tried valiantly to thread them with theme and order, and must be allowed reserves of endurance not granted to most of us.

Finally, Douglas Gibson of McClelland & Stewart is a marvel of persistence and a martyr of (my) procrastination. His stay in whatever purgatory awaits him (and all of us) has surely been abbreviated by the long charity he extended me. It may, in fact, such was the burden carried, have been abrupted altogether.

Note: The publishers acknowledge the cooperation of the *Globe and Mail*, the *Ottawa Citizen*, and the CBC's *The National* in compiling this volume.

Introduction

It may be the mark of a distressed childhood, or perhaps *exotic* is a more careful word, but one of the most vivid memories from my early days is of Joey Smallwood. Not a tramp on the barrens picking bakeapples; not a visit to St. John's (the first visit to St. John's is almost Jungian for most Newfoundlanders, a collective horror induced, I hasten to add, not by the sight of the city but the state of the damn gravel roads of the time); not some offshore excursion; but Joey Smallwood on television in full rant.

Memory has a few mercies, though, and I cannot now recall what was Joey's target *du jour*. But I do recall that everyone I knew was eager to talk about Joey's latest rage the next day, and were prepared and eager to go over its finer points, appeared actually hungry for disquisition. Can it be, I wonder, that Newfoundland children, so unlike their counterparts on the wide land mass of the mainland, didn't have normal childhoods? Didn't play cowboys and Indians (or cowpersons and aboriginals – let us contemporize) but found pastime and pleasure in political discussion?

Well, we weren't *that* strange. But it was surely a characteristic of life in Newfoundland that politics, and most particularly its grandest impresario in those times, Joey himself, was something much more than elections and legislative debates. Newfoundlanders had a way of viewing the sad and frustrating conduct of their public affairs as something of a continuous stage play, a running entertainment. I think part of the logic that informed this set of mind was that we were paying for this strange and (inevitably) despairing performance, and that it was best – and a cushion for the collective sanity – to look upon it as, at least partly, a diversion, a brittle amusement.

So all of us were, so to speak, reviewers, connoisseurs. Newfoundlanders are learned observers, lay scholars, of political foibles. They have strong memories and stronger stomachs. The details of politics – who ran where and when, why so-and-so got into politics the first time, the more inventive ruses of certain campaigns (I remember the case of the lapsed Catholic, the lost rosary beads, and the by-election) are the nourishment of avid recall and passionate debate.

For all that, Newfoundlanders were not then and are not now serious about politics in the way I find that the Canadians of other provinces are. I think that Newfoundlanders begin their understanding of politics with a presumption that all politics is futile, a deceit and a vanity, and that all politicians, until ever-so-rarely proven otherwise, are weathercocks of their own miserable ambitions and nothing more. This is as much a defensive attitude as a streak of genetic cynicism. Disappointed so often over their long, tormented, devious history, Newfoundlanders are deeply chary of investing hope in the promise of electoral actors.

We, they – we – have decided it's a game, or a form of play, and that it is best to "take" politics as an imposed spectacle, and to derive some satisfaction from its unfolding in the zestful scrutiny of its plots and players. Watching politics in Newfoundland is a casual art. Our age lives in dread of stereotypes – the dread itself has become a stereotype – but heedless of that, I think it is the Irish strand of the Newfoundland imagination, that strain of hard humour put up as a shield against large or overwhelming realities, or at least to deflect or contain their operation, that has converted politics into a game. Some lines of Yeats, though their original context is much too strong for what I intend here, hint at this disposition:

> We lived like men that watch a painted stage.
> What matter for the scene, the scene once gone:
> It had not touched our lives.

I do not know if this explains my own relish for public affairs, or accounts for my fall – it was more drift than decision – into the less nutritious peripheries of journalism, commentary, and comment. But I do know that some of that early zeal for watching the great play of Newfoundland politics, and the peculiar Newfoundland attitude of watching with detachment and an ear cocked for niceties of performance – for the style of the beast – has remained with me, and has trained or determined the manner of my response to the larger, though not richer, panorama of current national politics.

I do know that "current affairs," which is the unsatisfactory term for all that happens in the life of a nation which is thought necessary, useful, or sufficiently interesting to report or televise, always calls to me, not just for the substance of what is being reported, but equally for its off-glances, for the quality an event (or the actor in it) contains, which speaks to something beyond the event or its actor. Looking over the pieces in this gathering, I see – to take one example – that the passing of Pierre Trudeau, surely a high moment in itself, was also truly remarkable for how it spontaneously summoned a pause in the nation's life.

The five days or so of mourning Trudeau stayed the nation. And certainly we were all arrested by the leaving of a rare great man among us, but Trudeau's passing was singular in that it seemed to call almost every Canadian to an act very like public contemplation, a response, large though Trudeau was, larger even than he.

That was a monumentally weighty moment. The day-to-day of journalism is built into its very etymology. And the more normal fodder of comment or column is inevitably the day-to-day. But, at least to me, it is the day-to-day that stitches the texture of our common experience, and what is finally remarkable – there is a touch of paradox here – is not the remarkable but the common. We are not defined by the exceptional and the rare, we are grooved and coloured by a million commonplaces. It is by this understanding that journalism is a kind of diary of the "all of us."

Even the everyday can index or signal a larger current. An MP berates a senior citizen, who (the senior) is also a veteran, because the MP doesn't like to be bothered with letters from citizens who have not voted for him. This little episode, which was a subject for a "Points of View" on *The National*, said as much about a part of our politics as a barrel of degrees in political science. Likewise, Immigration Canada's difficulties with a live-in nanny (*who worked too much*) spoke pitiful volumes about the confusion of some immigration policies, even before the sombre events now known by the grim numeric of 9/11.

September 11 is the dominating event of our times. It shadows us even now, two years since the planes executed their murderous path into the Twin Towers of the World Trade Center, the Pentagon, and (foiled by the passengers) into the earth of Pennsylvania. Canada felt that wound, not as deeply as our American friends, and certainly not as directly, though it is not underlined enough that twenty-five Canadians were murdered in those same towers.

We have been attempting to realign our relations with the United States ever since, our government, executing none too clearly, and not without spasms of confused and at times insulting rhetoric, a policy of support and reassurance for the Americans – emphatically so in Afghanistan – while attempting simultaneously a clearly independent, visibly Canadian attitude in foreign affairs generally. Witness the Iraq war.

The effort has been clouded, not only because it contains some measure of self-contradiction, but also because a larger part of what the government does these days is an expression of a fractured government. The Liberals live a singular administration, in which the most powerful man, the prime minister, holds only part of its authority, the remainder inexorably collecting in the hands of his almost-consecrated successor, former finance minister Paul Martin. We're back to Newfoundland territory watching this drama, politics as a fusion of power and theatrics.

I like to believe that current affairs is a wide basket, that it is not, as perhaps it was in the antique days before truly mass media and near-universal communication access via cable television and the World Wide Web, bounded by the frolics on Parliament Hill or in the legislatures of provincial or territorial capitals. The public's business is, loosely, whatever catches its attention, whatever intrudes into general consciousness, or is pitched by the seductions of advertisement or marketing for our broad consumption. Pop culture frames us at least as much as politics. From the bestseller to the blockbuster, from Mr. Clinton's mad carnal shenanigans to

Oprah's latest foray into mass therapy, these are all signatures of how we live now, and all leave prints, of varying taste, on our experience and imagination. As will be obvious from what follows, I watch far more television than is good for me – I believe Oprah has infiltrated my shivering soul – but the play of what is ever so loosely called popular culture is both an index of our common sensibility and a relentless pressure that shapes it. There are two Homers, the cartoon and the bard, and the one in syndication (reluctant alas!) is the guy with the doughnut.

It is in the nature of column and commentary that it is only the events and people that star on any given day, or in any given week – the exceptional, remarkable, novel, or consequential – that are most suitable for broad treatment in print or on air. You choose to talk about what people are talking about. A subject, or a topic, is under the imperative – it is as much courtesy to the audience as concession – to reach as many people as is possible. The purely local piece may have as much substance and more intrinsic drama than what is in the national headlines at any time, but within the confines of four minutes on air, or less than a thousand words of print, to build the context necessary for the purely local story, supply the details, and then offer observation or opinion, is a freight, at least for me, too heavy to carry.

Gretzky retiring will always do, Ralph Klein is a gift always waiting to be opened, British Columbia politics so bursts its natural frame as to be always available for national savour, the delectable scandals and outsized personalities of American politics are as succulent to Canadian epicures of gossip and overreach as they are to Americans. Long trawling in this half-light of journalistic practice almost builds an instinct for what people may find interesting, contentious, amusing, or electric, and it is my hope that the selection within these covers matches at least one of those qualifiers.

POINTS OF VIEW

An Ode to a Leader (Huh? Where?)

We remember Martin Luther King, Jr., primarily, for a speech. The "I have a dream" speech.

The oration was delivered at a moment of moral urgency in the United States. Dr. King was magnificent that day. It is neither romance, nor nostalgia, nor the great grim shadow of his assassination so soon afterward, that powers our estimate of the vivid force of his words, uttered with such melody and suasion in front of the memorial to Abraham Lincoln.

A great cause – civil rights – had found the human being to speak it. There was, in the twenty or thirty minutes it took for Dr. King to peal those scrupulous phrases, something of a grand intersection. The man had met the moment, and both had found their words.

Martin Luther King was a leader.

The most particular memory I have of Pierre Elliott Trudeau is a very early one, in the 1968 election, which in retrospect wasn't so much a campaign on his part as an extended flirtation. George Gallup filtered through *ars amatoria*.

He was striding towards a microphone, in the insouciant manner that was exclusively his patent, and wearing a grin of such sovereign self-assurance that it makes the present-day smirk of George W. Bush seem like a late essay sent from his brain to his lips.

The crowd was randy with the partisan fevers and good-natured delirium that was christened Trudeaumania.

It was not what he was going to say – he said very little that day, beyond the usual tepid confections of an election-stump speech (it was like hearing

3

a Steinway martyred by "Chopsticks") – that had the audience electric with pleasure and anticipation.

It was just that he was there, and they were there with him.

Pirouetting at a conference, sliding down a banister, truculent and defiant on a balcony in Montreal, "Just watch me" during the crazed menaces of the FLQ and the riposte of the War Measures Act, these and other moments form a pool of common images from which the character, austere and flamboyant simultaneously, flashed into focus and memory.

Pierre Elliott Trudeau bristled with charisma. He was a leader.

This week, John Paul II, in the Catholic Church's jubilee year, wanders the common territory of three of the world's great religions.

Here is this man, whatever may be felt of the policies and doctrines he holds as adamant to his papacy, after a time in office in which he brokered the fall of communism, survived an assassination attempt and forgave the assassin, rounded the globe more frequently and with fuller houses than all its rock stars combined, who is still fired with such moral force that he pushes his tired shell of a body to yet one more intensity of endeavour.

John Paul II is a leader.

All three of these men embody, each with his discrete, emphatic signature, a term that has been floating by greatly unballasted lately – leadership.

The great mandarins of the Liberal Party have spent most of this week, and their considerable ingenuity, in unravelling the brittle façade of party harmony on the leadership question they spent the previous weekend constructing.

The Liberals' idea of putting something behind them bears an uncanny resemblance to a grudge match at Wrestlemania.

Elsewhere, conspicuous only by its stealth and remove, Reform-Alliance (it's as slippery to lead as it is to name) is beginning its leadership workshop, where, very soon, Preston Manning will discover if he is himself the light or has come to bear witness to Stockwell Day's.

To speak of leadership in reference to Dr. King, Mr. Trudeau, or John Paul II, and then use the same word to canvass the ructions of Paul Martin and Jean Chrétien or Mr. Manning and Mr. Day, brings a little of the same uneasy chill as when we speak of the novels of Jacqueline Susann and then, staying more or less on the same planet, speak of the novels of James Joyce. The words may be the same, but they've clearly crossed some invisible and frightening frontier.

Leadership, as we speak of it now, is a much-shrunken concept. With the Liberals, it is not much more than changing seats at a table and, aside from its spare dividends as political gossip, has little to offer a bemused or indifferent public. And the joust to decide who heads Reform-Alliance is so self-contained, so fixed and centred on the contenders themselves, that I am not sure it is polite to watch.

I don't think Canadians are waiting for an "I have a dream" speech from any leader. Something more spacious than "My turn" or "Hey, I'm new" might charm them, however.

– Globe and Mail

The Man Who Refused to Strut

"Why, man, he doth bestride the narrow world, like a Colossus." Preston Manning did not "bestride" anything, and has never been mistaken for a Colossus.

Mr. Manning's reluctance to strut, to strike the leader pose, or yield to the inflated sense of personal worth that seems genetically incident to the assumption of high office, was one of his more attractive qualities. Even when, after musing that Stornoway should be turned into a bingo hall, he moved into the desolate waiting-room glories of the Opposition leader's official residence, I don't think his hardest critics felt that he was putting on airs.

Mr. Manning didn't pitch himself as that much-appealed-to and venerated hypothetical, the common man. He has the diligence, intelligence, and industry that places him very clearly in the camp of the exceptional. He was a practising élitist leading a populist movement – the enduring paradox of his entire tenure. He planned meticulously, to the point where he (almost) controlled events, and yet continually invoked the almost mystic authority of the spontaneous popular will.

The common man responded to Mr. Manning's dedication, seriousness, blistering commitment to the job at hand, and, most of all, to a perception of his fundamental decency. There was the link, this decency, that earned him the respect of many of the electorate and – this is a triumph for a partisan politician – something very like affection as well.

His arrival on the national scene had to be the most difficult period of his career. From the moment Reform was a force in national politics, he and the party were more freely open to the amateur insults and smug dismissals of a galaxy of observers. Both he and some of the issues he championed were the objects of the lofty ridicule that only the truly sensitive are capable of larding onto their inferiors.

He was a rustic fundamentalist, which, for some of the wise and worldly, is a life form little higher than a beach rock. He had a sheaf of issues – immigration, law and order, smaller government, Western alienation, separatism – that to the enlightened clearly came from a quiver marked Bigotry and Racism. And, of course, he came from the West, the very badlands of regressive thought and repressive morality. Being dismissed in so peremptory a fashion has to be painful on any occasion; being so dismissed by the self-designated cognoscenti of tolerance must have had the added charm of being extremely funny.

There weren't many, on either side of the House, who could have taken the hammering. He could and did. And, over time, the battering began to work an opposite effect to what was intended by the batterers.

To revise Hemingway, courage is grace under scorn. A lot of people who were not Reformers and who would never vote the Reform agenda came to regard the man who lost the charisma sweepstakes to Joe Clark as someone they nonetheless admired. People also began to see he was that elective *rara avis* – someone who read and thought. The House is not crowded with these; on a given day, the amount of intellect that passes through Question Period couldn't sustain a promo for Ed the Sock.

The most profound display of nerve that Mr. Manning presented was last spring's demolition of Reform for the sake of Alliance. He wanted Reform's demise to midwife Alliance's arrival, and in pursuit of what he saw as that necessary goal, put his own future in the balance – with results we now know, and which led, ineluctably, to this week's announcement.

I called this nerve, but daring is the better word. Mr. Manning made something out of nothing. He spent thirteen years in the hectic, dirty, exhilarent byways of politics and put it all on the line in the service of the logic and principles of a cause. Lost, finally, and didn't play the sore loser. And now seems to have found the good sense to leave a game that is powered so much, and so compellingly, by vanity that some can never leave.

The irony is that his own "core" replaced him at the very time that his appeal had started to blossom. It was his gamble, but they unstitched what he and they had woven. And it is not at all certain, under the wavering leadership of Stockwell Day, whether the project that Preston Manning began can continue without him.

– Globe and Mail

The Barefoot MP: Splendour in the Crass

What's the difference between a beer commercial and a press conference by the Leader of the Official Opposition?

Less and less.

Well, there is one difference. The beer commercials are more upfront about what they're selling: gas, water, and yeast. Whereas the Leader of the Official Opposition, when he roared across the scenery on his way to his first press conference as an elected MP, tried to pass it off as a bid to highlight the natural splendours and scenic wonders of his new B.C. district.

David Hasselhoff used to argue, with equal transparency, and wearing much the same rig that appeals to Stockwell Day, that people watched *Baywatch* for the plot. If Mr. Day were intent on highlighting natural splendours and scenic wonders, I'm willing to wager they were those of his person, not that of the Okanagan.

Please do not mistake me. I'm not one to mock the dutiful science of body sculpture. I start each day bench-pressing a couple of hefty sides of bacon and combing an extensive collection of old Participaction ads for some pellets of masochism I may have missed on the first go-round.

I'm writing most of this while rock-climbing, with a laptop strapped to each ankle (helps aggravate the glutes) and sixty pounds of Hansard in the backpack. I set aside two whole days of the week for nothing but ab crunches. I wolf down more Müeslix than Norway in Lent.

I'm so aerobically tuned that, sometimes, in a light wind, I float.

So it's not Stock's love of the burn that arrests me. We're brothers beneath the Lycra. It's his eagerness to mix the physical regimen with the

9

political regime. So far, the only clear message we've received from the Leader of the Official Opposition is the novel, "I'm buff. Make me your prime minister."

Now if that were a really compelling theme, I think the Americans would have picked up on it first, and Al Gore would have gone with Suzanne Somers over Joe Lieberman as a running mate. Or more likely, Suzanne Somers would have gone with Al Gore as hers.

We've had the Sea-Doo. We've had the Karate Kid. And we've had Rollerblader Day. What's the message here? That a yuppie commitment to toys and calisthenics is a signal of New Age virtue. Or is the message a little more subtle? "Just look at me. I'm so much younger than Jean Chrétien."

This strategy is not without risk. The voters may reverse the question, and ask themselves not whether Jean is too old, but whether Stock is old enough.

There could also be a concern in the Day camp to shed the last residues of Reform and Preston Manning. I cannot conceive, even in the most obliging reverie, of Mr. Manning showing up barefoot and in stretch pants for anything. That is a just one push-up too many for even the most strenuous imagination.

So maybe it is the gravitas of his predecessor, rather than the all-too-often-exhibited haleness of the prime minister, that Mr. Day is seeking to supplant with these displays of friskiness and frolic. Mercifully, I don't think it has anything to do with his other rival, Joe Clark. Mr. Clark, whatever his shortcomings, is simply not to be engaged on the aquatic sportswear front. And good for him.

I will give Mr. Day this: zipping off over Okanagan Lake aboard his high-tech water jet after the "newser" on the beach certainly cleared my mind of any other images. Including the point of the press conference. I seem to recall his beginning by saying that the Chrétien "vacation" was over. If so, it was truly a daring way to frame that message. I do know he called for a four-day workweek for MPs, presumably to extend their opportunities for mountain biking, marathoning, and skydiving – all necessary for hip photo ops and a trim caucus.

It did, however, present the question of what might be next. Handstands in Question Period? Rappelling into caucus. Maybe a little tightrope-walking during the budget debate. It may be we will have to start turning to the sports sections of our newspapers just to keep up with the latest in politics. Which probably will not be to the advantage of sports or politics.

Well, in the States we have seen a wrestler turn into a politician. Jesse Ventura has demonstrated how easily the categories of entertainment and politics can fold into each other. Until a few years ago, the idea that throwing chairs at people and inflicting mayhem was an apprenticeship for public life would have been a highly dubious one. But times change and, alas, we must change with them.

But I would not like to see the process in reverse. I do not want to see people enter public life as a preparation for a career in professional wrestling.

Now I know, in Stockwell Day's case, that it's the furthest thing from his mind. Pro wrestling is undignified and crass.

Beach volleyball, however . . .

– Globe and Mail

Tom Wappel: The Veteran and the MP

There are ways to get worse publicity than Tom Wappel, the MP who wrote an eighty-one-year-old, a veteran, legally blind and partially deaf, and told him, sneeringly, in effect to get lost, because the old man had not voted Liberal. The *Toronto Star* broke the story yesterday.

Here are some:

- You could nail a five-day-old kitten to the floor and use it as a doorstop.
- You could cut off the heat to an orphanage in winter, and insist the little ones dance for stale biscuits, and then not give them any.
- You could take a chainsaw to the last redwood that was also the home of the last eagle and have it fall on the last panda.

Outside of these cringing options, however, Mr. Tom Wappel has more or less cornered the market in the Olympics of obnoxious behaviour.

It's important to remember the target in this affair.

Mr. Wappel wasn't bringing the weight of his discount sarcasm against some monster corporate invader, or tossing off a snarling letter to George W. Bush on Star Wars, or savaging some foreign dictator.

Mr. Wappel, the MP, was bringing the Big Bertha of his laser-guided scorn to fire on an eighty-one-year-old.

An eighty-one-year-old who actually fought in a war, to make sure that people would always be allowed to vote, so that things like MPs could continue to exist and would have parliaments to go to and offices in which to write sour-cute nasty little letters to their constituents and then get better pensions when the MPs retired than the veterans who fought for them.

Mr. Wappel says he's puzzled – puzzled that the vet would ask him, his MP, for help, when Mr. Wappel knows the vet voted Alliance. Mr. Wappel is merely puzzled. The rest of the country – all of it – is suffocating in amazement, staggered almost to the point of coma that Mr. Wappel thinks he owns the right to represent only those he knows voted for him.

As the letter reveals, he has it on record. That, Mr. Wappel, was the other reason for that silly war: the *secret* ballot. When Mr. Baxter, the veteran, was running around the coastlines of Europe dodging U-boats with the Canadian Navy, essentially what he was up to was offering the chance of losing his life for the right of all the rest of us later on to vote – in secret – and, dear God, as it turns out, in some cases for you.

We are puzzled, Mr. Wappel. How do you know? Why do you keep records? Democratic representation is not to be confused with a filing cabinet in some MP's office with the names of those who are loyal, and those – whether blind or deaf or old or not – who are not loyal.

Mr. Wappel has apologized. The blitzkrieg of outrage since yesterday was obviously too much for the courage of an MP to contain. But it's only because his charmless attitude is known that he's sorry for it; only because not even his Liberal colleagues can abide that attitude that he repents. When it was just him and the eighty-one-year-old, as the letter proves, things were so different.

I think this is a little too deep for a forced apology. And I can only hope Mr. Jim Baxter and his wife, after this gust has blown over them, have the strength to put the apology in the same wastebasket as the letter that made it necessary.

– *The National*

MP Raises

We're told that nothing is faster than the speed of light. It's one of the unalterable laws of physics. Among others, the genius Albert Einstein established this as the speed limit for the universe. Einstein claimed that nothing could move faster than light. But then Einstein never saw Canadian Members of Parliament when they decided to give themselves a raise.

The speed, in parliamentary terms, with which the raise is moving through the House of Commons may undermine our entire understanding of modern science. After Don "Make It So" Boudria, the House Leader, gets this raise through the Commons in three days, I expect him to head down to NASA and let them in on the secrets of intergalactic travel.

Has anything else been proposed, debated, and passed the Canadian House of Commons in three days? Tom Wappel can't post a letter in three days. The endangered-species act was first proposed in 1996, and this law on which the fate of whole species depends was proposed again in 2000 and again in 2001. That's five years. And still no bill.

If they could've linked the fate of the bald eagle or the duckbilled platypus to the hourly rate of MPs, I dare say by now this whole country would be one great park and preserve from sea to sea, and baby seals and auks would be the new Canadian flag.

It's not the amount that bothers me. In a world where the moronic output of Adam Sandler earns him millions and where Tom Green, the Ottawa cow-suctionist, even earns a living, where hockey players make fifty times what brain surgeons get by on, and rap artists wear more gold than they ever found in the Klondike, the amount seems almost irrelevant.

It's the speed, it's the haste, it's the timing. Three days, just before summer break, after an election. I have no objection to the idea of a parliamentary quickie, but must the only one on record have to do with their pay? There's human filth pouring into the harbours of Halifax and St. John's, and that's been talked about for decades. There is health-care reform, which has been on the agenda so long, it may show up next on the *Antiques Road Show*. Native treaties, Burnt Church, peacekeeping missions, school reform, parole legislation, these are topics that go to the House of Commons with all the momentum of a jammed glacier. How about immigration law? There are some hearings and appeals that have the pace of continental drift.

No, what's unique here is the quite wonderful intersection of the monetary self-interest and material well-being of those who are in charge of the parliamentary machinery. What it tells us – and this is the lesson we must all learn – is this: when MPs really think something is good, when they really want something to pass parliament, parliament is a Ferrari on a road made of greased lightning.

And next time you hear them say, oh, it's in committee, we have to study that, we are having trouble in the amendment stage, you will know that really what you're hearing is they don't want it to go through.

Now, if we could only tie that endangered-species act to the hourly rate and overtime.

– The National

The Sublime Ralph Klein

Remember the great ruckus in Florida after the American presidential election? Magnifying glasses, microscopes, and squinting scrutineers. If George W. Bush wants some advice on how to achieve a decisive result, I advise him to go to Alberta. Pronto.

They don't hang chads in Alberta. And if there's a dimpled ballot anywhere in that great province this week, I expect it's hiding out. When Albertans mark their ballots, they stay marked. Or else. Welcome to Ralph's world.

We could say that Ralph Klein and his Tories "won" on Monday night, but that's rather a puny way of putting it. When a steamroller passes over an ant, or a locomotive meets up with a Volkswagen, you don't say the steamroller "won." Or the locomotive "did pretty well." For the scale of this Alberta victory, I believe you have to understand that, given a couple of more votes and a favourable wind, Ralph would very likely have carried Saskatchewan as well.

Two NDP got elected. I think we must put this down to carelessness on Mr. Klein's part or the impulse to decorate. Just as easily, it could be an attempt to foreshadow the soon-to-be-called election in British Columbia, where two, now that I think of it, might be a little optimistic. The Liberals were decimated. Their leader, Nancy McBeth, fell before Ralph's smiling juggernaut. They have only seven seats. Seven. The same as the Biblical years of famine. Seven Liberal seats against Mr. Klein's Tory seventy-four.

This is not an Opposition. It's barely a genetic pool. Bernard Landry from the cultured province of Quebec must be looking westward with longing envy. If Bernard Landry were as popular as Ralph Klein, as in sync with Quebecers as Klein is with Albertans, Stéphane Dion would now be ambassador to the Republic of Hull. With all this talk of human cloning, I'd keep a close eye on Ralph Klein. If he falls into separatist hands and they run off a copy, I think the jig is up.

Some will write off this landslide as a function of Alberta's prosperity. With oil at its current price, so the theory goes, the Tories could run a lug wrench for premier and win hands down. Well, not so fast. If this were Ralph Klein's first victory, it might be explained as a fluke. If it were his second, it might be read as part of the unfathomable human appetite for sequels. But this vote, on the third time out – either Ralph Klein has figured out Alberta, or Alberta has figured out Ralph Klein. Either way, the Alberta agenda – a possible mixed health-care system, more powerful provincial input into national policy, more of Alberta for Albertans – is now an endorsed fact of Canadian politics.

A number of weeks ago, five or six Alberta academics and pundits called for the province to build a firewall around Alberta. This is seriously unnecessary. Alberta already has a firewall and it was massively reinforced on Monday night. It's called Ralph Klein.

Bernard Landry, eat your heart out.

– The National

Brian Chiding Jean for Sleaze: Sweet!

It was sweet, in the way that only certain blends of irony are, to hear Brian Mulroney this week call upon that now not-so-familiar, but still quite splendid baritone to deliver a fierce rebuke to the government and its embattled prime minister.

Mr. Mulroney, it is the opinion of many, left office before he was chased from it. More than anything, it was the taint of scandal and spectacle of patronage and its attendant mischiefs clouding his administration that made the public turn on the Tories and place Mr. Mulroney in some special place of intense opprobrium.

Kim Campbell brought her own formidable ineptitude to the campaign she headed after Mr. Mulroney's departure. But her contribution to the subsequent Tory obliteration, while impressive in itself, was secondary to the consideration that people voted against her because they had no direct way to vent their disillusionment on Mr. Mulroney.

It may not be comfortable for Mr. Mulroney now to admit that it was distaste for the practices of his administration that was the most compelling dynamic in the election that followed his departure. The Liberals at the time knew it well, and made very much of it, none more so than Jean Chrétien, who campaigned with great zeal on the idea of restoring "integrity" to politics, ending the "corruption" of the Mulroney years. Mr. Chrétien's instincts were sound. The people were weary and angry over the tawdriness that many associated with the Mulroney era. Jean Chrétien benefited greatly from donning the mantle of reformer, and the pledge to restore honour and integrity.

Now Mr. Chrétien is being lectured for his deficiencies, the scattering of patronage and the carelessness of his ministers – by Brian Mulroney. The gods of irony have been working overtime on this one, and they've had their best people on the shift. It's like some wonderful old melodrama, where the streetwalker, finally, gets to lecture the bishop.

A little syrup on this already-too-delicious saga falls from the consideration that the former prime minister raged against the dying of the ethical light – at a Conservative fundraiser! Earlier this same week, the current prime minister, busy purging his cabinet because of ethical reasons, found it impossible last Sunday to attend – a Liberal fundraiser!

A more significant irony is also at play. One of the central points of the now-forgotten Red Book, upon which Mr. Chrétien built his campaign post-Mulroney, was the pledge to appoint an independent ethics commissioner reporting to parliament.

Once elected, Mr. Chrétien did appoint an ethics commissioner, but he castrated the office by having the commissioner report not to parliament but to him. This created a delightfully vicious circle. When the Opposition, or the auditor-general, or the press suggest that a minister of the government is in a conflict of interest, the ethics commissioner is asked in effect to determine whether the government, through one or more of its ministers, is acting or has acted improperly.

Howard Wilson, the commissioner in question, was appointed by the prime minister and reports to the prime minister. He is a creature at both ends of his function – appointment and reporting – of the head of the government he is being asked to oversee and adjudicate. Mr. Wilson is a living embodiment of the idea of conflict of interest.

So the man, or the office (in this case it is difficult to see the separation), centrally placed to determine conflict of interest is in permanent, or structural, conflict of interest.

It is no wonder then that the Liberals are having difficulty getting this storm to move offshore. They have built suspicion of the process into the process itself, and the creature designed, one assumes, to give some distance or deflection from questions of ethics or scandal is itself a generator of cynicism and disillusion.

Pitching Art Eggleton out of cabinet on a Sunday afternoon and demoting Don Boudria must have seemed to Mr. Chrétien six days ago as moves both bold and swift. He must have reckoned that such decisiveness and dispatch would impress the voters and disarm the Opposition.

It has achieved neither. It was seen by most as a nearly desperate improvisation, and by hardly any as radical surgery. Comparisons between this moment in Mr. Chrétien's tenure and the end days of the Mulroney regime were making the rounds well before Mr. Mulroney himself appeared on the scene to give the reminder more potency.

Mr. Chrétien's government is now, in tone, practice, and style, the mimic and mirror of the one he campaigned to supplant. The irony is complete: Brian Mulroney is lecturing Jean Chrétien on the tawdriness and arrogance of a government too long in power.

– Globe and Mail

Newfoundland's Cod Fishery

It's difficult to credit, at least I find it so, that it's a full ten years since Newfoundland felt a shock, the cultural explosion of the collapse of the cod fishery. The cod fishery has been given, let us call it, a ten-year rest. But the news so far, at least, is not good. The most recent reports are that the stocks have not renewed, and there is still some puzzlement over fundamentally what went wrong.

An age that prides itself on its scientific and technological prowess is not as knowing of some things as we'd like to believe. I think Newfoundlanders, the ones that are still left in the fishing communities – and there are other fisheries than cod – have absorbed the news, which is by no means the same thing as saying we have accepted it.

In ways that it is difficult for outsiders to grasp, the fishery has wound itself into, penetrated every aspect and contour of, Newfoundland life. It is intrinsic to the history and drama, song and speech, the politics and settlement of the entire province. It colours how people think where I come from, the way they see things, how they see both themselves and other people. So it wasn't just an industry that collapsed, it was something much more fundamental to the spirit of the place that suffered an assault.

People knew that, after the fishery shut down, Newfoundland would continue. But the real fear, spoken and unspoken, was whether there had been subtracted from Newfoundland an element of its essence, that something had been removed that went to the heart of the province's temper and being.

It might be worth noting that something like Newfoundland's experience in this regard is happening in other parts of Canada: the threat to the

21

family farm out West, the closure of Cape Breton's great mines, the decline in population of many rural communities in many provinces are all connected with the passing of traditional and historical occupations.

Fishing, farming, mining, and forestry are not just occupations or jobs – they are some of the foundational activities of this entire country. And beyond the mere business of supplying work, they have been in many parts of this country the nurseries and shaping activities of how Canada came to be and evolved some of the values that are at its centre.

It's just that the blow in Newfoundland was so large, sudden, concentrated, and central that made its effect there so vivid. Ten years later, the province is still in a cruel suspense about whether the fishery will be re-undertaken. And even if it is, it will not be the same fishery. It will not turn on the same rhythms, even if it returns.

And the gap of ten years has meant many things. A great tenacious continuity has been broken. There has been a kind of limbo imposed on many of the traditional outports. Many people have left and many towns have declined. The officials of the province now turn to the offshore or Voisey's Bay or some other strategy of development to underwrite the future of Newfoundland.

The future of Newfoundland, however promising any or all of these developments may be, without the fishery, without the patterns and echoes of motions of its most ancient craft, is a different and, to my mind, diminished future. It is unfashionable in the technical age to speak of the soul of a place. But I know that Newfoundland has one, and what vigour and humanity that Newfoundland may claim emerges out of its long, often bitter, but – always in a low-key way – noble encounter with the waters and elements of the North Atlantic.

It isn't that Newfoundland won't be the same. It is that inevitably, in a way that is defiant of expression, Newfoundland will be less. The closing of the cod fishery was abrupt and brutal. It shattered something that was so long in the building and that was for all its mixed fortunes unique and immensely to be admired: the way of life of a singular people.

– The National

Crop Cycle Versus the Spin Cycle

Premier Roy Romanow, with others, came to Ottawa last week to argue the case for some crisis relief for small farms on the prairies. They were told, in essence, that they didn't know what they were talking about. After all, they only live there. And if there is a crisis in the farms of Saskatchewan, well, obviously a periscope in Ottawa is going to pick it up a lot quicker than a government in Regina. I think, however, personally, Mr. Romanow is right. But then I have got the disadvantage of having been out to that province a couple of times. And I may be further contaminated by having talked to a few farmers, who gave a wonderfully realistic impression of being people at the end of their tether. But enough of sentimentality.

It may be that Mr. Romanow has jumped aboard the wrong wagon train. They should have placed the farmers' problems in front of a human-rights commission and tried out the doctrine of equal pay for work of equal value. After all, if the principle of this doctrine is a basic human right, there is no special reason to limit its heroic reasoning to a portion of the federal civil service.

Small farmers are a wonderful test case. Many of them are gender-balanced, for one thing: husband and wife, so there'll be no need to rack up the sexist determiners. It'll be a straight comparison: Is twelve to sixteen hours a day planting, growing, harvesting, year in, year out, in flood and drought, equal in value – and this is the key – to

(a) the work of an assistant deputy minister;

(b) the work of a member of parliament;

(c) the work of your favourite senator?

We could compare then, as is the way with these things, patronage plums with more arduously gathered produce; ask whether the deputy minister's round of endless meetings is work of equal value to swathing night and day before a frost; whether sweating it out year in and year out in the face of American and European subsidies has the same job stresses as an MP's having to sit at the back of the caucus room, ducking the party whip's eye. It's the crop cycle versus the spin cycle. Simply put, the question would be whether the work of producing the nation's food is of equal value to producing the nation's politicians. Is a hired hand the job equivalent of a press flack? These are wonderful questions.

I encourage Mr. Romanow to enter sector comparisons as well. Human rights these days are very much a group thing. Well, does the farm community of southern Saskatchewan perform work of equal value to, say, the Bloc Québécois? Now it may turn out that a human-rights tribunal will find that, on average, forty farmers don't work as hard as forty senators. But then again, as the saying has it, some day pigs may sprout wings and horses take up knitting. On the whole, though, I think it's a safe route.

And considering that the most recent pay-equity triumph netted its stake-holders $3.5 billion, Mr. Romanow will very plainly realize that going to Ottawa for a paltry $1.3 million was pure timidity and small-town thinking of the most deplorable kind. It's those prairie skies: makes a man humble.

The farmers in need in this country work day and night and, at year's end, either break even or lose money, while supplying the most fundamental human need – food. Under my scheme, and with the backing of the appropriate tribunal, there's no need for a single man or woman of them not to net at least the take-home pay of a backbench MP. Equity? What do you think?

– *The National*

The Romanow Report

F inally, a Royal Commission you can bring home to mother.

Most Royal Commissions are creatures for hire. They're meant to buy time rather than pleasure, and they mainly work as servants to politicians who want to avoid, defer, or deflect an issue. They exist to escape a problem under the guise of pretending to explore one.

Mr. Romanow's commission is different, either because of its timing, his skill, or the accumulated exasperations most Canadians now feel about the health-care system. Maybe all three. It is one commission report which will foster debate rather than choke it.

Its recommendations may be accepted or rejected in part or in full, but they will not be ignored. Its release has intersected with the public mood for change and reform in health care. It will be praised, it will be damned, but it will not be ignored. That's point one.

Secondly, Romanow should be commended for putting all his cards on the table. He views the Canadian system of health care as more than just a system – much more. He argues it is central and defining to the contract we have made with each other and to the Confederation, that it embodies one strand of national values that are at the centre of how we regard ourselves and how we wish to be regarded.

Health care, he states, is as much a symbol as a system. And symbols are not hollow metaphors. They command loyalty and commitment.

On this point, Romanow is right for good or real. Our health-care system is the litmus for one strand of Canadian nationalism. Romanow's report is the strongest assertion of that strand of nationalism to date. He sees health care in a larger context as central to the idea of Canada. That sounds large, only because it is large. The scope of his claim is at once the great strength of the report and at the same time its weakness.

It is a weakness because we undertake to measure the efficiency and the practicality of a system not by how well it deals with individual sufferers, with patients, but by an exterior standard, how it comports with our civic ideals. It shields health care from direct and brutal scrutiny on whether, as a service, it gives fair, equal, ready access to people in pain and illness.

But he puts the argument out there – it can be debated – and that is a virtue.

Finally, money. If his philosophy and the commitments that spring from it are adopted, governments (federal and provincial) are going to have to spend and spend hugely. Believe this, with an aging population and a sophisticated universal health-care system, $15 billion is just a down payment. It is a mere instalment.

Canadians, if they love their system, if they value it as patriots and as patients, are going to have to pay for it. And if they say, "Yes, we want to pay," they must know that it is not a choice made in a vacuum. The scale of the commitment will make incursions into how much we dedicate to the armed forces in a time of terror. It will affect how much money goes to universities and how tuition fees rise. It will mean much for schools, highways, and municipal government. It will ask how serious we are about the environment, about Kyoto in particular.

Romanow's commission makes the strongest possible case philosophically and rhetorically for a national health-care system, publicly funded in its entirety, expanding in what it will cover and remedying the most gruesome present deficiencies: the waiting lists, the crowded emergency rooms, the absence of family doctors, and a vastly overworked staff. It sets the table for a grand political and economic debate. The poles of the argument are that health care will either save this country or it will devour it. A Royal Commission that throws down the gauntlet. Who would've thought it?

– *The National*

Brrrr-ing on That Global Warming!

I've been patient, more than patient, for a long while now. We've had bulletins for years and years, each one more sanguine that its predecessor, that change was imminent, that a bright new shining day – a really shiny day – was about to blossom. But here I was yesterday, on the fifth day of April, in Toronto, a mere hour's drive away from the lush vineyards of the Niagara Peninsula – one of the true Edens of our ancient green earth – and it was snowing.

I can take a bit of snow. I come from Newfoundland, a province not unacquainted with snow. We have an anthem, the "Ode to Newfoundland," that warbles in one of its less-menacing stanzas of "Winter's stern command." The "Ode," if I may be allowed this foible, is not just whistling Dixie here.

Newfoundland winter is a bitter, melancholy, protracted, soul-testing season. Indeed, if memory serves, that old grim harridan Mother Nature sometimes began her winter tune-ups down home as early as September. A sprinkle of hail here, a grotesquely premature snow squall there, a snap of frost on the Avalon, the bakeapple marshes rimed, their sad berries congealed – all this months before the lying calendar allowed it was winter.

The great flood that swallowed the earth was said in the Biblical account to have lasted forty days and forty nights. A mere tease, a sprinkle, a flash, compared to the eon of snowfall in St. John's last year. The snowploughs, the few not buried, lost, or burned out, were still at it in May. The worst winter, they said, in 130 years.

And now it's snowing up here in tropical Ontario in April. As I say, I've lost patience. If we're to have our global warming, I want to know when and how soon. It simply isn't enough to keep promising that the world, and our part of it in particular, will be a warmer place.

Global warming isn't the GST. It's not a promise to be broken with impunity. A lot of us have pinned our hopes on the thoughts of a sultry February, our own little bit of Victoria's early blossoming – a March without Gore-Tex and ice boots, temperatures in April that don't skulk in lower single frigid digits. But despite years of "warnings" of global warming, conferences and conventions hyping its imminence, it seems to me that we are as far away from that sunny utopia as ever.

If I were of an activist bent, I'd start a movement: Global Warming – If Not Now, When? If Not Here – To Hell With It! But it's too cold to be thinking of marches and demonstrations. And, more to the point, I don't think the political will is out there for a Make the Earth Warmer Real Soon movement.

I notice, for example, that David Anderson – a *West Coast* politician, let it be noted – is leading something of a cabinet charge to sign on to the mischievous Kyoto accord. I'm not up on the science of Kyoto. But when you mix politicians and environmentalists – choose any beaker you like – at a world press conference, the very last thing that is likely to crawl out is science.

Still, unless I am very much mistaken, the thrust of the Kyoto agreement is to *lower* world temperatures. Is this what Mr. Anderson would have us sign on to?

He says that enforcing these Kyoto protocols will cost us *only* $10 billion, almost as much as Canada's $12-billion defence budget. What in the name of Mother Earth has the amount we reluctantly spend on our armed forces got to do with Kyoto? (They might be a lot cheaper, by the way, if the odd snowfall in Toronto didn't tempt Mel Lastman to see the Canadian army as an extension of his City Works department.)

More to the point, spending $10 billion to go along with the fricassee of activism and apocalypse that we know as the global environmental movement – in an effort to make us even colder than we are now – is, in my view, a reckless defiance of our common Canadian yearning for a warmer world.

After me: "Global Warming: If Not Now, When? If Not Here – To Hell With It!"

– *The National*

The Walkerton Ceasefire

We live in an age of rising expectations and declining trust. Governments are not what they used to be. They are necessary, but in many ways people do not trust government. Whether this springs from any particular source – the media, the various ways politics itself has changed, the cynicism of the times – is in one sense not important. Just think about how we view elections. Most people see the noise and rattle of political campaigns much the way they watch a wrestling match. Most people don't, at any fundamental level, believe what they're seeing.

Elections are an end game. Politicians can make speeches, yet how few of those speeches really, any more, buy the honest conviction of the voters who, to be truthful, only half listen to them?

This is not just a problem with a single level of government, or a single political party, or even a single politician. True, some governments, some parties, some particular politicians are less trusted than others. But in the main, it is the structure that's under siege. The process of politics does not have dignity and respect in the minds of most people. At a fundamental level, we expect very little from our governments and give them a lot of slack on a very great deal.

But that basic core that people do expect, and expect without exception, tamper with that, disappoint there, and you have a real problem. At the level of really basic services, the fundamentals – fire, hospital, police, water – people are unwilling to cut any slack at all. This is the centre of people's real response to Walkerton and the deaths and the contaminated water in that town. Mess up on promises, play the silly games of partisan politics, do the attack ads, play politics in all the other areas as much as you want.

But here, at the level of things that truly count, and that people fundamentally need, and have to have, there is no room for error, or game, or excuse. The public doesn't care which level of government, municipal or provincial, was responsible, doesn't care which administration may have changed some or part of the regulations, or which level may have been more responsible than another. It just says, on something as fundamental as the water supply, this is why we have governments. And at this level of truly basic service the politics stops altogether. Get these basics right, give truly guaranteed service here, have no games at all for the truly core needs, and we'll forgive or overlook all the other charades and half-dramas that we call politics.

But mess up on something as absolutely vital as the reliability of the water people trustingly drink, well, then you mess up in one of the few remaining areas where we agree that we must have government at all.

The inquiries that are promised will come to particulars. But Walkerton has a challenge beyond the discovery of the particular facts of the particular situation. Walkerton extends the public's declining respect for the purpose of government itself. If ever a situation called for a ceasefire in partisanship and a real promise never to see the like of this happen again, then for both parties, citizens and their governments, Walkerton is that situation.

– *The National*

Canada Must Be Made Safe from Live-in Nannies

Yesterday was Valentine's Day. As you can probably guess, it's not a crowded day on my calendar. But for the rest of the world, it's an opportunity to show they have a heart. Even in Ottawa. Let's see if they do. You've probably seen the story out of Edmonton of the Filipino woman who has been hiding in a church on and off for the last six months. Hiding from the relentless and efficient forces of Canadian Immigration.

Just in case you haven't, let me tell you that Nancy Latetia – which means "happiness" – Cables is not a people-smuggler. Not one of the dreadful "snake eyes" who traffic in the misery of the poor or persecuted of other countries willing to "buy" their way into Canada. Nor is she some high-powered ne'er-do-well or scofflaw who arrived in Canada with a clothesline full of previous arrests and then proceeded to tie up the immigration service and the courts for years and years till our system began to look like a joke.

Nancy Latetia Cables is neither desperado nor mastermind. She is that most obnoxious of new arrivals: a live-in nanny. She is, in other words, one of those people almost exclusively female and from the Third World who make life so much more comfortable for the upper-middle classes and pro-fessionals of the First World who are both male and female. Evidently Nancy Latetia didn't understand one part of the rules of her stay here: that she was to be a nanny only to one family in Edmonton. And her employer, a lawyer, is said by her to have advised her it was all right if she did other work as well.

Nancy Latetia, in the spirit so lacking in the First World, actually committed the offence of doing work in a second home. Her mistake was

31

innocent. Her motives were simple industry. Her error: exceeding the work quota for a live-in nanny. Well, naturally Canadian Immigration is not going to stand idly by while people come to this country and work harder than expected, who try to get ahead, who set an example by not bleeding the welfare services or mocking the courts or arriving by the hundreds as camouflage refugees.

This poor creature has sought protection from immigration authorities by the desperate medieval gesture of seeking church sanctuary. The local MP wants the minister, Eleanor Kaplan, to show mercy. The local church obviously wants the same thing. Edmonton in no way feels threatened by Nancy Latetia Cables, and from all accounts – I was there recently – would like her to stay in their cold but friendly city.

What's the worst that could happen? Canada become a magnet for over-industrious housekeepers? But Ms. Kaplan whose department is a byword for unending hearings, judicial delays, and for hard cases getting the royal treatment, will have none of it. Canada must be made safe from live-in nannies who work too hard. Ms. Kaplan can spare Nancy Latetia, introduce a little happiness to her tormented and frightened existence, by exercising ministerial clemency. She can look at this lonely woman hiding in an Edmonton church, whose only crime is wanting to stay here and earn her keep, and say Nancy Latetia Cables, you do us honour by fighting to stay. Welcome.

But Ottawa is a cold city, and it isn't friendly. And evidently ministers in that town do not have a heart even on the day after Valentine's. Ms. Kaplan wants Nancy Latetia Cables deported pronto. If Eleanor Kaplan changes her mind and lets this woman stay, I'll write the minister a Valentine myself.

– The National

NEWFOUNDLAND

Between the Rock and a Hard Place

It was fifty years ago this very day, "just a few minutes before midnight" on March 31, 1949, that Newfoundland and Labrador joined Confederation. But only by chance.

It was supposed to be the next day. A timely alertness of the delegation to Ottawa accelerated the signing of the documents to avoid the event coinciding with April Fools' Day. Considering the later growth of the Newfie-joke industry, this was prescient.

It was no joke at the time.

Within a small, close, intense community, the battle over Confederation enlisted all the pride and fury and passion Newfoundlanders have always brought to their sense of home and place.

From the larger Canadian and British perspective, whether Newfoundland, the plaything of a decrepit Empire and a beggarly island remnant of 350,000 souls, would choose or not choose to house its destiny, finally, within the neighbour federation did not greatly agitate the slumber of the chancellories. In the great scheme of things, one way or the other, it was just constitutional tidying-up.

Newfoundlanders knew otherwise. They had endured their spell on a pitch of rock in the North Atlantic amid the heartbreaking inclemencies of weather and wave, and the deeper miseries of fitful and feudal government, since time out of memory.

They combed a living from the sea, gallantly teased spare sustenance out of an even sparer soil, and in the great coastal chain of tiny settlements that ringed the mad indentations of harbour, cove, and bay, built a way of being all their own. This was not a "lifestyle."

What they were was all they were.

The question of 1949 was instinctively known to everyone: "This is our own, but can it continue?" The Confederation debate was a struggle with goodbye.

At home, it is a story too familiar how a combustion of public maladministration and the bitter mischiefs of an almost arcanely inept and corrupt politics had led Newfoundland to the suspension of self-government in 1933 and a return to the limbo and indignity of colonial administration for the next sixteen years. This interlude of self-inflicted life support was known, with saturating eloquence, as the Commission of Government.

But the horrors of Newfoundland politics were, emphatically, not original to the pre-Confederation period. They've been a dark carnival of mischance and almost creative incompetence since Sir Humphrey Gilbert planted the British flag in a mound of earth on Duckworth Street overlooking St. John's Harbour in 1583.

In those far-off days, pirates visited other territories to conduct their proper business, to loot; they came to Newfoundland as to a finishing academy or a spa for the profession. More for study than rapine, they bent themselves to close watch of the Order of Newfoundland Politicians – the platonic originals of freebooting and sleeveenery.

(Note: While the Irish had the first grab at "sleeveen," with its dense cargo of "craftiness, malice, malingering, pettiness, spite, and perfect good-for-nothingness," the word has become Newfoundland's by force of local illustration.)

Our politics, then, were mad long before bankruptcy and misfeasance climaxed in the utter collapse of all politics in the 1930s. However, even during the lethargy of the Commission, the furies were stirring in the beguiling genius of one man who would engineer the most signal event in Newfoundland history since poor John Cabot stared up from the *Matthew* at the rock welcome of Bonavista.

Confederation unleashed Joey Smallwood. He had been a smouldering volcano denied a vent, a compact mass of banked energies awaiting purposeful explosion for most of his adult life.

Just for contrast: at the same age that John F. Kennedy was elected U.S. president, Joseph R. Smallwood was raising pigs and selling army-surplus blankets somewhere outside Gander. He had been a journalist, author, broadcaster, publisher, union organizer, and a kind of multi-purpose propagandist, whose career (and he would have scorned the prissiness of that term) was all tangents and no arc to rest them on.

Primarily, he could talk. He could talk fence posts into the ground, and sell satellites to the executive of the Flat Earth Society.

He was a natural without a game. Confederation changed that. Whatever the after-theories of Newfoundland's joining Canada, and there has been a stew of them, it was an event that would not have been – when and how it occurred – without Joey Smallwood.

On the rostrum at the national convention convened to determine Newfoundland's future, on wharves and in town halls. Mr. Smallwood pitched security and opportunity against independence and pride, played the "sons of toil" of the outports against the "aristocrats and merchant princes" of St. John's.

Aside from his demonic fluency and energy, he had one other more subtle, but equally persuasive, advantage. He was like a cracky dog. Newfoundlanders will understand that description immediately, and see it more as tribute than dismissal. It mainly stands for sauciness, persistence, and fearlessness against any odds.

He was a comic, bizarre, rough-hewn, enthusiastic, outrageous man, unscrupulous and sublimely manipulative in combat, a hustler and a showman, yet somehow very private, remote, and even shy. Everything about him seemed half-finished and improvised, except his determination and his pride, which were sovereign.

Mr. Smallwood both articulated and personified Newfoundlanders' defensiveness and pride, and, finally, he gave shape and voice to the almost intolerable love in all circumstances that Newfoundlanders have for

Newfoundland. They would not have surrendered their dominion under any other leadership.

In any event, it was less than full surrender: 78,323 votes for Confederation against 71,334 for a return to self-government.

Fifty years have passed since those wild dances of manoeuvre and debate; our scantily achieved admission into the fraternity of provinces and the high mysteries of Ottawa has had five decades to weather and wear.

Mr. Smallwood is gone, but still a presence. We have had four other full premiers (five if you count the flash tenure of Thomas Ridout, a local edition of Kim Campbell but without her legendary staying power): Frank Moores, Brian Peckford, Clyde Wells, and Brian Tobin (the dilettante, the incendiary, the cardinal, and the conquistador).

It is impossible to catalogue, let alone rehearse, all that has happened, all that has changed. There are themes and touchstones.

Economic development. We've been up and down that ladder so often we've forgotten where the wall is. Our entry into Confederation gave us both more security to attempt development and something to brace us when, as frequently we did, we failed.

Even on an anniversary, there is no gainsaying the folly and adventurousness of some of the attempts. Mr. Smallwood's rubber-boot factory and hockey-stick plant have passed generously into that region of myth where dragons speak English and princesses kiss toads.

Mr. Smallwood specialized in toads that stayed toads. There was Come By Chance and its oil refinery (our own Isthmus of Kuwait overlooking Placentia and Trinity Bays). And the Upper Churchill hydroelectric development, a double miracle: the building of it and the monstrous alienation of its revenues (by us, we did it) to Quebec.

This is an embarrassing rosary, but it surely would be a sin not to go one more bead and call up Mr. Peckford's sublime vegetable fantasy: Sprung, the twenty-seven-million-dollar hydroponic-cucumber greenhouse – a horticultural and economic depravity that bends the mind.

Of course, it hasn't all been the strange island of Dr. Moreau, not by a long shot. The search for economic self-sufficiency was in part driven by considerations of dignity. More than is comfortably acknowledged, the cartoon spectacle of Newfoundland as a receptacle for bailout programs – begging bowls with acronyms, the LIPS, the DREES and DRIES, UI – scorched our pride and rebuked our heritage. Some stumbling was just a haste for virtue.

And there has been the offshore, sane excursions into the new technology, more exercises of individual enterprise, and, despite its current torments, the find of Voisey's Bay. Newfoundlanders do want to make their return on the bargain. Confederation, in this sense, is far more stimulus than narcotic.

It may be questioned whether Confederation was the singular precipitating agent of the changes Newfoundland has seen in the past fifty years. Separating what would have been inevitable anyway – passage of time, change of common perspective, the slow evolutions wrought by each passing day – from that which Confederation instigated is like unwinding a ship from its voyage.

These things I know proceeded from the long-procrastinated linkage with Canada: the suspension of the claims of pure physical want, which had always been the harpy attendants on the life of the common Newfoundlander. After Confederation, and because of it, Newfoundlanders were never, to anything like the extent of their foreparents, exposed to the distresses and brutalities of extreme exigency. The happy Newfoundlander of myth was often – too often – hungry behind a defensive grin.

The introduction of twentieth-century supports in the business of everyday life. The great trinity of "roads, hospitals, and schools," the very perquisites of any decent life, were within a generation of Confederation, for the first time since Cabot, available to the mass of Newfoundlanders.

Elections during this period were like some demented ballot-box Christmas: the heavens spewed forth bulldozers and graders, it rained pavement and concrete, and Santa Joey ho-ho-hoed to victory after victory.

"Let me fish off Cape St. Mary's." This is one of the more delicate vocal lyrics in the rich Newfoundland canon. We used to sing it as a love song. Now, it's a dirge or a prayer.

The devastation of the cod stocks was the grand psychological and social event of post-Confederation Newfoundland. It snapped a psychological continuum that set the boundaries of our being here. It was an event of complexity and social force equal to Confederation. In an especially acute manner, it may have completed, may have forced on us, that journey away from ourselves that is the undersong of Confederation.

We Newfoundlanders are more complicit in the cod crisis than we like to admit.

The fish were ours to watch and to keep, and we didn't. We may argue and rail to our angry heart's content about the depredations of the Spaniards, the assault by the factory trawlers, and the somersault science that kept multiplying quotas in the face of exponential decline. We may crucify federal management for its torpor and incompetence, and we should.

But nothing will remove the simple consideration that the great spawning shelves of the Grand Banks, and the great fish stocks of the North Atlantic, were the inheritance of the Newfoundland generations. We were the stewards. We were the keepers. And we failed.

I do wonder, though, whether that fatal carelessness would have been ours without the umbrella of Confederation. In the dreadful lingo of the brokers (and, for that matter, the weathermen), we were no longer exposed.

The various and generous federal breakwaters against the hard life, what all comprehend now by the social safety net, welcome and necessary as they were, benign as they are, may have slowed the perception and numbed the intuition of a historical default.

Without Confederation, we would not have survived the death of the fishery. But without Confederation, fearing more precisely the price of a lapse, we might perhaps have watched more and not have had to taste the ashen consolation of "surviving" it in the first place.

"Outport" is the characteristic Newfoundland word, the place removed and away, half sanctuary and half exile, sea-dependent and sea-conditioned, generous with challenge, scant with opportunity, a place at once of intense welcome and hospitability and yet desperately exposed, precarious, and vulnerable.

Newfoundland doesn't have outports. Newfoundland is the outport.

This glory of Newfoundland history also has been our confinement. We take our exuberance from what we've endured. The history of this place, for all its hardships and austerities, is eerily affecting. It's a strange music that binds us.

We forgive Newfoundland a lot, and (why not be candid one day in fifty years) we can overdo it. We have a taste and an almost Irish flair for reported misery. We were not sealed in a box, or walled in a marine cave, till the Great Doorman ushered us into the world and the Canadian way.

But it resists all the prowess of overstatement to tell how greatly the idea of belonging to a larger and more stable entity contributed to the potential and opportunity, to the imaginative tracking, of Newfoundlanders after Confederation. The intense, freighted, circumscribed, and close world of Newfoundland was suddenly – larger.

The popular genius for talk and song, the festal inventiveness in the teeth of bleak circumstance, the carnival buoyancy and vitality of Newfoundlanders, for all its vivid allure and charm, have always seemed to me something of a willed and desperate gaiety, the brave face of a disguised lament.

The great tragedy of Newfoundland history has always been individual and nameless. The loss was in the territory of the soul. The generations before Confederation were rock icons of pride and self-sufficiency; they detested whining and victimry as a kind of suicide practised on dignity.

However, it is impossible for a Newfoundlander of today not to feel in one's blood how much was lost, how much was not seen or done, how much talent and character and life were foreshortened and amputated in the steel circle of toil, necessity, and denial.

Lost opportunity is the phantom spirit of Newfoundland history, its uninscribed legend: Had To.

Confederation with Canada was the necessary turn.

We've joined with a generous people and we know it. And generous is probably, in its full sense, the finest word in civil language. It's a very Canadian word. So we know how fine it has been.

But I know why that vote fifty years ago was such a scalpel phrasing of our intent. It had to find the space between heart and mind.

Confederation was necessary, benign and sad.

– Globe and Mail

Bardot and the Other Cleavage-Scientists
Sealed Our Fate

I was tempted to take up the cudgels on behalf of the Newfoundland seal hunt, except that there really isn't much of a hunt any more.

Perhaps more to the point, just as I was about to take them up, I realized that I really didn't know much about cudgels, save that in any sentence I have ever read they are always being "taken up." They are the "purple cow" of my vocabulary. "I never saw a purple cow / I never hope to see one / But I can tell you, anyhow, / I'd rather see than be one."

Isn't poetry wonderful? I have a feeling that the "cudgel" is the purple cow of English diction, a word as opposed to a thing. Does Canadian Tire sell cudgels? Have you ever borrowed one from a neighbour?

A little checking reveals that even the great *Oxford English Dictionary* betrays some exasperation when it comes to sourcing the word. That most worthy compendium of all that is known or can hope to be known about the words we use and where they come from strikes a very odd note when commenting upon the roots of "cudgel."

After suggesting it is an Old English term "cycgel," the dictionary slips into pure speculation – "of which the old Teutonic type would be kuggilo" – and then collapses into pure bafflement with the confession, most remarkable for the *OED*, that "nothing is known of it in the cognate languages."

So what's the point in taking up a phantom word to defend a phantom hunt? For the great and glory days of the Newfoundland seal hunt have long since been over. When it was fallen upon by the spluttering environmentalists in the 1960s, it was already a carcass. In those mad days, the ice floes were mainly a stage set for the publicity virtuosi of Greenpeace and the International Fund for Animal Welfare.

They came in the full armour that is only available to the absolutely righteous. What they knew of Newfoundland or Newfoundlanders was perhaps only equal to what they cared for either – a corpuscle, infinitely compressed. They were the new missionaries, steaming into the backwaters of ignorance and barbarity. The Newfoundland fisherman was the easiest of targets – the poor bastard didn't trail clouds of "the Other," so there was no minefield of political correctness to tap dance through. He was by sensibility reticent, so unlikely to go confessional and teary on camera, and therefore unlikely to mount a defence in the idiom of the times.

Mostly though, he was dazed and confounded by the circus of know-it-alls and busybodies who were suddenly interfering with his livelihood and traducing his reputation to what seemed like all the world. A crowd of loud strangers who were quite theatrically making a full nuisance of themselves while he was only going about his business had burst into his backyard.

It was always, in my judgement, more, much more, about fundraising and achieving profile for the environmentalists than it was ever about the seals. And that is surely all it is about now. For the environmental juggernaut, the seal hunt was the rain forest before they discovered the rain forest.

It was because publicity was its motor that they found it so easy to lure the lollipops onto the ice floes. Every fluffball from second-rate sitcoms and B movies was willing to do a walk on the ice to "save the seals." The day that Brigitte Bardot, Madonna of the Ice Fields, came trailing clouds of glory, and linked her expertise to the agitated consciences of the animal-rights brigade, we knew the game was over. As I recall, Yvette Mimieux was the other cleavage-scientist to offer herself for the requisite photo op.

There was never any winning from the fisherman's point of view. He was the anachronism, they were the future. The seal hunt was neither worse nor better than any other practice whereby we humans have filled our bellies or clothed our backs. But its optics made it insupportable. Cute animals – seal, panda, or porpoise – and organizations that are cuter still are, as a combination, irresistible.

It is over. The seals are in no danger; they never were. Now they're like rabbits in a Viagra factory. The only thing the seal hunt really achieves nowadays is that it still sends a current up the spine of the environmental warriors, and solicits Farley Mowat's never-sleepy muse.

It's a wonderful piece, his *Sealer's Song* – kind of Alexander Pope filtered through the artfulness of Hallmark. I really liked the refrain: "For we're the fellows picked by God / to kill the seals, and save the cod!"

An ode for the ages, though I don't know how "God" got into this. Maybe rhyming dictionaries aren't what they used to be. But as poetry, why it's right up there with the purple cow. The metrics are a little rickety. The metronome must have stammered.

– Globe and Mail

My Favourite Place: A Cove of Inner Peace on Newfoundland's Cape Shore

Two of my favourite poems are by Coleridge: "This Lime Tree Bower My Prison" and the exquisite "Frost at Midnight." Both are consummate pictures, nature cameos, meditations grounded in wonderful evocations of the scene. Of course, if you're pals with Wordsworth, romping great distances on foot every day through the Lake District, and a magisterial poet yourself to boot, then the ability to "catch a place" in words is not all that surprising.

I know where my favourite place is. And I could take the generic "you" there. I can locate it on a map and, even as I write this, can see its serpentine coastline road in the eye of what I am pleased to call my mind.

Newfoundland's Cape Shore road, for the purposes of this selection, begins at Point Verde, a proud outport lighthouse town just outside Placentia, the ancient French capital of Newfoundland. Placentia is roughly 115 kilometres (highway distance) from St. John's. The Cape Shore ending in St. Bride's is, as the name indicates, a coastal road of about fifty kilometres, punctuated by a scattering of very small, or just small, towns: Little Barasway, Big Barasway, Cuslett, Angels Cove, St. Patricks, the jewel of which is not a town at all, but a cove, pure and simple – that of Gooseberry.

It is a small cove, and it has a beach, which Newfoundlanders are willing to claim is a sandy beach, though the effete who have tasted Florida littoral, or the great expanses of Tofino or Hawaii, might quarrel with the description. Sand in those places is small, smooth, and sultry. Gooseberry Cove's sand is much more masculine.

It is a perfect cove. Cove means more than a coastal inlet. In Old

English, it carries the cozy connotation of being an inner chamber, and with the proper attributive it carries the meaning of spirit's chamber or breast. The word, like the place I refer to, speaks of quiet, "innerness." A cove is a spiritual condition as much as a geographical marker.

I cannot describe Gooseberry Cove, and Coleridge is dead. But I can tell you what it is like to be in that place, at evening or in the early morning. As I have said already, it is the jewel of the Cape Shore, and that is a diadem in a matchless crown. I can supply some measure of its transaction with the spirit of the visitor. Not in my own words of course, but those of Gerard Manley Hopkins, who, under a different imperative, wrote these lines:

> I have desired to go
> Where springs not fail,
> To fields where flies no sharp and sided hail
> And a few lilies blow.
>
> And I have asked to be
> Where no storms come,
> Where the green swell is in the havens dumb,
> And out of the swing of the sea.

The effect of these lines is the reality of Gooseberry Cove.

I've visited in all seasons and all times of day. I've seen it buried in fog, the waves whipped up following a fall hurricane, in mauzy June and bleak December. No matter. The external climate is irrelevant. Gooseberry Cove is the very isolate of tranquility.

The going to it, and the coming from it, over the splendid wilfulness of the Cape Shore road itself, is the only thorough justification for the invention of the automobile that has yet been hit upon. But the arrival upon it, and the staying at it – well, weld your favourite Beethoven adagio to that tease of Hopkins above, and you have a foretaste.

– Globe and Mail

Alas, Joey Smallwood Was Larger Than Fiction

The Colony of Unrequited Dreams
by Wayne Johnston, Knopf Canada, 1998

Wayne Johnston's new novel, *The Colony of Unrequited Dreams*, has as its protagonist Joey Smallwood. That is some of its strength and most of its weakness.

It is a novelistic biography, perhaps most precisely a novel whose spine is a biography of Smallwood's life and times, enwrapped in a fiction, purely of Johnston's device, of Smallwood's (unrequited) love affair with his school chum, journalist Sheilagh Fielding.

Fielding, the fictional character, and Smallwood, the real one, remain unattached; they never truly mesh as characters. The surgical graft Johnston attempts doesn't take.

This isn't her fault (or his). It's Smallwood's. It's a problem Smallwood had in his real life that I now find persists in his fictional one. He refuses to share the stage. He wouldn't be Smallwood, real or imagined, if he did. Ask John Crosbie, whose autobiography, *No Holds Barred*, bears something of the same burden. Putting Joseph R. Smallwood in any book is bad news for the other characters.

I suspect Wayne Johnston knew this when he started, and I admire his courage in ignoring the insight. But if you were standing on a street corner when a grand piano came tumbling out of a high-rise, I might admire your courage in thinking you could coax a little Chopin out of it before it met the ground. If I knew you, I'd attend the funeral too.

Smallwood will not be contained. *The Colony of Unrequited Dreams* tries to, or so it seems to me, but drains and diminishes the Smallwood that so many Newfoundlanders still remember, producing a pastework substitute. The fictional Smallwood, the Smallwood whose thoughts and voice are rendered here, this sensitive, love-conscious, and tormented Smallwood is (the adjectives are unavoidable) smaller and more wooden. Fictionizing an inner life and inventing a love interest has shorn Joey of the vigour and elemental charisma that were the magnetic signature of the original.

He never sounds right. This Joey muses and broods. He's formal and balanced and judicious. He remarks the feelings of others, that quiet inner voice that Johnston posthumously invests him with churns on with low-voltage precision. This Joey – and I'll roast in hell for saying this – is almost a '90s kinda guy.

This is more than a failure of fictional ventriloquism. The complaint isn't that Johnston is an inadequate mimic. "Doing" Smallwood was social traffic for half the office and bar wits in Newfoundland for years. The inner and private life that Johnston has composed doesn't fit the character. Fielding, as the story almost always refers to her, as an exterior co-sharer of the Smallwood history, just doesn't belong. She collides with what is known of the real story. And, if I may put it like this, she's over-made. She's a journalist. She's his friend. She's his critic. She's his witness and his mate.

None of this can be. Smallwood had only two real love affairs outside his marriage. They were with himself and Newfoundland. Those were his passions, and they were so huge, so full, that there simply wasn't room – time in the day, space in the psyche, urge in the heart – for any other. Smallwood's public life was his private life. Politics was his mistress, his wife, life's work, career, hobby, and rest. He never slept. He retired to count votes with his eyes closed.

Finally, he was his own best fictionist. Smallwood wrote a lot. He was a journalist, loosely defined, before and after his premiership. By fictionist I mean he "wrote" his life in the scramble and rush, frustration and elation, rapture and decline of the Newfoundland political event. He composed the personality "Joey" with the same calculation and inspiration that is the mixed chemistry of every born writer. In this sense, and though it was on the small stage of the orphan colony, Newfoundland, he was a great writer.

But does this matter to a novel? An author is free to combine and invent as he or she chooses. Just so. But a reader is also free to feel a disappointment if the original is within reach of memory and experience and the created version is less persuasive, or compelling, or present. To those who have never heard of Joey Smallwood, or the Confederation campaign, or the delicious vagaries of pre- and post-Confederation Smallwood politics, will this matter at all? Yes, greatly. It is only with the real, historical Joey Smallwood that the story, the fable, of *The Colony of Unrequited Dreams* can oblige a serious engagement.

This is my central contention with this book. And it is not any on-the-other-handness that makes me want to add other considerations. There is one space of soul when Wayne Johnston may meet Smallwood more as an equal. This book is inevitably a romance of Newfoundland, the place. And Johnston has written here as feelingly and as well as anyone of Newfoundland's dilatory and bitter jaunt to the twentieth century. He is as fervid an imaginer of Newfoundland and as complicit in getting her story out as Joey was. He is acute in response to her melancholies and meanness, shrewd in the telling of her arbitrary and inexplicable gifts and denials.

The book is romantic and realist at one and the same time. By a curious twist, if you leave Smallwood the character out of this book, it is almost the kind of chronicle Smallwood, if he had spoken a lot less to others and a lot more to himself, could have written.

But Smallwood was always talking to others. That dialogue of self with self, the great conversation of life for normal men and women, did not offer the kind of auditorium that Smallwood found congenial. This story, much like Judge D.W. Prowse's *History* (Prowse is the Gibbon of Newfoundland and this book's other great presence), was beyond Smallwood.

It's worth saying this in conclusion: Smallwood would have liked *The Colony of Unrequited Dreams* – "for the Newfoundland bits," he might say. But there'd also be a less than reserved satisfaction at this almost Euclidean exhibition that there's no Newfoundland story in which he's not the hero.

– Globe and Mail

Fratricide, St. John's Style

"It is a terrible thing," the Psalmist urges, "to fall into the hands of the living God."

I do not really believe that it reaches to the level of Biblical thunders to fall within the rhetorical crosshairs of John Crosbie, but it does have its own distinct and not unimpressive angst. As the country goes through something of a blizzard of leadership conventions, the presence of John Crosbie in the *Globe*'s pages a few weeks ago awakened the thought that, across the entire span of political parties, the rhetorical charge of the current batch of front-benchers is very much not what it, even very recently, used to be.

Mr. Crosbie was engaging in a set-to with his Meech Lake nemesis, Newfoundland Supreme Court Justice Clyde Wells. The tone of the *Globe* exchange was not up to the charge of those high days when both men were at the top of their game over the Meech fiasco.

Mr. Wells was then, as all will recall, premier of Newfoundland, and Mr. Crosbie was that eminence known as "Newfoundland's man in the federal cabinet." I do not know if this latter is a term of art, but it has always been the case that Newfoundland's man in the federal cabinet was a potentate at least equal to its premier, and depending on the artfulness of the occupant, and his access to patronage and prime-ministerial benevolence, sometimes the premier's superior.

The Wells-Crosbie debate of recent days was seen by some, and by no less a legal observer than Clayton Ruby, as a "settling of scores by old men who should know better." I think this description, for one thing, vastly underrates the vitality of the debaters in question, and as for the requirement that they "should know better," that's a rubric that has force for all of us, at every stage of life.

The young have their follies in equal measure with the old: the only real distinction is the energy of the former, and the avidity of the latter, in pursuing them.

The timeline of the Crosbie-Wells engagement, its continuity and endurance, is one of the most interesting things about it. I am flooded with melancholy that the esoterica of Newfoundland politics are not on the mental fingertips of every Canadian citizen. It is probably not the case that most people know that John Crosbie and Clyde Wells entered public life at the same time, when both of them were invited to join the cabinet of the Great Pharaoh of Newfoundland politics himself, Joey Smallwood.

For the vast Canadian audience of today, Mr. Crosbie is as much an emblem of Progressive Conservativism as the Smith Brothers once were of cough lubricants. John Crosbie, however, began serious political life – I am tempting grim fate here – as a Smallwood Liberal. So did Mr. Wells. In fact, Mr. Wells was enfolded with such Smallwoodian exuberance that the patriarch of all partisans extolled young Clyde as "keen, keen as mustard."

I don't know if then or now Clyde Wells appreciated the condiment compliment, but in its compression, repetition, and earthiness, it was a tidy sample of the Smallwood manner. Regardless, they were hardly on the premises when they revolted. And they were – this may surprise some readers – a team. It will be no surprise that, as a team, they were formidable.

For Newfoundlanders, when Clyde Wells took the stringent and lone stand he did on Meech Lake, and held out against the imprecations of 90 per cent of the country's élites, the prime minister, *and* John Crosbie, it was not a surprise. They had seen him "fall into the hands of the living Joey" and withstand a whirlwind of attack and scorn that would have felled oaks and withered diamonds.

Mr. Smallwood and the Wells-Crosbie team fought it out for over a year. Mr. Smallwood, eventually, lost. But they, in any clear sense, didn't win. They made Mr. Smallwood weak enough for Frank Moores, however, to beat him cleanly. In a way, they made Mr. Moores premier.

It was during the great upheaval that one other sea change occurred.

Prior to this match, John Crosbie was among the least confident and most tedious and unimpressive public speakers that the nation, never mind Newfoundland, has ever endured – Paul Hellyer without the wattage. But one could not challenge Joey Smallwood, the Mount Etna of political oratory, and not be a public speaker. The need to survive that contest, and his own sometimes frightening determination, turned Mr. Crosbie into one of the most effective combat-orators this country has produced.

So when I see Mr. Wells and Mr. Crosbie at it in the daily prints, I do not see spent warriors wasting their time. I see, instead, the splendid inertia of two divergent temperaments, who whether they wish to admit it or not, have shared a career. It's a Newfoundland Zen: All is one, finally.

– Globe and Mail

Newfoundland Calls to Amend Constitution

The last time there was a real Wrestlemania match between Newfoundland and Ottawa was way back when, as they say, giants walked the earth. Joey Smallwood and John Diefenbaker had a wonderful go at each other over one of the terms of Newfoundland's union with Canada. There were more sparks that flew out of that match than Churchill Falls has been able to generate ever since.

Today, another Newfoundland premier – one that, as he would be willing to admit, doesn't have quite the voltage of Joey Smallwood – threw down the glove at Ottawa, and the current Liberal government, over Ottawa's handling of the Newfoundland fishery.

Roger Grimes went quite a distance. He wants no less than a renegotiation of the terms of union. At issue is the continued closing of the Newfoundland fishery. But contained in Mr. Grimes's announcement is a good deal more than just the fishery.

The premier very clearly states that there exists a broad and deep feeling that Ottawa doesn't understand the consequence of its policies for Newfoundland, that there is a growing resentment over what he has called Ottawa's high-handedness when it makes decisions affecting Newfoundland that go so much deeper than the bare economics of those decision.

Ten years ago, the historic Newfoundland fishery was halted. Since then communities have been gutted of young people and the middle-aged. Some outports have dwindled into shells of their former vitality. Each year of the so-called moratorium – and there have been ten of these years – has seen the gradual, slow atrophy of the cardinal signature of Newfoundland's way of being. Closing the fishery was not the same as closing a chain of drugstores, or a string of Kentucky Fried Chicken outlets.

So there is a background sentiment for what Roger Grimes announced today. And it is taking on some extra power from what is going on simultaneously in the New Brunswick crab fishery. That sentiment may be stated as follows: a growing sense of distance from Ottawa, the feeling that the whole East Coast, not just Newfoundland, is an item in the bureaucratic administration of Canada, rather than a living component of Confederation.

It's my feeling that it isn't the decisions in themselves or the facts behind them to close down the Gulf cod fishery or limit the crab fishery that have so angered fishermen in both provinces, but that they are issued from the federal Fisheries Department and a federal government from some high distance, unburdened by a real feeling for what these decisions will mean for those who have to live by them.

Roger Grimes is heading for an election soon. Without a doubt, he is taking the dramatic step he has taken impelled by the advantages he sees for him politically in taking it. Politics never sleeps in Newfoundland. That much is unchanged since Joey Smallwood's day.

His political advantage aside, he is also mining a very real perception: that the oppositionless government in Ottawa is no longer as careful as it should be with the texture of people's lives in what we call so easily "the outlying regions of this country." And that the feeling of being left out constitutes one of the soft fractures of this Confederation, as alive in Newfoundland and the East Coast as it is, depending on the time of day, say, in Alberta.

I don't know if what Mr. Grimes launched today will have a real benefit for Newfoundland fishermen. But he has done one real service already: he has broken the spell of complacency that thinks just because the government in Ottawa doesn't face any real opposition, there's not real opposition to the government in Ottawa.

– The National

THE WAY WE LIVE NOW

Why People Get Fat

The federal government has announced it will spend fifteen million dollars to research why people get fat. I'm very glad to hear it. It's about time.

Why people get fat is one of the last great mysteries. We've made a dent in the big bang, peeled back black holes, and opened our understanding even partway to the origins of conscious life and the popularity of Oprah Winfrey. But science has twiddled its thumbs far too long on the last real hidden riddle of the cosmos. Why people get so damned fat.

I'm not a scientist myself – I'm putting in far too much time on global warming to make that claim – but if I may, I'd like to suggest just a couple of lines of inquiry.

Now this may be radical, but I think they should look at food. Nor should I wish to prejudice the experiment, but I think the amount is important. Just a guess, I know, from a layman, but take a look at food and the amount of food.

And if there's anything left over of the fifteen million dollars, perhaps they could have a look at eating, too. Eating food, I mean.

I suggest they eat out a lot for science. I know how little work has been done in this area, but I suspect that, if they designed the right experiment, say a controlled study involving Boston cream donuts, vats of deep-fried chicken, and chocolate-chip ice cream in buckets, they're going to find a connection between fat, food, and eating.

Lots of eating of lots of food.

It's only a hunch on my part, but I'm willing to speculate that people who eat a whole lot will on average weigh a lot more than people who eat only a little. A hummingbird weighs a lot less than a pig, and guess which one eats less.

I know this is pioneer stuff, obesity and dieting are the great *terra incognita* of the natural sciences, but whoever connects the dots here or fastens the waistband will be a Galileo for our time, the Einstein of girth science.

Donuts. I think they should pay special attention to donuts, especially Tim Hortons. This is after all a Canadian study. Honey-glazed, chocolate-coated, and the aforesaid Boston cream. If a person consumes his weight in donuts once a month, I'm willing to hazard that, in the following month, to do the same, he will have to consume more donuts. Donuts may be the primal soup of weight gain. Homer Simpson has done a lot of good work in this area. After this study is over, they'll be naming hospital wings after Homer.

Cake and steak, worth a look. A couple of pounds of steak a day, a few porterhouses, for example, every evening after work, followed by a chaser of beer and a chocolate cake or two may put a little tension on the pantyhose. Folklore has it that a great intake of beer could take a washboard stomach and turn it into a barrel of guts.

The point is really we just don't know – why people get fat, I mean. It could be climate change. Those greenhouse gases could be puffing people up. But I think it's deeper. My money is on food and eating, especially in combination.

And, oh yes, lying about the house.

I grew up with someone. She was an aunt. And she didn't, of course, have fifteen million dollars to refine her views. But I still remember her marvellously subtle injunction to all of us layabouts and deep-eaters, which was stop stuffing your gobs and get out of doors; Participaction before its time.

She was as thin as a rail, smoked like a chimney, and didn't have but grade eight. In a different time, she would've been a research consultant.

In the meantime, I say three cheers to the federal government on this one. Fifteen million to unriddle biology's last great puzzle, mere chump change. Fat and food, eating and weight, is there a connection? Stay tuned.

– The National

My Rage Against the Machine

Question: What is the difference between purgatory and hell? Answer: Hell never ends.

According to my decaying memory of the Catholic catechism, purgatory is a place of torment and pain, but it has boundaries: It is not eternal. Whereas, "Out of hell there is no redemption."

It is the hope of release, the knowledge that it will end, that makes purgatory endurable. Conversely, it is the knowledge that hell is of infinite duration, rather than the particulars of any of its inventive and excruciating horrors, that is its most terrible torment.

Hell – eternal; purgatory – bounded. It is on the basis of this distinction that I suggest that trying to call the help line of any large corporation – an airline, a computer company, a power corporation – is not a hellish experience. It is merely (oh! what a "merely") purgatorial. "Help line" can also stand in for customer service, information numbers – you know the list.

Before I illustrate this distinction, I wish to offer a general proposition, a law for the times we live in: the more we multiply the means and speed of our communications devices, the greater will become the difficulty of ever talking to anyone. The corollary is: while the possibility of talking to a real person in any large corporation is very nearly infinitesimal, the possibility of talking to one in *any company whose business is communication* does not exist.

Have you ever tried to phone the phone company? I rest my case.

Airlines Winter is coming on, the season of storms. The greatest lie on earth is routinely buried in an injunction we'll all be hearing frequently from now on. Whenever there's a storm, all the news broadcasts will "urge passengers" to "please call their airline before proceeding to the airport."

Trying to call an airline or, for that matter, an airport during days of deep tropical calm, during days of such atmospheric torpor that leaves do not stir, bumblebees take siestas, and all of Nature is in stasis, is a marathon of voice-mail menus and near-interminable waiting. Trying to call during a blizzard is an act of sheer incontinent dementia. No one answers an airline phone during a storm: this is a law of physics.

Computer companies   The rule is, they can call you, but you will (almost) never get through to them. I had a call from Dell Computer this week. They wanted me to pick up their warranty for a second year. I have a few weeks left on the current one. I also have a minor problem with my computer. So I asked, before signing on, that seeing as they were calling me, could I be switched over to the help line to discuss the current problem under the current warranty? That couldn't be done, even after I gave them the understanding that getting through to someone would be a really big consideration towards spending another hundred dollars for a second year of "coverage."

I called the "help" number, endured the purgatorial "menu," the bilingual repetitions, the commercials, the Muzak, and was duly at the end of those torments "put in sequence." I did this three times, waiting ten minutes each time, and had someone else do it three times more. Never got through. Not buying warranty.

I also had another purgatory with trying to phone Dell to check on an order for a new computer. I would rather run barefoot through a field of thumbtacks than go through that again. "Dude, you're getting a Dell" is now a line out of Dante. I'll be fair here – I'm sure Dell is no worse than any other company. And Adam Sandler is no worse than David Spade.

Power companies in Ontario   The Tories in Ontario are finished. Ernie Eves should pack his bags and go. If Ontario's citizens, after jumping to one power company or another, have tried to get "customer service" to talk over their arrangement with the company, or have a bill explained, then they have had a private bath in purgatory. The power companies have the manners of Attila and none of his charm.

Readers will have their own examples of the "fires that burn but consume not" and the voice-mail menus that extend to eternity. In this wretched age of super-communication, of voice mail, cellphones, beepers, e-mail, Web sites, help lines, and customer service, you have an arsenal of means to communicate, and no one to talk to.

It is all a lie. They don't want to talk to you. They don't even like you. You are a nuisance. Once you've bought the toy, signed on to the service, plugged in the computer, given the credit-card number – *you no longer exist except as a piece of grit in the gears of their machine*. Their time is precious; yours is (like you) worthless.

This is purgatory, and you are in it.

– Globe and Mail

If You Need a Cop, Just Light Up

Morality should be symmetrical. If we're beaten with a stick for one vice, then we should be beaten with a stick of equal length and flex for a vice of equal allure.

This isn't one of the rules of equity gnawed over by youngling lawyers while they're still filing their teeth in law school. Its evident even-handedness and clarity might be thought too much, possibly traumatic, for the little sharks-in-diapers of a profession that thrives on the obscure and the sinuous.

I'm sure that when Allan Rock attended law school, the rule of symmetry wasn't posted as part of the coursework. And judging from the remorseless pedantry with which he continues to run his health jihad against smoking, it hasn't polluted his mind.

Mr. Rock is now campaigning to remove the signals "light," "mild," and "medium" from the packaging of cigarettes. The dental porn and knee-slapping impotence jokes, together with the apocalyptic health warnings that now brocade every cigarette pack, are evidently not enough for the cause. Why stop with "light" and "mild"? Why not ban the alphabet? And while he's at it, forbid the purchase of cigarettes unless patrons enter a store and point at them mutely, while standing upside down on a case of beer and reciting an ode to tofu.

The federal government is poised to legalize marijuana as an all-purpose relaxant. It watches without a furrow in its health-caring brow as "the greatest health-care system in the world" has waiting lists metastasizing, and ambulances chased away from emergency rooms.

It sits, mute as moss and twice as lethargic, as explosive campaigns for beer depict to the young the paradise of fornication and stupor that awaits them with every cold and gassy swill. The roads still have their quota of crashes, manglings, and wasted lives – inextricably linked to the access to and misuse of booze. In this, it's business as usual, and the advertising in all its fleshy glory owns half the television time, three-quarters of the sports teams, and all the best billboard space in the country.

Crack, cocaine, heroin – all the dreary life-wasters – hardly ever get the same glory of teeth-gritting declamation, or the intense piety of exhortation, that burdens the softer narcotic. Vancouver's East Side (holy Vancouver, so smoke-free an "environment") is still the pestilence it was five years ago, with hookers and heroin and dereliction. The health minister is not out on the East Side trying to rid Canada of that visible scourge.

The federal government will do everything about smoking except the one thing that would wash its hands: stop receiving revenue from the vice. It can't preach out of one mouth and ingest the swelling revenue with the other.

Toronto is going smoke-free. Again. In Toronto – I do not know what it's like in other smoke-free cities – you may have your car broken into, much damage done, things stolen, and if you report it, you'll get voice mail. Leave your name and number. If you're lucky, maybe within five days of leaving the message – long after the villains have fled the scene, perhaps the city – you may get a callback. This may pass for therapy in an Oprah age, but it is not police work.

No one will show up the same day to – what is that word I'm looking for? – oh yes, investigate. There is not even a pretense that some mauling of your property, invasion of where you live, or theft of your possessions will actually trigger police work in Toronto.

Light a cigarette in a restaurant, though, and a bevy of smoke beadles and *Drabble* graduates will be on you with the speed of a broken promise and the attitude of Tom Wappel. Offend the anti-smoking despots in Toronto, and the law in all its ridiculous abundance and insolence is there before the second drag.

The message here is simple. Pass laws, levy fines, execute rigorously for trendy moralistic novelties. Ignore pillage, intrusion, and good old-fashioned criminality.

Drench the nation with booze and its blandishments, the feds and Mr. Rock are inert, vacant, and unstirred. Zero tolerance for one vice, 100 per cent tolerance for the other.

Someone smashes up your car and steals your goods – that's your business. Light up a cigarette – that's everyone else's.

Fix the health-care system, eliminate the scourges of hard drugs and street misery, moderate the flood of booze commercials – then, maybe, Mr. Rock will have the standing to debate "light" and "mild."

Send a cop when your car is broken into – then, maybe, people won't be lighting up in sheer frustration and anger over a city that has time for trivial things but doesn't give a rat's rump about what counts.

– Globe and Mail

You're Sick and It's All Your Fault

It's too bad the federal government let Roy Romanow loose to study health care before this story broke: a Winnipeg doctor has announced that he will no longer treat patients who smoke.

In that decision, and the logic that supports it, lies the remedy for all that ails the nation's troubled health-care system.

There are two central principles at work in the doctor's decision, which, if followed with rigour and consistency, will, in an instant, reduce the demand for universal health care, unburden its staff and facilities, and save immense buckets of money.

The first principle is patient culpability. Are you sick or injured because of something you did? Wrap the car around a tree because you were on the cellphone? Don't, repeat don't, dial 911. If the illness or injury is your fault, the pain is your own, the suffering belongs just to you, and your doctor may shut the doors of medicare in your face.

Smokers' illnesses are their own fault. And cutting off smokers from the health-care system will immediately eliminate 30 per cent of its clients. Roy Romanow, go home. Problem solved.

But, though smokers are legion, they are only a subset of the addicted class. Alcohol addiction is a gold seam of maladies and injuries, both physical and mental. Cutting off the alcoholics will trim the lines in the emergency rooms, and an overburdened health-care system will finally start to hum and buzz like the hygienically oiled machine it's meant to be.

If one addiction takes you off the health-care rolls, obviously, another will as well. The hard and soft narcotics, painkillers and cough drops, prescription and non-prescription pharmaceuticals, the rock of hash and the kick of crack – all of these have an energetic and toxic following. There are whole armies of doped and hooked people out there whose pursuit of their own addiction brings them to the waiting rooms of our clinics and the taxed attention of clean-living medical staff all over the country. Off with the addicts.

The good doctor's wisdom extends beyond addiction. Culpability for one's own malady is the rule.

AIDS is a demanding disease. We will have to discriminate among AIDS victims. Those who suffer its afflictions through unsafe sex clearly fall into the category of "those who have brought it on themselves." Under this new regimen, "Go home and moan" will be the watchword.

It is too easy to list the obese, the reckless, the sedentary, the fast-food junkies, and the extreme-sports freaks – but they fall into the grab bag of those who bring pain, injury, misery, and unwellness unto themselves. To the fat cardiac or the maimed snowboarder, let the call go out: "The doctor is not in."

And here is the second principle: physician rule. Sick people have had the run of the health-care system for too long. Medicine, like war, should be left to the professionals. Doctors, acting on their own, should decide which of the sick and dying are worth their time.

A doctor-centred health-care system, one that leaves the doctor to make a preliminary moral decision on those who stumble or fall at his door – before engaging his attention or calling on his skills – is so much clearer, so much cleaner, than this dreadful relic of state-supported, universal, tax-payer-borne, free-for-all, patient-centred freak show that we have now.

Before a patient is even asked for his or her medicare card, the scrupulous physician will bend over the maimed and halt with just one critical inquiry: "Is this your own fault?"

A "yes" answer, and the wailing hulk is wheeled out to agonize untended, and rage alone at the dying of the light. Cruel, some might say, but what's a continent of cruelty against a doctor's right to choose?

There's only one refinement I can think of to improve on its near perfection. Our nation's hospitals, ambulance services, doctors, nurses, paramedics, and psychiatrists should push this artful reform one more mile.

The sick are the number-one burden on health care. The Eastern mystic and the Western psychiatrist have long suspected that the sick are complicit in their own sad condition. Doctors should – and on the principles outlined here, they will be on solid ground – refuse to treat anyone but the completely healthy. Medicare for the healthy – don't you like the sound of that? It's so tidy.

Well, maybe "treat" is not the right word. How's "mingle with"? In this brave new Hippocratic world, the hospitals and clinics will be near-empty. Doctors and the very well will have to invent reasons to see each other. I suggest a weekly party. A smugfest. They'll have the space.

Poor old Tommy Douglas. He thought health care was for sick people, doctors served patients, and medicine was for those in pain. Damn deluded socialist.

– Globe and Mail

Air Rage? Nope, Just Another Fool

Remember that ape (and I apologize to our evolutionary kin for the slur) who raised a drunken ruckus on an airplane and defecated on a food cart before being restrained by the crew and some passengers.

I believe the incident took place in what is called "executive class." Whatever. He was surely a first-class nit, and if this were not such an elegant newspaper, I would gladly call upon more earthy and, in this context, more appropriate terms to describe him.

Making a nuisance of oneself, being a loudmouth and a boor, bullying servers, and being heedless of everyone and everything except one's own imperious whims and wants – this is the classic description of the self-worshipping egotist.

Egotists and boors have always been with us. The mannerless are legion. It's just that, in the age of laptops and jet engines, they have a greater range of venues in which to unleash their obnoxiousness.

There was nothing clinical about the jerk's behaviour. As far as I know (outside of certain television productions such as *Temptation Island*), there is no genetic foundation for the desire to void one's bowels in public because someone doesn't jump when you holler, or, for that matter, no biological riddle behind the apparent need of some people to harass, humiliate, and torment airplane crews.

In fact, the venue – the airplane – has nothing to do with it. This jerk was a jerk before he rolled out of bed that day. A jerk when he shaved, and a jerk when he hauled on the pants he was later so odiously to lower. A jerk before he left his hotel on the way to the airport. A jerk in the taxi that took him there. A jerk in the lineup before he got his boarding pass, a jerk in the waiting lounge, and a jerk when he lowered his busy rump to the moderate comforts of the executive seat. If I had the time, and you had the patience, we could extend this catalogue right back to the sad moment when this jerk's parents – I presume, somewhat hesitantly, they did it in private – decided to romp in the act that eventually brought him into the world. He was, as they say, a jerk from the get-go.

Unfortunately, we have given a name to this desperate kind of behaviour, a name that somewhat unhitches it from its simple vulgarity and quintessential tackiness. We call this kind of stuff – when it happens on airplanes – "air rage."

I don't know what "air rage" means. But I do know this: deciding that the codes of civil behaviour do not apply to you, that you can be a mean-spirited son of a bitch, a loud, hectoring, foul-mouthed, intemperate, insolent, miserable sack of arrogant ignorance has *nothing* to do with where you are – on the ground, in the air, or, for that matter, at sea.

It may be unpleasant sometimes to travel by air. But we have manners, if we have manners at all, to negotiate those moments when unpleasantness is thicker about us than usual. Furthermore, it is a good bet that, when unpleasantness occurs, it is very likely occurring to the person behind you and the person in front of you. In other words, we are not alone. And the adult or civilized person is willing to hold in check his or her annoyance so as not to add to the common annoyance of all. This is not only good manners; it is good sense.

But the jerk or fool (you will note that I have upgraded him) thinks his annoyance is more important than yours, surely more important than the feelings of clerk or steward or fellow passenger, and thinks it licenses him to vent. Little Tommy must have his tantrum.

But, I repeat, it is not "air rage," any more than the inconsiderate blasting of the horn, the cutting in front, tailgating, cursing, giving the finger, by the fool on the ground in the car is "road rage." Both terms are meaningless therapy-speak. When some idiot rams another car, or runs over a pedestrian, merely to save a couple of seconds, all we have, *pace* Freud and Oprah, is a fool in a car.

Let us not prissify the world and life. Let us not confect dainty and trendy terms to "explain" what does not need explanation. The loudmouth two rows in front of you berating the stewardess (please, not "cabin attendant" – this is a plane, not a fishing lodge) hasn't got a "condition." And the lunatic who nearly side-swiped you is not suffering from "road rage." He's a little coward who's convinced that his car and anonymity morphs him into Clint Eastwood on wheels. It's old-fashioned, unclinical rudeness.

(I just cut myself on a bookmark. I swore and cursed most valiantly. Intemperance, bad manners? No. It was a clear case of bookmark rage.)

From all of which I offer the following maxim: We do not classify the condition of being an idiot after the venue in which his idiocy is made manifest. Repeat after me: On the road or in the air, he's a fool anywhere.

– Globe and Mail

Cellphones

There may be more obnoxious agencies of human misery and torment than the cellphone. But they are few:

- Being mistaken for a wheat field by a cloud of locusts.
- Being buried alive with a loop of the soundtrack from *Titanic*.
- Attending a constitutional conference; being mistaken for a pundit.
- Interviews from film festivals.

In Toronto, which is the vanguard of so much of what we recognize as true human enlightenment on this planet, there is a movement to have the use of cellphones in cars banned by law.

I'm not so sure that this is altogether such a healthy idea. The wonderful dexterity and nimbleness of Toronto pedestrians is one of the glories of the globe. Watching a group at any crosswalk in this city is like being in your own *National Geographic* special. Cheetahs are sluggish, gazelles are clumsy, in comparison with the Toronto pedestrian staring down a Porsche, a yuppie, and her portable hand-held.

Every person who crosses a street in this city knows that the BMW bearing down on them is really a mobile telephone booth with a licence to kill. Everyone knows that, if it's a choice between keeping one eye on the road and one out for pedestrians, or hitting the speed-dial to negotiate the finer points of the divorce settlement at 140 kilometres an hour, the cellphone is going to win every time.

It's helpful to think of the great highways leading into this city, the 401 and the Don Valley, as essentially a giant switchboard on radial tires, and of the people behind the wheel on these highways as so preoccupied absorbing information from their stockbrokers, their mistresses, or their nannies, as to have no time at all to acknowledge the information that they've just cut off an eighteen-wheeler transport truck, and are about to vacuum up some poor Ford Taurus under the bonnet of their chattering SUV. "Reach Out and Touch Someone" is such a vivid little slogan.

The windshield in any car with a cellphone could just as well be made of lead as glass, for its only purpose is to maintain the privacy of the call, not to clarify the direction of the car. And now that cellphones also have Internet capacity, to the wonderful ability to talk and drive at the same time we may add the pleasure of authorship; composing witty e-mails while whizzing through the red light and nailing the bike courier, is such a higher function of the human brain which, as all will acknowledge, is simply wasted merely keeping track of the traffic and people in front of you.

Some people say cellphones are as bad as alcohol. I think this is a slander on booze. Alcohol is something which, when added to the human mind, makes it lazy, and careless, and stupid. Cellphones in cars gravitate to those minds that are that way already.

Should we ban them? I think Mothers Against Drunk Driving should open a subsidiary. I may give them a call.

– The National

Time for Closure

There was a time – oh, it's so long ago now – when "closure" was a fancy term for going out of business. I seem to remember too that people used to say the word when they were buying houses. "We're pretty near closure on the deal." It made people who were buying twenty-thousand-dollar bungalows feel like they were slip-sliding with the Eaton's and the Bay Street crowd to say they were near "closure" with the real-estate agent.

I don't know what "closure" means any more, but it's everywhere. Closure is a psychobabble term, the kind of word people use a lot on *Oprah* and *Sally Jesse Raphael*, after the third course of chicken soup for the soul and after mortifying a studio audience with some dreadful narrative of high-caloric dysfunction or repressed memory. "I'm seeking closure now," someone says, and the audience gets misty-eyed and they release a flock of seagulls in slow motion and John Tesh hammers out some New Age mush on a white piano somewhere, mercifully off in the distance. And then Oprah, like the good therapist *manqué* maitre d' she is, remarks: "Thank you for sharing that. I feel empowered just thinking about it."

Well, closure, I am happy to report, is going the way of the inner child, that fuzzy little ferret that was the rage of the therapists and the healers and the darling of people who practised hugging strangers for a living just a few short years ago. Well, he's gone now, moved out, found alternative accommodation. The new rage is grief-counselling. I don't know when grief-counselling happened, but it's very clearly the Microsoft of pop therapy. Grief-counsellors are everywhere. Well, who are they? Where do they come from? What do they do?

After that terrible devastation in Columbine, we were informed that grief-counsellors were on standby. When the jet plane crashed off Peggy's Cove, same thing. They grief-counselled the relatives. Makes sense. Then they went after those who helped after the crash. And finally, they were interested in grief-counselling the reporters who covered it. The end of this Kleenex chain, I presume, has to be that the grief-counsellors are then themselves grief-counselled, and so on and so on and so on.

Is there a button somewhere someone presses after every tragedy to let loose the grief-counsellors? Well, it may be an antique idea, but most people who have suffered the loss of a dear one or been ground down by some personal tragedy already know how to grieve. And they don't need therapy to get them to grieve. In fact, as a moment's reflection will confirm, you don't need therapy to grieve because grieving is the therapy. Human beings grieve to absorb the shock of loss, accommodate their anguish, and regain their equilibrium after genuine trauma. We remember; we mourn; some pray; and we return. The experience is intensely personal, deeply intimate, and, most of all, private. It takes place with varying intensity within families, among friends, and with community. Strangers, however well-wishing, are not wanted unless called for. The presumption that grief-counsellors are part of the rituals and privacies of mourning is both undignified and arrogant. How we seem to have reached the point when grief-counselling is automatic perplexes me. When people suffer personal loss and tragedy, they should be left alone to mourn with those they know and care for, and those who know them and care for them. If professionals are wanted, let each individual or family make the choice. I say it's time for closure – on grief-counselling.

– The National

The Blue Box of Paradise

When we speak of indulgences these days, most people think of extra-sweet desserts or shopping sprees. Personally, I think of chocolate cake as one of life's necessaries, just behind air and the works of Vladimir Nabokov, but this may not be the majority opinion. I do know it is an effective antidote against the impulse to jog or lift weights, which visits almost all of us in our weaker moments and, now that Stockwell Day is running those all-too-robust ads – splitting wood, running – threatens to become epidemic. "Chocolate cake – our friend" is my motto.

But I digress. Indulgences have a much worthier pedigree. In the far-off misty time when the Catholic Church was the empire of the world, her majestic sway was not a little assisted by the practice and policy of the sale of indulgences. This was a time when those within the embrace of the Church and her doctrines accepted unfailingly that a life lived in serious, or mortal, sin led to an afterlife burning in hell's steady flames. And that those who did not trespass mortally, but trespassed nonetheless, would be offered the sweetmeats of purgatory's tormenting fires. The stay in purgatory was no trifle; it could last for thousands of years.

That purgatory had an end – sometime – was what made it purgatory. But the ardent believer, who lived in venial sin, carried about a lively conviction that, when he or she went to Judgement, something more than summer camp was waiting on the other side.

The Church sought to remit the anxieties of the living, and to swell her own treasury, by the practice of selling indulgences. This policy could be looked on as the great-granddaddy of the frequent-flier programs and, indeed, had its own version of what are now known as élite and prestige categories. The kings and nobility could commit atrocities on the grand scale, then jump the queue to heaven by the purchase of the powerful indulgences to wipe out their misdeeds on earth. The poor and merely mischievous peasant would have to perform feats of pilgrimage and turn over a life's paltry savings just to clear the warden of purgatory.

Well, indulgences, at least in this advanced corrupt form, left the world, together with the other charms of medieval life, such as plague and superstition, and we are sadder for it.

Or have they? I have long looked at the practice and policy of recycling, and its great emblem, the blue box, as a revival under suitably modern auspices of the ancient religious get-out-of-jail-free card.

Environmentalism in all its grand enthusiasms is surely the great doctrine of our time. It has its shrines and holy places. What is the rain forest but Lourdes for supermodels and Sting? It has its bizarre rites and eerie rituals and holy words. "Ecology" has long since slipped its intellectual moorings and is now an all-purpose airpuff, signifying purity of purpose and advanced reverence for the earth. The word itself is more (organic) incense than meaning. What is Greenpeace but St. Paul with dinghies of high outboard capacity, and rechristened, tellingly, Zodiacs. People perch in high trees for months and years, much like the ancient eremites sat atop high and piercing rocks, both as signals of a faith that has passed to feverish rapture.

Ordinary mortals, of course, cannot wander with the energy of the zealots. But to be environmentally unfriendly is surely the mortal sin of our time.

What else is this great festival of discord over Toronto's garbage but a holy war? It is the believers versus the unbelievers, the elect versus the sinners. The "science" of the argument is a cloak for a more mystical encounter. An environmental-assessment procedure, for example, is best thought of not as a weighing of evidence but a purification ceremony.

What those who deeply oppose the Toronto plan are truly wrought up over is that Toronto is producing any garbage in the first place, not that it wants to move it out. Hence the calls for more recycling.

Some people have the folly or the simplicity to believe that recycling is about tin cans and bottles. But, of course, it is really a purely spiritual affair.

It is the plenary indulgence of our age. Outside a monster home – complete with SUVs in the driveway and evidence of conspicuous consumption all about – one lonely blue box, with its pop tins and Evian empties, is a sign of the sinner saved. Should there be a compost heap in the backyard, the occupants within will get two harps when they go to ecology heaven.

Buy, consume, possess. Ravish the earth to support all excess. Park but one blue box on the curb, and chant "ecology" twice a day in front of a favourite tree, and you have bought your way into paradise.

You are this day, my son, environmentally friendly.

– Globe and Mail

Is There an Expert in the House?

I forget where I heard that "an expert is someone you call when there are no adults in the room." There are experts, alas, on everything – from dieting to DNA – and I take a dim view of most of them. All the experts in the world didn't help the O.J. Simpson trial. In forensic quarrels, the expert's opinion seems to be seriously influenced by which side summons, and pays, the expert. Which suggests that it's the expert's reputation, not the truth, that is for hire.

Lifestyle experts are a contradiction in terms. Those with a life don't speak of lifestyle. *Oprah* seems infested with them, and they all seem alike – the soft shamans of New Age therapies. I live for the day when there's a crisis on *Oprah* and someone shouts: "Is there an aromatherapist in the house?"

Bookstores are littered with the bound gush of "relationship experts." John Gray, author of *Men Are from Mars, Women Are from Venus*, is the most famous astrologer of the human soul, his fatuities having racked up sales that probably overwhelm those of almost any author other than J.K. Rowling. Ms. Rowling's success is all the more impressive in this context; for all of Harry Potter's wizardry, the Potter oeuvre has more of real life than John Gray's planetary slush.

The downfall of the expert is nowhere more cruelly indexed and exposed, the currency of the word more devastatingly debased, than on – drum roll, please – *Entertainment Tonight*, the news show for people who cannot spell "news." It was on that show a few weeks back when everyone's favourite talking chipmunk, Mary Hart, announced that *ET* would be featuring Richard Hatch as the program's resident "expert" on *Survivor II*.

Mr. Hatch, most will recall, was the corporate trainer who outweaselled everyone else on *Survivor I* to win one million dollars and enter the fast-food pantheon of modern celebrity along with such worthies as Darva Conger, the mercenary bride of *Who Wants to Marry a Multimillionaire*, and Hugh Rodham, the *pardonista* brother-in-law of Bill Clinton.

I can accept Richard Hatch as an expert on . . . Richard Hatch, an accomplishment of limited appeal and even more limited utility. The mind, however, rips itself from its moorings and screams for the nearest exit at the thought that *Survivor I* or *II* (a) constitutes a subject that can support an expertise, or (b) that Richard Hatch, with his clothes on or off, represents a body of opinion that even *Entertainment Tonight*, the very flotsam of flotsam, would represent as expert.

I know there are people even now finishing doctoral dissertations on Archie comics and *Leave It to Beaver*, but these are monuments of substance and erudition compared with an "expertise" on *Survivor*. There are, forgive me while I impale myself on a pointed bra, "Madonna studies." And for all I know, there are universities busy setting up whole departments of Krameristics and Seinfeldology. I'm a *Drabble* consultant myself.

Time was when there were real experts. People who roped off an area of inquiry or interest of consequence and weight, and made themselves, by a splendid combination of industry, enthusiasm, and intelligence, masters of that subject. Some were, as we should say, professionals. The great scholars of the humanities or sciences fill this category. About some things, they knew all that was worth knowing, and then some. They are cruelly and ignorantly parodied in today's pop-culture blizzard, when Regis Philbin, the impresario of *Who Wants to Be a Millionaire*, quizzes some sullen greed-monkey on whether Tom Selleck or Tom Cruise is Rosie O'Donnell's public crush. Give me a lifeline, please.

The other experts – to my mind, the more attractive – were the great amateurs. One of them used to ornament these very pages. Eugene Forsey kept up a stream of letters to the *Globe and Mail* for years on points of English usage and parliamentary procedure, each one of which was a sparkler of wit and reasoning. He was inevitably described when he appeared as a speaker or panellist as a constitutional expert. What he didn't

know about the arcane and (to some of us) forbiddingly tedious constitutional history of this country or the nuance of House of Commons procedure, only an equally rare and passionate learner could tell.

I like to think we could apply to Mr. Forsey, somewhat kindly, what was
once written, rather mordantly, of the Master of Balliol College, Benjamin
Jowett:

> First come I, my name is Jowett
> There's no knowledge, but I know it,
> I am the Master of this college:
> What I don't know, isn't knowledge.

I can only hope that his kindly shade will forgive me housing him in a
column with Mary Hart and Richard Hatch – both gravel against his
marble. But then, Mr. Forsey was an adult even before he was an expert. I'm
sure he'd understand.

– Globe and Mail

IN MEMORIAM: SIX CANADIANS

John Munro Ross
(1928–1999)

Family physician, teacher, husband, father, grandfather, Order of Canada recipient, 1994.

To know, in a specific immediate sense, we are about to die has to be the greatest terror, the most eminent trial of our dignity and fortitude. For most of us, it would be unbearable.

I do not want to say that the capstone of the physician and friend John Ross's life was his manner of leaving it. But it was a marvel.

He knew he was dying, and wrote me to say so. He was diagnosed with colon cancer, determined – in consultation with a doctor he himself had trained – it was as well to forgo available treatments. That determined, he set about to make his goodbyes. Even, calm, courageous, and dignified. And with his closest, his family and his wife, Doreen, loving.

It was the stamp of purest character. Only a truly good man could have died with such steady ease and perfect courtesy, offering others the rest in peace so soon he knew to be offered him.

There's a wonderfully benign complicity in people's recollections of him. All circle around finally to his instinctive, unremitting kindness, a presence of decency that almost amounted to an emanation.

I am not stealing an opportunity to exert the raptures of hyperbole here. John Ross was good. And "good" is as large a word as our kind has ambition to register. It's difficult to avoid big words when writing about John Ross. And I do not mean long words or unusual ones. Decency, kindness, humanity: these are the biggest words we have. Sometimes, as in the life and practice of this man, the clean, core meaning of these fierce terms are given as rich a force and as full a rendering as they are permitted to have.

His sympathy was more than an inert and vague harmony with the sufferings and agitations of others. It was the principle of his life. A friend and colleague, Elizabeth Davis, R.S.M., caught it when she wrote that John Ross "walked a spiritual path with practical feet." He gave vigorous, consistent illustration to the consideration that medicine is a traffic between two human beings, and that respect for the sick is more sovereign than anything to be found in a black bag.

I would not injure his memory, or offend (even posthumously) his sense of humour, by portraying him as a shell of piety. In the 1960s, during his appointment with the cottage hospital in Placentia, Newfoundland, he was enough of a humorist not to see Joey Smallwood as perfect. He sometimes gave public voice to this insight, which startled partisans, and was rumoured to have puzzled and perturbed the Liberal emperor himself.

When he went from Placentia to the family practice at the Health Science Centre in St. John's, many people muttered he had been driven out as being perhaps a closet Tory (which in the Newfoundland of the time was simultaneously a term of art and a redundancy, maybe even a failure of mental hygiene). Now, in the higher moments of Smallwood's sway, it was not indictable to question him, but it was not prudent, either. John Ross was distinctly untroubled by either consideration.

Having a wide concept of neighbour might be the definition of a civilized human being. On that count, he was surely more civilized than most of us can wish to be. His neighbours could be the people of Placentia, Shea Heights in St. John's, or in the last glorious instalment of his career, young physicians in Uganda.

John Ross had two extracurricular passions that are fundamental to my recall of him. He loved music and poetry. Music and poetry may not make people better people. But it is surely a truth that the lovers of either or both are hoping always to be so. John Ross was a piece of poetry and music himself.

– Globe and Mail

Mordecai Richler
(1931–2001)

Mordecai Richler was here. He had quite a span in fiction and quite some marvellous creations, from Duddy Kravitz to Jacob Two-Two and Barney Panofsky, but to my mind the most emphatic and compelling character on or off the page was Mordecai Richler himself.

He was so there, I think he had his own climate zone. He had a temperament, and this is a lot to say, at least as large as his talent. There was a whole lot that went to make up that scrutinizing, mordant, mischievous, playful, earnest presence. He was not hospitable to folly in any of its demented guises. He had a bristling acute intelligence that called every garden implement a spade just in case, whether the current mania of pseudo-sensitivity, victim worship, and cocktail-party censoriousness that goes under the name of political correctness, or the artful contortions and blazing contradiction of the more eager Quebec separatists, or the prim, tight-lipped, ethereal self-regard of grant-hungry writers. If there was a balloon inflated by pretense or hypocrisy, it were best not to launch it if Air Commander Richler's scourge of prudes, politicos, and propagandists had been granted flight clearance.

He was an adult Canadian. I doubt very much he bowed his head at the mention of maple syrup or grew syrupy every time he saw a Canadian flag. In the presence of things that matter, however, excellence of earned achievement in any of the pastimes or pursuits that betoken this nation – from high-wire prose to the parlour ballet of snooker – he was as prideful as the most misty-eyed patriot waving Sheila Copps handouts on Canada Day.

He admired that other austere undemonstrative master with whom – and it honours them both – he deserves to be bracketed, Pierre Elliott Trudeau.

Both were men of deep sentiment who loathed its charlatan cousin, sentimentality. I think he believed in what he did with the same unshowing
intensity as Trudeau, in his different case, believed in what he did.

Mordecai Richler believed, of course, in words. This is a difficult faith
to maintain. It can only be maintained with great scruple, discipline,
exactness, and passion. These are all of them virtues of character and
mind. And for all the projected dishevelments of Mordecai Richler – the
rumpled get-up, the loitering cigarillo, the lingering Scotch – nothing was
allowed to interfere with that which counted. He believed in writing as an
art, that art exists for its excellence, and that from that excellence, rather
than from some pre-attached agenda, it did its good work for men and
women everywhere.

He expanded the frontier of Canadian presence in the world. As a com-
mentator and essayist, he was among the most fluent, engaging, trenchant,
and humorous that there is anywhere. *O Canada, O Québec* is great political analysis and observation; it is more importantly a great satirical romp.
The novels have weight, character, feeling, and craft. They are the pedestal
on which all else that he did was supported. Both the novels and his other
writings hinged on his truly remarkable and unflinching ability, so rare at
any time, to see things as they are and to say them with force and precision.

I would not move to end this little farewell without remarking on one
other outstanding virtue of the man which some will find at odds with the
script that has been written so often of him. He was among the most cour-
teous and civil of human beings. And behaved with such delicacy and
chivalry towards those within the circle of his affection, close friends,
family, Florence, his beloved wife, as to serve as a model for the very
conduct of affection and friendship.

How are we going to remember him? Novelist won't do. There's nothing
wrong with writing novels. At its worst, and I'm sure Mordecai Richler
would agree, it's a victimless crime. But novelist can't contain him. He was
a generous man, generously gifted, who by his presence and his craft gave
more pulse and heart to the days we lived with him. He broadened Canada.
He expanded its legacy and he was more fun to have around than should be

legal. Mordecai Richler was here indeed. He gave the art of being Canadian the bite and savour it so sorely needed. Mordecai, the warrior.

We are sad to hear he's gone and, on this cruel day, we wish his family well.

– The National

W.O. Mitchell
(1914–1998)

The practice of W.O. Mitchell offers a most interesting variation on one of Shakespeare's most compact observations. As Shakespeare had it the "imagination of a poet" gave to "airy nothings . . . a local habitation and a name." In my judgement W.O. Mitchell worked that famous transaction in reverse.

He gave to "local habitations and names" a residence in the minds and imaginations of thousands. It was the province of his distinct genius to take the local and the particular, something immensely familiar to him – a boy, the prairies, a family – and to fashion that material so that it awakened recognition across the entire wide territory of human response from Alberta to Zanzibar.

This is not easy stuff to do, to set out characters, and a setting, and an account of how things were, and have it settle so naturally, so fittingly, into the experience of so many others, some of whom are vastly removed from the particularities of what is being told.

Who Has Seen the Wind. That string of words now fits so inevitably and easily into the mind, with its Biblical overtones, prairie evocation, and mix of bitter and sweet nostalgia, that it's as if it were one of those pieces of phrasecraft or melody that sweep into us from the air. It is startlingly right.

That is one other thing about W.O. Mitchell and his masterwork. This quality of being so startlingly, so beautifully – for *Who Has Seen The Wind* is a beautiful work – right.

There is in the very best writing – I am speaking here of extended prose, short story or novel – a signal from the very beginning that everything is in tune, that everything is working in perfect cooperation, which radiates the entire work from the first letter to the very last. There is almost behind the words a presence of integrity and fitness, a tracing of the sureness of touch of the writers' perfected instinct.

Who Has Seen the Wind is aglow with that instinct, with the enchanted harmony of a story perfectly told. It sings the melody of language, when language, as it so rarely does, reaches perfect design and execution.

It truly is amazing what Mitchell's so extended and fertile career managed to accomplish so early.

Now, Mitchell was a writer – everyone will give him that – but he was more. He – I was going to say worked, but I'll change that – he lived in a variety of public guises, extra-authorial incarnations let us call them: lecturer, performer, stage raconteur, friend of a legion of fledgling writers, and not least broadcast familiar, that, even outside his writing, he made himself a presence in the life and minds of Canadians. I do not know if there is such a thing in Nature as a one-man ambience, but W.O. Mitchell unarguably was a felt and vital constituent in the distinctly Canadian way of seeing things.

Which is really what all the very best writers ever do: they do not teach us, so much as guide us to ways of seeing *and* feeling. And the absolute best, the handful of consummate artists, not only expand the repertoire of *our* seeing and feeling, they also add to – these words are Johnson's – the public stock of harmless pleasures.

W.O. Mitchell: he multiplied our delights; he gave comfort and strength to the Canadian imagination; he lent his full playful authority to the trade and craft of writer-storyteller. The life and example of W.O. Mitchell are a sweet Canadian greatness.

– *Cross Country Checkup*

Pythons, Misfits, and Canadians – Gzowski Talked to Us All

T he most vivid encounter I had with Peter Gzowski was not on radio. It was during his purgatory with *90 Minutes Live*, the attempt – perhaps before its time, certainly before Peter was really fit for it – to build a late-night TV talk show in Canada.

The guests that night included (a) a klatch from *Monty Python's Flying Circus*, who came on in women's clothes, and one of whom was in that state of advanced ossification best known as ape drunk; (b) a professional impersonator of the Queen, who, in contradistinction to the real Queen, acted imperiously when in role or out. I remember her ordering a taxi when the ordeal was over, with the tone of voice that suggested execution for the publicist should a taxi not appear – soon. She was not so much an impersonation as someone possessed; (c) the Duke of Ook (I am not making this up), a "pianist" – the scare quotes are emphatically necessary – who strode to a studio piano, hit a few discords, and then jumped up and down in the manner of an ape, while furiously scratching his armpits; and (d) me.

This tea party took place in St. John's, which explains my presence in the conclave of horror and madness. It was a novel experience for me, being the only person that could even pretend to normalcy. My anxieties of having to navigate this witches' brew of live television were trivial compared to Peter's. After all, he was the host. He had to endure them all, for ninety minutes, in front of a studio audience and while being beamed to a fascinated – I suspect mesmerized and maybe even fearful – Canadian public.

This was not an occasion that geniality could save. It may seem now just a trifle ungracious to offer the anecdote when the themes of Peter's life and work are being, as they should be, rehearsed with gratitude and fondness by so many people whom he genuinely touched, and by whom he was much admired.

Well, he did endure. What is more, insofar as such a congeries of misfits and neurotics – myself included – could be held at bay, he did it. It was a moment not of great polish but of admirable valour. It reminded me that Peter, besides the other virtues for which he is now being celebrated, had a performer's fortitude.

His real presence, of course, was through and on CBC Radio. Radio was his element. The tone and fact of public broadcasting received its key signature from this one performer over the life of his career at the CBC. He was a friendly champion – if this adjective doesn't quite nullify that noun – of a certain idea of Canadianism. His career and inclination led him to the study of this country as a country.

It will be remembered that his first major program was called *This Country in the Morning*. His taste and evangelism on behalf of Canadian letters was always part of a fuller campaign to find the best and most distinctive of Canada, and to give it notice and celebration.

He had an in-studio presence that was formidable, a beguiling quality – both of voice and manner – that hid a deep earnestness with the job at hand. He worked to prepare, he had goals when he set out to talk to someone, and he was professional in the way we say musicians or actors are professional – they labour to acquire skills that they equally labour to conceal.

His connection with what may be fairly called the CBC constituency was deep and intense. It is remarkable what his three-hour stints each morning achieved over time. The subjects he chose, the emphases he gave to certain ideas and people, constituted a soft agenda for a type of Canadian pride.

I think this was all to the good. We Canadians are too loose in our apprehension of this country. We too infrequently take the inventory of what we are, who we are, and why we matter. Peter Gzowski was a goad to Canadians' complacency about their country, and a genuine, necessary, and intelligent booster of this country's virtues.

Add to that, he was a zealous friend to Canadian letters, and to the men and women – academics, novelists, essayists, and publishers – who hold

Canadian letters in their care. He had that fundamental insight that the arts, broadly understood, are the nurture of a citizenry, and he as a national host (in his case, that term has a double ring) was there to introduce, diffuse, and praise the arts of the country to the country.

This is – was – a large consignment for any career. When I saw him last, just some months ago, he was still at it, in his capacity as chancellor of Trent University. This was a large, skilful, serious man, an example to anyone in the broadcast profession and a very jewel to those who care about Canada.

We shall miss him.

– Globe and Mail

Glenn Gould
(1932–1982)

*T*he *Silence of the Lambs*, the movie that introduced the world to the cannibal serial killer Hannibal Lecter, had one quiet un-grisly moment. It's when Lecter is sitting in that suspended cage of his just before he does an escape. He's listening to classical music, and it's J.S. Bach and it's the *Goldberg Variations*. That's Glenn Gould's playing and that was Glenn Gould's doing.

Gould made the *Goldberg Variations* his signature piece. He recorded it at the beginning of his career and at the very end. And such was Gould's way with the music of Bach that he propelled this austere, intellectual, but always beautiful music into popular consciousness. Even Hannibal and Hollywood caught it.

September 25, 2002, marked the seventieth anniversary of Glenn Gould's birth, hallelujah – and October 4 the anniversary of his death, alas. But as I hope this little anecdote about Hannibal indicates, he may be gone, but it was great that he was here and he's surely not forgotten.

Glenn Gould is one of this country's utterly unfailing icons. He is the most singular celebrity this country has produced in modern times. He was an eccentric, a loner, an individualist. He achieved celebrity – not that he sought it as such – the hard way. He had a remarkable early fame and decided to shun the vehicle that bestows fame, giving up the concert stage and the public spotlight for the soundproof walls of a recording studio. His musical vision was also, in many cases, at odds with his peers in the classical world.

But he rewired the world's consciousness of the music of Bach. Bach was his bible, but no one before him and no one after played Bach in that very particular, always masterful, passionate, and fervent way that Glenn Gould played Bach. He was very near a total recluse in an age of publicity agents, star turns, and endless hype, but his deep devotion to the great glory of playing a piano as well and as profoundly as a piano can be played earned him an eminence to rival that of the most gaudy, fame-addled superstar.

The one feature of his playing familiar to everyone who has heard of Glenn Gould recordings is a combination that shows up on most of them – the sound of his creaky chair and the further sound of Glenn Gould humming along to his own playing. You are never alone in a room when listening to Glenn Gould. Gould has weathered very well since he left us. I think, if I may be a little irreverent, he's actually grown on us since then.

Outside the CBC Broadcast Centre in Toronto is a wonderful sculpture of Gould in his perpetual overcoat and hat, on a park bench. The statue is very good. It's lifelike. It has, though, what Gould in his life did not have: a very beckoning sociable quality. When tourists or Torontonians walk by, it's not at all uncommon for them to stop, walk to the bench, and sit down with Glenn, or more hastily, pat him on the shoulder as they're going by. It's all marvellously familiar and friendly – my buddy, Glenn Gould.

I think it's a wonderful thing that a performer in the relatively inaccessible world of classical music did what he did so well and so individually that people still feel his presence twenty years later, still feel his presence and even something of a kind of kinship or bond with him. All the heroes that this country has produced don't lace on skates. What Gould did for the piano, for his beloved Bach, and for the idea of rigorous excellence in the pursuit of sheer beauty makes him one of our most remarkable and most distinctive Canadians.

It is, as I've said, twenty years since he left us. Three cheers for Glenn Gould.

– The National

Pierre Trudeau: He Has Gone to His Grace, and That Leaves So Much Less of Ours

The sad vigil the country went on a few weeks ago this afternoon reached its inevitable conclusion. The largest, liveliest, smartest, fiercest, and most graceful public figure that Canada has had in modern times, and probably ever, has made an end.

He walked outside the boundaries of expectation in almost everything he did. He was intense, private, and reserved, and gave himself to the one profession, the one vocation, that most depends on exhibition, attention, and continuous display.

He was radiantly intelligent, a full intellectual, powered with Jesuitical resources of argument and reason, yet – on so many occasions – was the most visceral and passionate of our public figures.

He hailed from the province that, with reason, nursed doubts about its place in Confederation, was burdened by fears of its future and destiny. Yet he of all Quebecers was the one most powered by the certitude, by the absolute confidence, that Quebecers were larger by being Canadians, and that a lack of confidence was more a failure of nerve than a matter of politics.

He bore a symbolic relationship with his time. This angular, complex, multifaceted personality seemed to say things to this country outside the words of his speeches or his policies. There was some element within him, or of him, that acted like a summons to the Canadian imagination: to live a little larger, think a little more carefully, or bring more courage or daring to our dreams.

Pre-eminently, his life and his public career revolved around the idea of Canada. In any turn of crisis or act of state, from the storm of the FLQ to the patriation of the Constitution, Pierre Trudeau acted from a conception of the whole country, and a determination to give body to this country's often vague and drifting sense of itself.

He paid the country the deepest tribute a real politician can: he believed in it with his brain and his heart, and gave the wit of the one, and the heat of the other, to enlarging and enlivening its possibilities and our citizenship.

He was no neuter. It is one of the grandest things we will say of his memory that, at times, he antagonized as much as he inspired; our affection for Pierre Trudeau was turbulent and always interesting. If citizens of this day lament that leadership is a game of polls and cozy focus groups, there will always be the example of this man to remind us that convictions can be set in bedrock, and that adherence to principles is the most enduring charisma.

Canadians first admired Pierre Trudeau, halted before his presence in a kind of happy awe. Over time, as we learned him – and if it is not presumptuous, he learned us – the admiration melted into, I think, a dignified affection.

He left politics larger than he found it. He added to the dignity of public life and did not subtract from it. His life and career spoke to everyone of the sheer power of excellence as an ideal. In this wide, mixed, and imposing country, for the time he was with us Canadians knew they had one touch of grandeur outside the landscape.

Passion, intellect, honour and courage were his hallmarks. He was, in public life, the best that we had. It was an honour and a joy that he was around, and a real grief that today so much, so very much, of what is best about us, has made farewell.

He has gone to his grace, and that leaves so much less of ours.

– The National

THE POLITICS OF LANGUAGE

That's "Fisherman" to You, Son

NEWS ITEM: East Coast Fish Crisis Called Off. Reporterpersons Get Job Description Wrong: Lobsterman Has Identity Crisis, Says, "I Didn't Know All This Time I Was a 'Fisher,'" Weeps at Town Meeting.

"I've been a Fisher all my life."

About the only person who can make that statement without cringing, and with some fidelity to things as they really are, is someone like Eddie, the sometime tagalong of Elizabeth Taylor, back in those spare days when Liz was marrying people, and staying married to them, for what seemed like months at a time.

Fisher is a perfectly good surname, and I'm sure poor Eddie was very proud of it. Nonetheless, I don't think Eddie, even with the surname, ever pretended he was a lobsterman.

It's not a sentence – *I've been a fisher all my life* – you will hear very often on the East Coast. I've wandered the outharbours and inlets of Newfoundland many a wide year, loitered on wharves and traipsed through fish plants, and never heard it escape the voluble lips of a single bayman. Not from the men in their boats, not from the men on the shore, not from their wives, not from their offspring.

I suppose it is possible they whispered it a lot when I was out of earshot. But I don't really think so. Fishermen are sly, not shy.

I haven't heard it, because the noun it carries – this prissy "fisher" – is not one they're familiar with or inclined to favour.

But lately I cannot turn on the television or pick up a newspaper without the word clanging its nerve-grinding way through editorial and on-the-spot report. The crowd I work with, the CBC reporters, can't seem to get enough of it.

The ugly week in Burnt Church, New Brunswick, has been remarkable for some real news. It's also been remarkable for what appears to be a conspiracy on the part of the entire news media to rename the people they are reporting on.

Fishers? Have the reporters asked permission of the fishermen for this re-baptism? Isn't there enough already to unravel on the East Coast, with the strife and stress between aboriginals and local fishermen, without going into a fit of yuppie word-washing and lexical cleansing?

One would have thought so. But report after report, editorial after editorial, TV stand-up after TV stand-up has been a constant drizzle of "local fishers," or "non-aboriginal fishers." (This last clumsy clutter is surely a long way around *something*, God alone knows what. *"What do you do, my son?" "I, sir, like my father before me, am a non-aboriginal fisher."*)

Now, I have no doubt that in the emancipated corridors of the federal bureaucracy and on certain university campuses, such lingo – precious, creepy, and condescending as it is – is coin of the demented realm. Not calling things what they are called is a specialty of the bureaucracy and the academy alike. Obfuscation, false delicacy, and cowardice in the face of feminist stylistics hangs in the air like fog over the Grand Banks. The fog, at least, belongs.

But reporters and editorial writers are not freestyle sociologists sponge-bathing in the murk of political correctness. And they surely know that the sensibility of the people they are reporting on is at least as important as the putative sensibilities of some smidgen of people they are reporting to.

Is it the fear that some urban assignment editor is going to have a fit if they say "fisherman"? It should be noted, and it is worth noting, that Quebec is not the only place where they have language police.

The dread of using nouns that are not gender-neutral (a term that in itself manages to be ugly, hollow and Orwellian all at the same time) rattles reporters who have brazenly walked through war zones and urban riots. Courage is a very mixed phenomenon.

It will be noted that everyone has given up on "fisherpersons." That was tried for a while, but the "persons" bit at the end made it too obviously concessionary, too obviously a flag calling attention to the genuflection to fad and preciosity. "Fishers" is more gutless. It's politically correct without having to at least announce itself politically correct. It's sly political correctness.

Let's make a deal. Within the precincts of the broadcast buildings and editorial houses, let's keep on with camerapersons and soundpeople, copypersons and newspeople. But when you go out "where the fishermen gather," call those people what they call themselves. Fishers? Stop it. You don't believe it yourselves. It's hypocrisy and condescension.

– Ottawa Citizen

What Fools These Moralists Be

I can't count – and I am a great counter – the number of times that, after reading *Macbeth*, I went out looking for a Scotsman to spit at. Dirty Scotsmen. One of them killed that sweet Duncan. And, of course, the wretched Shakespeare gives the villain, and his harpy wife (now there's a piece of goods – are all Scottish wives harpies?), the best lines.

I do so hope the Scottish Anti-Defamation League (warning: ethnic stereotype ahead!) gets the wind up its kilts and rousts every production of *Macbeth* from here to Albania.

Maybe, too, it could follow the example of that worthy bunch – this is a mouthful, so be patient – the Council on American-Islamic Relations, Canadian division (CAIR-Cd), and distribute a one-page pamphlet on Scotsmen to those empty heads who still traipse to see this travesty of the most surly, penny-pinching race of mumblers on the face of the earth.

The CAIR-Cd is planning a little pamphlet on Islam for the unenlightened attending *The Merchant of Venice*, because it doesn't like the way the Moroccan Prince in that play has been cavorting.

I gather from an article in Thursday's *Globe and Mail* that this most minor of minor characters has been prostrating himself rather too promiscuously for CAIR-Cd's taste. I'll assume the information handout will have an appendix on the Salman Rushdie fatwa, and the inaesthetics of authoricide.

CAIR-Cd protested. And the pliant diplomats at Stratford (Stratford used to be known as a theatrical venue, but it has branched out into international relations and conflict resolution), where *The Merchant of Venice* is playing, agreed that CAIR-Cd may hand out literature prior to the audience's being mauled by Shakespeare's.

Will the pamphlet, I wonder, be in iambic pentameter?

Will it be read by someone wearing bells and a strange curly cap and playing a lute?

Shakespeare was very fond of clowns, and it strikes me that something as ludicrous as what is essentially a sensitivity-training seminar being loosed on the theatrical public ought at the very least be conducted in shreds of motley.

When they run *Hamlet*, I plan to picket and distribute anti-suicide tracts. And maybe an ad or two for an assertiveness-training course – "gloomy Danes, half-price."

Shakespeare was such an ignorant, insensitive putz. *The Tempest*, a slander on the First World. *Lear*, a house of woman hatred. *Othello*, a bad dream in pre-civil-rights Georgia. *Timon*, a cauldron of roiling, indiscriminate hate. *Titus Andronicus*, Ted Bundy's favourite bedtime story. The history plays, saunas of chauvinism, warmongering, and hatred of the French.

Shakespeare, now that I list it off – I think we should ban the bastard. He subsumes, in one way or another, every unfashionable bigotry, stereotype, insult, and mischief that this delicate, prissy, stainless, Rwandan, Pol Potian, Bosnian, Northern Irish, Middle Eastern age abhors.

Indict the Elizabethan fiend. There must be a tribunal somewhere with a hole in its docket. Maybe the one that so far seems to have missed Idi Amin.

Exhume the rancid cretin scribbler. Flay his mangy bones. Ban his portrait from the *Globe*. Save the children. Charge the chauvinist, misogynist, racist, imperialist creep with laying land mines of cultural insensitivity for four centuries.

Shakespeare the polluter. Shakespeare the child-abusing monster ("I would have plucked my nipple from his boneless gums, and dash'd the brains out"). Shakespeare the running dog of imperialism. Sexist, white, English, and dead. The one-man chilly climate of Western civilization.

Close him down, I say. Pulp every line and verse. Expurgate him into oblivion. Smash every witticism, and strangle every precious simile. Throw Juliet off that balcony. Stuff Lear with Prozac. Put Hamlet in therapy. Make

Shakespeare conform to every sensibility randy to take offence, every cultural study seminar, and every yuppie human-rights commission. "All germens spill at once," indeed. Blot the odious bugger until he vanishes.

We in this sweet moral age cannot have the stench of these timeless creations come "betwixt the wind and [our] nobility."

This is the golden age of nitpickery. We have arrived at that pinnacle of cultural supremacy where the past merely exists as an open-pit mine, wherein we dig to find examples of our superiority, in contrast with the rampant depravities of those moral midgets who trailed the careless earth before us. O brave new world!

The plays of William Shakespeare are on this understanding the library of his cultural impoverishment, his grotesque insensitivity, his moral puniness – compared to us and our guardian committees.

This is the very delirium tremens of political correctness.

When or how we reached the point where the greatest expressive genius of the human race has to be filtered through the infinitely more narrow and arid sensibility of the grievance-mongers; where poetry has to genuflect – maybe even fall prostrate – to the squawking missionaries of race, class, and gender, the Holy Trinity of PC, I cannot tell.

But if Shakespeare offends your religion, well, Shakespeare *is* my religion. And he's a wider and more welcoming creed than are dreamt of in all our trendy philosophies.

Considering that we live in an age where taking offence has become an art form for some and a way of living for others, let me say that I have taken offence at your taking offence. I will picket your pickets, protest against your protests, see your cry of marginalization, and raise you a voice appropriation.

But not on holy ground. Get out of my church. Your leaflets are offending my god.

Write your own plays. Leave mine alone.

– Globe and Mail

Is There a Gender Doctor in the House?

The gender pontiffs have got their linguistic knickers in a twist over our beloved national anthem.

They're right to be worried. War, pestilence, or famine are as nothing when it comes to "language exclusion." The distress is mighty, and so it should be. Language bias is one of the most corrosive phenomena of our times. I never pass a manhole cover (personal-cavity disc) without a shudder. Why the lid on a steel chute to the sewer line deserves the male prefix I'll never know.

Therapeutic feminists have applied their healing arts to many outrageous and grotesquely insensitive texts, including the Bible and the familiar Lord's Prayer, and a wonderful business it has been. A conference in Texas, in 1999, put the revisionist scalpels to the "Our Father" and came up with a new take on the beginning of that prayer that is as close to lyric poetry, outside of Coleridge in an opium stupor, as we're likely to see: "Our Mother, who art within us, many are your names."

It's a bit loose, I grant you. Father is now Mother, he/she is no longer in Heaven but in us (which is not quite the same place), and, instead of the name being "hallowed" as in the patriarchal chestnut, we have a lisping Judy Collins kind of mushiness – "many are your names."

But, with a few candles, a smoking censer, and an atonal guitar hiccupping in the background, it'll do. Get John Tesh to oblige with the reading, and I think you've got a new church.

The problem with "O Canada," as every Canadian knows, is that it's riddled with sexism, one thick ungraceful stew of testosterone set to music.

No wonder they love it at hockey games. It must intimidate the Swedes. It's clearly time we got off the debate over health care, the sorry state of our armed forces, Quebec, the farm crisis, people living on the streets, prairie drought and eastern fog, and turned to what really agitates the Canadian citizenry: gender bias in the national singalong.

The offending phrase, which may turn out to be the root cause of anorexia, hives, and a multitude of other anxiety disorders (the wounded psyche is a spawning house of ills and mutilated self-esteem, a spiral of toxicity), is "in all thy sons command."

It has been spotted as committing a horror against "inclusiveness," and very likely transgressing against "diversity" as well. And to offend against either of these defining pieties – why, it were better a man (or a woman) tie a millstone around his (her) neck and throw himself (herself or themselves) into the sea.

The word "sons" is the problem, sons being, by definition, obnoxiously male. And even though sons have always owned to having mothers, and honouring a son always a proxy endeavour for honouring the mother, to the laser-eyed lynxes of gender stereotype, it's male, and it stops there. And they see sons, being male, as excluding all females.

This is, alas, only a part of the problem. Sons are not only not daughters, so to speak; they are also not mothers, not dads, not cousins, not aunts, not even the next-door neighbour. My point is that the noun "sons" excludes even more than just females. It excludes every other sibling relation, clan membership, casual acquaintance, and even passerby. "O Canada" is almost, by this reading, a virtual encyclopedia of exclusion.

So avant-garde language feminists shouldn't feel they're alone in their trauma. Think of the poor soul who comes into the Canadian world as a test-tube baby. Wait till he, she, or whatever wakes into full consciousness and finds there's no reference to the lab beaker in the anthem. Send in the clones. Canada's anthem is a minefield for thousands yet unhatched.

This is all pretty amazing. Here we were waltzing through the first years of the twenty-first century thinking that the dragons of separatism were the only threat to the permanent harmony of one of the most favoured nations of the earth. And there, lurking in the aural wallpaper of a jingle that most people know only for the opening line, is, as it were, the red worm, the semantic virus, waiting to dissolve our fealty to the country and render us unable to pass a maple leaf without somehow feeling left out, abandoned, and alone. Not even the beer commercials will save us now.

Is it too late? Can something be done? I doubt it. Good lyricists are hard to come by. I see Neil Diamond is making something of a comeback. The author of "I Am, I Said" might be able to blend together something of an inclusionary fricassee to meet the crisis. Or that jumble that put together "We Are the World" for Ethiopian famine relief might give us an anthem, which, even if terminally banal ("we are the children"), has the right low-frequency fuzziness and cosmic vacuousness that the grievance doctors find so sedative.

A song for the ages. One that includes so many, under every conceivable category, that it includes no one. That's what Canada needs. An anthem written by a committee.

I think we've just saved the country.

– Globe and Mail

Death Is Too Good for the Word Weasels

E very action produces an equal and opposite reaction. Britney Spears – Christina Aguilera. Dirty Old Bastard – Eminem. It's that simple. The axiom belongs to classical mechanics, by which I do not mean garage men with a taste for Vivaldi.

After the action, there is the reaction. It follows, so Polonius remarked in a different context, "as the night, the day." A person is active – one who takes initiative, is animated and dynamic; or a person is reactive – one who abides the initiatives of others, who stirs, so to speak, only when shaken.

Lately many of us are being urged by the jingoists of pseudo-therapy, job counsellors, personnel departments, and Oprah in all her phases, to be proactive. This does not mean, as one would suspect from the term, to be in favour of – pro – the active. It evidently does mean . . . just what does it mean?

Is it an inversion of classical mechanics, an invitation to take action, in response to an action, before that action has taken place? That, of course, would be the height of foolishness, not to mention impossible. It really would not do to cart the accident victim off to the hospital to have his wounds repaired before the sad wretch has actually passed through the speculative windshield.

Proactive is, rather, just a piece of sad, trendy verbal junk. If an employer, or friend, or counsellor wishes to recommend that a person take a stance of alertness towards the future, attempt to anticipate the curves of life, then they should say so.

There is no need to defile the laws of physics, the logic of semantics, or the grace of our mother tongue, and harangue the poor sod on the merits of being proactive. Proactive is verbal weaselry.

Officiousness, when it can cohabit with that tacky slut self-righteousness, is chillingly fertile. "We are pleased to offer you a non-smoking environment." If we account verbal clutter as a pollutant, then this tacky string of nonsense and unction is its own offence. There are three lies buried in the marshland of its officious euphemism: (a) the "we" in this noisome figuration are not "offering" anything; they are directly threatening fines, ostracism, and possible criminal sanction to anyone who lights up; (b) being "pleased" to offer whatever it is they are offering is what the wonderful H.W. Fowler would have called a "noxious genteelism," an effete avoidance of more direct, and honest, language. They are not merely pleased that those who wish to smoke cannot, under penalty of bylaw, smoke. They are insufferably delighted. Any honest airport or corporate building should break out into one of Lizst's Hungarian Rhapsodies preceding any non-smoking public announcement, which would be proactive; (c) what is a non-smoking environment? Environments – unless they are forests on fire – are not normally smoking to begin with. Is the St. John's airport, for example, expected to be on fire when passengers arrive, or is it normally on fire, to justify an announcement that calls attention to its non-smoking character this time?

The announcement does not mean that they are offering a non-smoking environment. In fact, come to think of it, an airport is actually not an environment at all. Airports are anti-environments, stations of limbo between the hell of the freeway that brings you there, and the purgatory of the sealed cigar case by which you leave. What the dried static of the overhead speaker is saying is that *you* had better be a non-smoking environment.

Someday, someone will do a study on the damage hygiene has done to grammar, or, if I may so put it, how hygiene has impacted (on) grammar.

There was a lonely time, long ago, when meteors came streaming out of the sky and made a big impact. I am your true antique, for I can recall when impact was not a verb. Nowadays, something is always impacting something else, and emphatically I am not talking of operations in the dentist's office.

Impact, the verb, is merely a pseudo-technical dress-up, a feeble attempt to make the obvious seem refined, or remote, or special. It is more weaselry.

"Bribing the purchasing officer will greatly impact our sales."

The world is littered with specious, useless, and annoying cant words and cant phrases. The most recent *Law & Order* episode embroidered the stale TV screen with a logo announcing that next week there would be an "all-new *Law & Order*." As opposed to those partially new episodes, which get so tedious after the fresh bits are finished: "This week the *Law* portion of our program is new; the *Order* you've already seen."

We will never fix this sad business. Only in a proactive (preferably non-smoking) environment can we be pleased to offer an all-new lexical pride and sensitivity and be impacted accordingly. It is a consummation devoutly to be wished.

– Globe and Mail

TO READ OR NOT TO READ

The Author Eater

You walk into any of the monster bookstore chains and you will find it. Head for the pyramid of Self-Help and Psychobabble, usually within the sightline of another pyramid of Diet Fads and Low-Fat scripture, and you will find a smaller, but more hallowed, hill. This is the Oprah pile.

"Oprah's Book Club®," says the poster on top. It's an unostentatious little sign, something like the little flag that successful mountaineers bring along with them to pin on the crest of Everest. When you've made it to the top of the world's most celebrated peak, you really don't need a garish banner.

Same thing with writers for Mount Oprah. Just to be one of that celebrated heap, to have been, along with your book, selected and elevated (there are no Sherpas on this climb; in fact, there's no climbing either – the goddess speaks, and you are there) is both the deed and the deed's advertisement. You've just won Talk TV's Nobel Prize. Your book and you are now part of the most successful franchise in all the history of print. You will be rich. You will be transformed. If you have a brow, prepare to have it middled. Once you were an artist; now you are a commodity. Once an author; now all Oprah-resistance is futile.

There are people who think Oprah's Book Club® is a good thing. These are people who think that books are a kind of spiritual oatmeal, a kind of low-fat diet for the soul, and for them Oprah's Book Club® is therefore a special-order meatless buffet for the soul.

There, you wander into a book wide-eyed with soft wonder over the power of "literature" to fulfil an empty spirit, teary with the approach of rapture promised by a "sensitive" author, overcome with finding your "story" in the writer's story, your life caught in that life, all the lessons you need set down neat as a laundry list, validation just around the corner, and empowerment swooping down like a Disney eagle to carry you off to some soft-focus Paradise Island where Wally Lamb and Maya Angelou strum ukuleles strung with their own slack prose, and Deepak Chopra is walking back and forth on the beach mumbling something about something else, followed by a clutch of smiling – always smiling – PBS ladies asking him to beg for them, and there are whole relay teams of strangers waiting to hug you, just because you are you. And look! Over there on the sandspit – isn't that Tony Robbins (teeth, power tapes) empowering the Buns of Steel queen (more teeth, more power tapes), and surely that is the author of *Seven Habits of Highly Successful People* (less teeth, more tapes) having a "meaningful dialogue" with the author of *Chicken Soup for the Soul* (can't see the teeth), and Robert Bly (beard, he may not have teeth) chanting verses that will someday be printed on a lucky subway men's room. Towards evening, Sister Wendy will be along to comment on the pastels in the sunset.

Not all the characters in my little fantasy are Oprah people. Wally Lamb, of course, is. And Deepak Chopra is an Oprah enlistee. Deepak is a low-hum, New Age spiritualist as far as I can tell from the few chunks of him I've seen on the beg-a-thons. He's perfect Oprah guest fodder in that he looks intellectual but is actually more the empathetic type. Maya Angelou and Toni Morrison have their own islands, but occasionally Oprah is willing to give them an upgrade to hers.

But they are all in the same business: the dreadful celebrity-amped, do-it-yourself home pseudo-therapy and self-sculpturing mania/industry of which Oprah is the TV universe's supernova. Books, as we know books, as the world used to know books, are not part of that soft-focus pan-pipe carnival at all. That is, books as literature, books as houses of art and difficulty, books as the registers of poetry and the wonder of language, books about some other self, any other self, than your self.

The books that make it into the high dominion of an Oprah benediction make it insofar as they conform to the other imperatives of the empire. Oprah's Book Club® is a mirror for the narcissists of self-help, healing, empowerment, and TV-studio redemption; they are all part of the passion-less passion play of yuppie image enhancement. It is no surprise that diet and exercise gurus are installed along with the mind stretchers, for the business really is the same. There's a shortcut to every plastic heaven, and *The Oprah Winfrey Show* is a one-stop convenience store for them all.

It's not a book club at all. It's one of many parishes of Oprahdom, where the myrmidons of the talk goddess unite to take monthly instalments of sacred writing. Normally, most gurus have to write their own material. That dreadful cluster of smarminess and unction, John Gray, for example, has had to bend his sheeny brow and rent a laptop to produce *Men Are from Mars, Women Are from Venus*. But this pseudo-sociological relationship slushbucket is at least John Gray's own pseudo-sociological relationship slushbucket. When Suzanne Somers, who used to sell bent and springy pipe for a living (and, let me add, gave dictionaries a whole new word – "ThighMaster" – for "chrome and padding that is squeezed between the legs of sitcom blondes"), decided to become a carbohydrate consultant, she had to write her own inanities.

Oprah is the only guru who doesn't have to start with a blank page. In the superhyped Oprah world, she's the guru who swallows the writings of all others. Her books are not books by other people; once they have been picked, they become hers. Oprah is the site. These books are just emana-tions from the oracle that has chosen them. In this sense they are all the same book.

Oprah's Book Club® is not about reading the books as much as it is about finding the Oprahness in everything or anything. Such was the wisdom of Jacquelyn Mitchard as recounted in an article in the *Citizen*, who ruefully reported: "If you send my name to the 900,000 who bought *Deep End of the Ocean* it will mean nothing to them. There's no carryover. You learn quickly Oprah's the brand name, not you." Talk about the death of the author. The chat-show host who swallowed Random House.

So let us put behind us all the spurious chatter about what a good thing it is that so many more people are "reading" because of Oprah, or how much literature is the better for the book club, or the publishers' delight over their spiked and gluttonous sales. As filtered through the celebrity-machine, mass cult marketing of Oprah, these are no longer books. They're pills in soft or hard covers, semi-literary pharmaceuticals, the print version of Prozac. And they are, even more fundamentally, just another piece of merchandise from the talk empire. Oprah cares as much about your mind as Martha Stewart does about your party.

If you want to read a good book, pick one yourself. Ask a friend, or take out an anthology from the library. Find your own way. You are unique, and independent reading will give you some small hope of remaining that way. The next time you find yourself in one of the big shops, don't just walk by the Oprah pile. Scorn it. Tell the clerk: "If I wanted to watch television, I wouldn't be here." That'll fix 'em.

– Ottawa Citizen

To Read or Not to Read

How to Read and Why
by Harold Bloom, Scribner, 2000

Why do we read? This is a profoundly simple question and one which will supply a million answers, each of which will do, and none of which is full or perfect. But if, out of such potential variety, we were to select a single reply and have the hope that it be fuller and less imperfect than the rest, I would eagerly nominate that of Harold Bloom, the American literary sage who has devoted a lifetime to reading – reading with care, affection, and with an abundance of informed response and relish. Bloom, very happily, has supplied us with a small book that speaks, judging from its title, to the question: *How to Read and Why*.

Before turning directly to Bloom, however, let us pause to fix the inquiry. What do we mean when we ask, "Why do we read?" Plainly, we read because, while it is not necessary to life that we do, life is much easier, more accessible, wider in its potential for those who can and do read than for those who cannot and do not.

There is, at literacy's atomic level, some very basic information in this world. We do not normally think of the medicine bottle or the highway sign as belonging, properly, to the world of print and the habit of reading. But belong they do, and life is a little less precarious when we are equipped and minded to read the small print or the large markings.

Warnings, instruction booklets, the names on buildings, concert bill-boards, maps, election signs, fat-content charts and mission statements, hospital admission forms and loan applications, *TV Guide*'s summary of tonight's episode of *Ally McBeal* – much that is useful, some that is decorative, and a very great deal of what is necessary comes to us in print. If we did not read, life would be more hazardous and living, surely, more cluttered. Mere proficiency in reading, then, bare literacy, makes us more ready for life, reduces its perils, and shortcuts many of our necessary encounters with experience. At this level, the question "Why do we read?" is either otiose or self-answering.

When the question is posed more seriously, there is implicit in the very asking that the inquiry has sidestepped the obvious and utilitarian, and opened instead to all the forms of reading that do not answer simple needs. Reading that is surplus to our needs is what we usually mean by "reading." We don't need to read the comic strip *Drabble* (though I strongly urge it) or *Moby-Dick* (even more strongly), as we don't need to read any of the hundreds of books that spangle in the altitudes of the bestseller lists each year, or the even more hundreds of established classics to which at least a portion of each generation makes intelligent and renewable recourse.

In reality, the question now is: Why do we read any material other than that which is purely useful or purely necessary? Why do we read books? Why do we read poems? These are not new questions. They have been asked since the days of the papyrus scroll and will survive the Palm Pilot. Francis Bacon answered that reading makes us full, ready, and exact, and which of us would not like to be all three? Bacon added to his table of reasons we read this plaintive caution: if a man "read little he had need have much cunning, to seeme to know that he doth not." No decent person wishes to be known for excess of cunning; reading spares us from the need to be sly.

Generally, the answer to the twin questions are elaborations on the classic formulation that has been with us since Horace. Literature teaches and delights; we read to learn or to find pleasure. It is the disposition of the individual reader that determines whether the emphasis is on learning or pleasure, utility or ornament. Either seems a sufficient cause, but despite the enduring tenure of this – to me – very satisfactory understanding of why we read, there has been an insistent pressure in Western thought to provide deeper or grander rationalizations.

The practice and pleasure of literature has called out defenders since Plato's jagged attack on the poets in his *Republic*. Aristotle's *Poetics* is as much a defence of literature as an anatomy of one of its kinds. The summoning of tragic emotions (pity and terror) and their expurgation or catharsis, by the spectacle of a great hero's fall and death, is not articulated merely as a version of aesthetic homeopathy. There is in Aristotle's clinical description always an undercurrent of implication that the tragic effect is spiritual in essence, that the representation on stage or in drama of a man *in extremis*, bent and broken by Fate or a tragic flaw, carries a virtue, a force of enlargement, to those who participate in the drama as spectators.

Many of the greatest writers have spoken in their own voices, or in those of their surrogates and creations, of why they have written, or what is the same thing, of why writing and art are valuable, worthy, necessary. *The Tempest* is a sly defence of poetry; Milton's *Lycidas* is the voice of poetry itself addressing the subject of the purpose of poetry. Philip Sidney, scatterings in John Donne's poems and prose, Dryden, Pope, Johnson, Shelley, Pater, Arnold, Eliot, Auden, Stevens – this is just a sampling of the great practitioners who have worried or celebrated the question of literature and why we read, and, indirectly, how we should.

In our more immediate times the work of George Steiner is a continuum of efforts to meet with full address the ancient question of why we read, and if reading, finally, has any value beyond the indulgence of epicurean appetites and onanistic connoisseurship. Steiner shadows his inquiry with the massive countercase of the Holocaust – the malign exercise, after all, of an educated civilization, inheritors of the richest traditions of the Enlightenment in philosophy, music, literature, and art, and yet "uninfluenced" by that enlightenment, Beethoven quartets pulsing decorously within the camps themselves.

Steiner leaves the question, I think, painfully agnostic about the spiritual utility of art, about its capacity to elevate or cleanse the human spirit beyond the capacity for atrocity. Art is not talismanic, it is not apotropaic; it is at best as uselessly neutral in the exercise of moral and political life as a soap opera or a football match. Art has better apologists than either soap opera or football, but if I may vary what Auden said about poetry, it emphatically does not stop things happening, and we are foolish, or mis-guided, to think that it does.

Scholar and critic Harold Bloom is one of literature's more ardent and engaged contemporary defenders. Bloom has been searing the atmosphere lately with some of the most spirited defences of the traditional under-standing of literature since Shelley and Arnold. His works on the great canon and Shakespeare can be seen as part of a full-throttle campaign to save literature from itself, or more precisely, from its ostensible guardians in the postmodern academy. He has now added a slimmer, more accessible volume, the very title of which announces that he intends to conduct the campaign at ground level: *How to Read and Why*.

Bloom views literature as under attack, in some cases hijacked by parti-sans for non-literary, even anti-literary, ends, in other cases tormented and desiccated by the abstruse imperatives of theory and pseudo-philosophy. In Bloom's increasingly anxious view, literature – the craft and play of words – has become a hostage of grievance-mongers, last-ditch Marxists, new puritans, and campus politicians of all stripes. So it is Bloom agonistes we have been reading lately; *The Western Canon* and *Shakespeare: The Invention of the Human* were his blast of the trumpet against the monstrous regiment of the new academy and its "school of resentment."

They were, as from Bloom's perspective they had to be, alloys of polemic and appreciation. He had to attack to clear a space for appreciation. And he summoned up the great practitioners, the canon of Western writing, to appropriate the spell of their achievement to the particulars of his case. Shakespeare he called up separately, because in the Bloomian cosmos Shakespeare subsumes all the rest, is the canon.

This new book winds up the campaign. In some respects, having read the two previous, I looked forward to the continuing struggle. Bloom is a large sensibility; his scorn, though affecting a weariness and now pre-dictable in its ranging, has its purely literary delights. His enthusiasms are large and contagious. He really is a critic who can inspire others to read, or to read anew. And he does hold his subject in clear view.

It is what has been written by the strongest and most gifted minds. The example of the very best invigorates our reading of what is not the very best, and the same example is part of the texture of most of those creative minds who write in our time. We read the old to better read the new. We read to multiply the savours of reading. Authors, with rare exceptions, are not islands. There is something to the conceit, explored variously by T.S. Eliot and Borges, to name just two, that literature is a cooperative endeavour, an accumulation of powers and effects which spans the generations of man.

But *How to Read and Why* is not the concentrated, laser-guided salvo that many will have wished for. Neither is it a stripped-to-essentials primer that honestly takes the very real challenge of providing a solid, true answer to this lasting question. It is a series of glancing observations and mini-essays on a cluster of very great writers (a few not so great) under the useful classifications of short stories, poems, novels, and plays.

It is always a pleasure to read Harold Bloom. His engagement with literature is nervous and alive. Literature is a passion with Bloom in a way, and with the same intensity, that we say love is a passion for most of humankind. If I were asked why Harold Bloom reads, I would answer, with very little rhetoric, "Because he is in love with books and words and in reading he finds happiness." That may be a saccharine gloss, but I think it true. As to how he reads, it is enough to say that he reads intelligently, fully, with great resources of memory and power of association, and with an intuitive comprehension that the art of literature is a component of our understanding of life, and a very large part of why life is worth living.

I merely wish this book had said so. Why Harold Bloom reads, and what, are truly interesting and important speculations. But Bloom has not written that account here, nor has he given as a substitute any real account of why we should read. There are hints, glorious offhand descriptions of the pleasures of particular works, *obiter dicta* of quite compelling attractiveness on a diversity of writers from Jane Austen to Cormac McCarthy. This is Bloom's chapbook and his enchiridion. But it is not what it says it is, and delivers much under its promise.

Reading is like music in that most people whose lives are engaged with either or both intuit a value from that engagement. We do not like to settle simply on the proposition that, like looking at a sunset, we are present at a scene of considerable gorgeousness. Even in the case of the sunset, we don't want to settle for that. It is not enough, however, to settle for mere intuition. Maybe it should be, but that is another question. Are these intuitions mere self-flatteries, a gathering of esteem over our own sensitivity, our relish of the fine. Fainting over Shelley is in its way something of a private Academy Award: "I'd like to thank my wonderful mind, and my beautiful sensibility." Is reading more than that? We think it must be. An exquisite hedonism is a pathetic defence of literature. So when Bloom signals that he is ready for an encounter with these questions, we attend. And, reasonably, are encouraged that we are going to bypass the stock responses of exuberant enthusiasm and the rhapsodies of windy response.

Milton is a very good place to begin. Milton is large, fierce, and for many, forbidding. Forbidding, in fact, was in a manner his life's work. "Why should we read *Paradise Lost*?" is a very good question. Why should we read a massive, complicated, and difficult poem, housed in an antique form, burdened by an anachronistic theology, and bristling with ever more remote allusions and almost impervious syntax? Why indeed? Bloom doesn't give much real help on this real question. The fragment on Milton mutters a little about Satan as a character, and suggests that a reading of the majestic marvel will extend our understanding of "the Protestant spirit." With all due respect to the Protestant spirit and its many fascinations, it is, I fear, the very last bait to lure the novice or the intimidated to an appreciation of the baroque glories and mainly unattended achievements of *Paradise Lost*. We should read *Paradise Lost* because it is very beautiful and we do not have enough of beauty. And we should read it because it manifests an almost unearthly collusion between the creative intelligence and language itself.

Why also should we read *King Lear* or *Hamlet*, Coleridge or T.S. Eliot? This book does not really want to make the fundamental engagement that such a question demands. There is a case to be made for reading, and it is as important that it be made in our busy, electronic days as it was when Plato started scowling at the poets. The humanities – the poor, tattered, limping humanities – have need of their defenders. Harold Bloom is surely one of their most vigorous and indefatigable, and it may be churlish, after he has done so much in other books, to whinge about this one. But the cause is so fine, and Bloom so capable, that we could not help but wish for more. For now we will settle with Johnson's axiom. We read "[the] better to enjoy life, or the better to endure it."

– Globe and Mail

Reading, Writing, and More Writing

The deep-wooded and pleasant grounds of the Governor General's residence, and the elegant mansion that shelters His Excellency Roméo LeBlanc, at 1 Sussex Drive in the nation's capital, exude charm and impose a subdued but confident dignity. Once we get past the masonry and trees, however, the Governor General's Literary Awards themselves offer a confused prospect. They are founded, I believe, on a conflation of what art is and what artists do, the function of writers and the value of reading. They are also a highly decorous smuggling operation, chauvinism cloaking itself in literature.

There is first the idea that artists exercise a benign social influence, that their "being here" is, of itself, uplifting or meritorious. This is not, of course, a localized Canadian phenomenon. Artists everywhere have been insisting on the idea of art as spiritual manna, and artists as singular dispensers of it, since haughty Modernism raised its tent. But there is more than a touch of the golden calf about the enterprise – art has a sacred function, invisible effects, transcendent value – and I think that, as with any self-advertised product, we'd be wise to hold the incense.

Artists are as pleasant as any other human beings, but not all artists, of course, are great. That would be intolerable. But such has been the success of the propaganda that most of us who are not artists (and our ranks, I fear, are diminishing – the advent of performance art, slam poetry, and video festivals having promiscuously swelled the definition of art and furiously democratized the profession) have taken it as writ that the more artists there are per acre, then the more enlightened and civil the country they inhabit. This is the fundamental idea behind the Governor General's Awards, and is the very elixir of being for the Canada Council.

But is this true? In what possible sense are we "better" if we self-consciously seed the land with authors than if we primed the pump for salesmen, plumbers, or short-order cooks? Why, if the country produced three hundred novels a year from the teeming brains of three hundred state-esteemed writers, is it in any moral or spiritual sense better than if we only hear from, say, thirty of them? We seem to be confusing worthiness with bulk.

More particularly, why do we subscribe with such conviction to the notion that nurturing Canadian writers is a socially beneficent goal? When did literature become the handmaiden of chauvinism, even a chauvinism as tempered and reluctant as this country's cautiously beating heart allows? The Governor General's Awards are not about writing. They are about patriotism. Writing and patriotism are each fine soups in themselves, but they are a terrible stew.

The other string in the bow reveals the bias of the Governor General's Awards. We hear it time and time again, broadsheeted and broadcasted, from the towers of the academy to the festivals on the street, that it is good that the hills (and valleys, outports and prairie villages, main streets and downtowns) are alive with the sound of heavy pecking on myriad soft-percussion laptops. This is the "more voices we have" doctrine, which is the Charlottetown accord of Canadian writing.

All literature, I think, suffered when we started talking about voices instead of books. The "more voices we have" doctrine is at best a mushy liberal sentimentalism, and has as much to do with the art of writing as the prose of corporate mission statements. The Governor General's Awards are very big on encouraging "voices" and insist that, the more voices we "hear," the better we are "as a people." This is cant. It's heartfelt and high-minded cant, but it's cant nonetheless.

The Sunday-school, civics-class piety of the Governor General's Awards is best illustrated by the last of its silent presumptions. By showcasing writers, and multiplying voices, the GGs will magnificently encourage more Canadians to read more Canadians. This is not objectionable in itself.

Reading is one of life's few innocuous pleasures, right up there with gazing out to sea, or staring into a fire. But Canadians, I fear, are dangerously close to believing that reading a book is (like joining a health club or adopting a highway) a virtuous activity, and more particularly a peculiarly Canadian virtuous activity.

The Governor General's Awards cannot be charged exclusively with responsibility for this curious state of mind. (The charming and former host of CBC Radio's *Morningside*, for example, has driven more people to the Canadian books section than it may be delicate, in print, to admit.) But the GGs are the most high-powered promotion of the idea, and the single institutionalized embodiment of it. The idea itself, however, is a piety masquerading as a revelation.

Why is reading automatically virtuous, and why have we subscribed to the notion that more Canadians reading more Canadians is an intrinsically Canadian civic virtue?

This can be but a sketch. Essentially, my objections are these. The Governor General's Awards are inscribed with three fundamental misconceptions: (1) Literature is good for us as Canadians. (2) The encouragement of Canadian writers is a shortcut to an enhanced Canadian consciousness. (3) Reading is a civic virtue.

None of these propositions is self-evident. A couple are half-truths. All of them are a mischief to real literature.

– Globe and Mail

Enough Said

There are times the mind needs to get away, far away, and I can think of no further verge than the distant work of a great, though little-known, seventeenth-century preacher and divine, Lancelot Andrewes. He was an ornament of the court of King James I, a principal in the assembly of literature's and Christianity's greatest book, the Authorised Version of the English Bible, and a writer and stylist of remarkable force and distinction.

In the 1604 Hampton Court Conference, the seminal event in the production of the Authorised Version, this man of "great holiness and great learning" was charged with the responsibility of the Old Testament books from Genesis to 2 Kings. There were forty-seven other scholars and divines enrolled in the commission, but no other of Andrewes's authority and assurance. In an age of fiercely learned men, he was exceptional: Thomas Fuller paid this compliment, that Andrewes "could serve as INTERPRETER GENERAL at the confusion of Tongues."

The A.V., or King James Bible, was published in 1611. It was worked on at the time William Shakespeare was writing the plays of his deep, language-intoxicated maturity; at the time that John Donne, the foremost love poet in English, was easing himself towards the decision to take orders, and to become, along with Andrewes, one of England's foremost preachers; when Francis Bacon was busy with his essays. The Authorised Version, in other words, was in embryo when the language itself, under pressure from some of the most gifted agents in all its history, was taking shape.

In that short, intense spread of years, the lexical imagination felt the full, high spread of its wings, and there is nothing that gives us pleasure today, as readers or writers, that does not carry some residual gift from that period. The core of that moment was the King James Bible, of which George Steiner has written: "No other book is like it; all other books are inhabited by the murmur of that distant source."

But it will not serve to urge people to read Andrewes if what he wrote for himself does not have its own and discrete charm and force. It will certainly not do when we are urging on them five-hundred-year-old sermons, sermons moreover of great density and knottiness, that even some of his contemporaries found stiff going.

A sermon by Andrewes is a word-by-word progress through a Biblical citation, a progress of fantastic discrimination and analysis, of winding and unwinding paths of meaning from each single word, and from the whole in combination. It offers a spectacle of logical and verbal gymnastics driven by what I will call a furious holiness. Reading Andrewes, despite our distance from his age and ethos, is exciting.

No less a poet of our time than T.S. Eliot, the magpie of Modernism, incorporated stretches of Andrewes, taken directly and with minimum alteration from the sermons, into some of his most inviting work. The opening lines of "The Journey of the Magi" have Eliot smuggling Andrewes into the twentieth century. Eliot's "cold coming . . . of it" was Andrewes's earlier phrase. *Ash Wednesday* has a like trawl.

In fact, it is mostly due to Eliot that, outside a circle of connoisseurs and specialists, Andrewes's name survives in our time. The 1928 essay "Homage to Lancelot Andrewes," in which Eliot ranked the prose of Andrewes "among the best of his own, or of any time," woke many a student to his existence, and served as a passionate and exacting recommendation for a neglected master.

The frequently remarked austerity of Andrewes is greatly overstressed. He is often plain and playful, frequently beautiful, with passages of astonishing simplicity and directness. We forget sometimes how much of what impresses us in Scripture is almost unutterably simple and direct: "Let there be light." "In the beginning was the Word." "Jesus wept."

A portion of that pristine, spare beauty is to be found in the thickets of Andrewes's sermons, a beauty that radiates all the more intensely for its context, a flower on a steep, bare path. I make the obvious comparison to introduce a passage from Andrewes that is lucid, ordered, plain, and affecting:

> It is now the time of flowers, and from flowers, doth the Apostle take his term. . . . Their best, their flourishing estate they hold not long, neither the flowers, that are worne, nor they, that wear them either: they, nor we: but decay we doe, (God wot) in a short time.

Rigour, beauty and cadence. Enough to stay our cascade into a new and noisome millennium. Lancelot Andrewes, seventeenth-century divine – just the best guide for such a journey.

– Globe and Mail

What Likeness . . . Through Yonder Window Breaks?

"Literature is news that stays news." The aphorism is Ezra Pound's, a poet acquainted with both. Pound was something of a self-appointed communications director for the Modernist movement as it was a-birthing in the early decades of the last century. This was a loose amalgamation of poets and artists, which wasn't political in any but the broadest sense, and anticipated the Canadian Alliance only in its fondness for manifestos, its indecipherable lust for faction and division, and its need to rain perplexity and confusion on its most steadfast well-wishers.

The Modernist movement gave the world great poetry and great prose. *The Wasteland* and *Ulysses* may be taken as its iconic achievements. I am not sure what the Alliance is going to leave us, except the less-than-poetic prospect – should they insist in continuing to disembowel each other in public (while shedding communications directors by the bushel) – of Jean Chrétien's unruffled entry into a fourth, even sixth, term.

What, will the line stretch out to the crack of doom? (*Macbeth*)

I do not know if Stockwell Day has read much Shakespeare during all his troubles, but if I may put it this way, Shakespeare as surely read him.

Upon my head they placed a fruitless crown,
And put a barren sceptre in my gripe. (*Macbeth*)

Shakespeare is our only true Nostradamus. Meaning, in contrast to that durable sixteenth-century Kreskin, the pet of cranks and quacks, that Shakespeare has the true prophetic or proleptic power. In his lines, scarcely a situation we know, or have come to know, has not been anticipated, represented, and expressed in consummate language.

I take this to be the principal reason for the deep and wide excitement to the *Globe*'s (the current paper, not the prior playhouse) presentation of what may be a hitherto unknown portrait of the most famous high dome in the world's literature. People want to read about Shakespeare because he seems, already and in advance, to have read them. Shakespeare is always news and, this week in particular, I am not at all certain whether, via the *Globe*'s presentation, the Avon bard was giving us a break from the Alliance; or the Alliance, via Ezra Levant, was feebly trying to crowd out Shakespeare.

The first truth about Shakespeare is that we're fascinated by him because, being human, we're fascinated by ourselves. He is not so much a seer as the most gifted eavesdropper in the history of the world. With this exception – that he heard all our really important conversations before we had them. This is what Harold Bloom was on about in his bestseller *Shakespeare: The Invention of the Human*. That Shakespeare, the dramatist, represented in his plays the vast repertoire of the human condition, and that Shakespeare, the poet, pioneered the language to articulate – gave us the words to express – the crises, joys and pains, and the everyday, of our human condition.

Shakespeare extended human consciousness. The claim is no less bold than that. So we are fascinated by Shakespeare because, more or less, he has been everywhere before us. This is why, for the deepest critics of Shakespeare – and this has been a phenomenon noted by everyone who has ever studied the subject – when they stare into Shakespeare, they find themselves staring back.

Coleridge reads *Hamlet*, and Hamlet emerges very like the dithering, sinuous, introspective Romantic poet-philosopher manqué, Samuel Taylor Coleridge. Keats reads *King Lear* and sees an image of a great "plastic" empathetic power, very like the sensibility of the young John Keats. Jorge

Luis Borges, a master reader and writer of our own day, encounters in Shakespeare a person who is no one and everyone, a person, in other words, very like the vague, shimmering omnipresence of the Borges persona.

But we are not all Coleridge (thank God) or Keats (a lesser relief) or Borges (we could only hope). And for most of the world, the thirty-something plays, the two narrative poems, and the sonnets, are not a breviary. We do not encounter him, perhaps, as frequently and as feverishly first-hand as did earlier generations. Nor are the great set speeches and monologues ("To be or not to be") or the clutch of truly famous sonnets ("Shall I compare thee to a summer's day?") carried, beyond the first line or two, in the living memory of very many. We store Seinfeld tag lines and lisp Oprah-speak.

But Shakespeare has burned through the literature and lives of four whole centuries, and far beyond the English tongue. His words, in citation, quotation, allusion, imitation, translation, parody – on stage, in film, transposed to other forms, novel, opera, or musical suite – as exercise, study, and meditation, constitute or have built a vast and inescapably present world of their own. Borges is right. He is everywhere. He is an environment. Part reef, part echo chamber, we say things back to him. The great part of all active literary life, writing or reading, is an acknowledged or unacknowledged archeology of Shakespearean presence and influence.

I mean no blasphemy, but much like the other Creator, the God of the Old Testament, he does not show himself. At most, we have the "hinder parts," which in Shakespeare's case amount, up to now, to those two, mostly featureless portraits – stark Droeshout, cold Chandos – familiar to most of us in reproduction. It is impossible to strain or sift his identity, "Shakespeare the man," from the plays or poems, because he is so perfect a ventriloquist and impersonator that we can never be sure that it is Shakespeare speaking through a character, or a persona.

Many have tried to claim him for cause or sect, on the basis that this or that line or text is his real voice, but he is quicksilver and ghost-quick:

> . . . started like a guilty thing
> Upon a fearful summons. (*Hamlet*)

He cannot be stayed. He is – till the promise of the picture in the last week – impervious to confident discovery.

So, naturally, we want to look at something that we can believe is him, at least something a little better than that bleak snowball of a head, with the few lapping hairs and what-me-worry eyes, which is the most common representation. A real picture of the real man, we hope and think, might offer a clue to the nature of genius, a hint of the soul that found those miracles of language with such dexterity and sovereign purchase. This is a major clue to ourselves, more real, at least to our imaginations, than all the unravelling of DNA.

Even if the picture is proven, and even if that defyingly youthful representation receives that gigantic authentication that the world (especially the irrepressible and thoroughly Oliver-Stonian Baconian heretics) will demand, we will have advanced, in one sense, no further.

He has been before us here, too.

> There's no art
> To find the mind's construction in the face. (*Macbeth*)

Given that these words file from the play whose hero is a Scottish regicide, one who believed in witches and thought that trees were pedestrians, they may not greatly inhibit our speculation.

If that's him, really him, we'll look. Again and again.

– *Globe and Mail*

The Real Dr. J Gets Stuffed

Samuel Johnson: The Life of an Author
by Lawrence Lipking, Harvard University Press, 1998

"I may surely be contented without the praise of perfection, which if I could obtain, in this gloom of solitude, what would it avail me? I have protracted my work till most of those, whom I wished to please, have sunk into the grave, and success and miscarriage are empty sounds. I therefore dismiss it with frigid tranquillity, having little to fear or hope from censure or from praise."

For the biographers and enthusiasts of two centuries, Samuel Johnson has been something of his own Falstaff, a presence that overwhelms and obliterates, by force of personality, all considerations exterior to that personality. Just as Falstaff drowns the plays in which he so copiously lives, Johnson the personality – essentially, Boswell's Johnson – overcrowds Johnson the writer. It has been the consent of generations that the prose-captured melancholies and summary adieu of the peroration (cited above) of Johnson's great *English Dictionary* reach the pitch and summit of artful human utterance. Johnson's writing at its finest – in the preface to the *Dictionary*, in *Lives of the English Poets*, in the *Rambler* and *Adventurer* essays, is articulation at its most intelligent and most beautiful. (In a corpus so luxuriant and multifarious, driven by exigency and the wavering importunities of the everyday, not all has the command of his best.)

For all that, Johnson's writings will never have the instant charm and approachability, the delicious gratifications of Boswell's transcriptions of the talker Johnson. Why hike when one can sunbathe? And I am not sure that we would wish that they do. The writings are, however, of incontestable worth, force, beauty, and persuasiveness. He is one of that small company of truly great writers gifted with a seemingly instinctive relationship with language, for whom words inhere with their very being. As Mozart is to music, so Johnson is to English prose. When, therefore, a new book appears which suggests by its title, *Samuel Johnson: The Life of an Author*, that the stress is on the author not the life, on the writings not the personality, our interest is seduced. Alas, it is a hope from which we soon awaken.

This book is not a disappointment. It comes close to being an offence. It has so little that is new to say, and says that little amateurishly and on occasion even vulgarly. An insensitivity to tone, an ear stopped to cadence and nuance, an unresponsiveness to the harmonies and disciplines of diction – these may not *absolutely* preclude one human being from setting up to take the measure of another who is preternaturally gifted in these registers. In sports, for example, judicious spectators are not necessarily athletes themselves. But surely, a sense of one's limitations should enhance prudence and caution.

I cannot swim, but I can *watch* those who do. However, it will be an eon hence, and a dark day in a cold hell besides, before I write a book about the techniques of flotation and propulsion. In these other, Johnsonian, waters Lawrence Lipking cannot swim either. However, on the evidence of certain passages, I am not sure he even knows how to wash.

"In 1729, when Johnson left Oxford for years of vegetating at home instead of trying his hand in London, authors were in bad repute."

This is Coles Notes, the lenient version. How precise it is. Was it just in 1729 when authors were "in bad repute"? Was there a reputational revival in 1730, authors suddenly coming into "good repute"? Which authors? Shakespeare, Pope, Elkanah Settle? Homer? Or the scribblers and witlings of party faction? Bad Sammy, "vegetating at home" when he should have been exercising an entirely different cliché and "trying his hand" in London. *Samuel Johnson* is pocked with such descents into the shorthandese of (dare I say this in the light of the next example) undigested criticism.

"Moreover the character of the Dictionary – as well as its bulk – depends on its omnibus illustrative quotations. . . . In this respect the book is literally patchwork. It devours and digests other books, which Johnson's rough handling often turn into mincemeat."

I'm not sure whether that sentence is intended to be taken literally. Given Johnson's celebrated gusto at table, it could be that Lipking has Johnson pegged as a bibliophage. Whatever the literality of the "mincemeat," what are we to make of the preceding observation (where we're clearly out of the Meat Section and into the Haberdashery Department) that Johnson's *Dictionary*, a work of genius and gigantic industry, is "literally a patchwork"?

These examples are not eccentric. *Samuel Johnson* is a compendium of mischievous and misplaced idiom, glancing and erratic judgement, and fundamental misappreciation. Its failings, other than stylistic, stem from what may be called a mistaken assignment. Lipking wishes to make a case for why Johnson became an "author" and what being an author meant to Johnson. Now, "author" is a slippery term in these times, and in this book. The times have become overzealous and supersubtle on a concept that, plainly approached – which is how Johnson would have approached it – is more blatant than subtle, and as close to self-evident as a large building or a rainy weekend. An author writes books, and according to the degree and kind of satisfaction readers receive from those books, an author is more or less esteemed and rewarded. Some write primarily for esteem, others for reward, most for a combination.

Johnson wrote quite clearly for reward: "No man save a blockhead ever wrote except for money" is one of his most famous expostulations. He wrote also for esteem, which meant winning some place in the file of great literature.

To these two plain understandings we may add a third, vital to the particular author Samuel Johnson. Deeply moral, Johnson realized and accepted that to have great powers was to be under a Christian duty to expend them properly. For his entire life he was lacerated by the consciousness of not properly employing himself, or falling short of what Providence could expect of him – this despite the *Dictionary*, the edition of Shakespeare, the *Lives of the English Poets*, the essays, the poems, despite a harvest of such plenitude and riches that any one alone would distinguish the life of an author.

This is nothing special in any arcane sense about Johnson as an author. Thus the luxuriance of Lipking's speculation and psychologizing to explain what for most of us can be taken as given are tedious. Among them: that variously, Johnson "exercised little control over his development as an author," that (guarding his own standing) he "polices the world of letters and warns the wrong sort of people – the lazy or unlettered – to keep out," that as author "he acts for the nation" or "is a surrogate for the nation." A steady drizzle of such formulations, printed with a splattering of politically correct usage, do not constitute a reading of Johnson or a genuine response to him.

It will be a sad thing if the unwary come upon this book thinking it will clear a path to one of the most sadly undervisited treasuries of English literature. For it is a bramble, obstructing a prospect of almost unaccountable beauty and life.

– Globe and Mail

Keen Memory Made Tender: Nabokov the Prodigy

Speak, Memory
by Vladimir Nabokov, Knopf, 1999

"I am an ardent memoirist with a rotten memory, a drowsy king's absent-minded remembrancer. With absolute lucidity I recall landscapes, gestures, intonations, a million sensuous details, but names and numbers topple into oblivion with absurd abandon like little blind men in file from a pier."

– Vladimir Nabokov, Strong Opinions

Vladimir Nabokov is a phenomenon among writers, precociously gifted, unconditional in his urge towards excellence, radiant in his resolve that art is a reason for being.

He achieved in a second language a sovereignty of articulation that many fine writers could not in a first. How it came to be that a Russian-born writer, forced by the deplorable fact of exile to work in the second tongue, leapt into so full and keen an intimacy with English is a question that wades into the shoals of psychosocial analysis, the "science" Nabokov scorned with such acid hauteur.

He was possessed of a verbal intuition of truly remarkable accuracy, range, and depth. His style works the most difficult alliance, that of precision and poetry. All of his books have moments when the reader stops reading, ambushed by perfection, or – since below the moon, perfection is not ours to be met – something as close to perfection as the art of writing allows.

In any of those moments, Nabokov will have fixed something so precisely, worked an exquisite balance of sound, diction, and rhythm, or fashioned an image crisp with newness and astonishing in its ingenuity or revelation, that attention to plot or story is subdued in admiration.

Speak, Memory, his one autobiographical effort, is almost a compendium of such moments. It moves from grace to grace, winds in and out of several keys – lyric, nostalgic, sarcastic, naturalistic – with unimpeachable sureness of touch. Alas, it is only half an autobiography, stopping when Nabokov flees Germany with his wife, Vera, and son, Dimitri, for the second exile in America.

I cannot think of a modern work in English that is its stylistic equal. *Speak, Memory* – and this is the simplest and highest tribute a book can receive – is at the front of the line of those few books we willingly, eagerly, reread.

It is the most accessible of all of Nabokov's work, the place for those who have yet to addict themselves to his bracing delights to begin. It is the one fully personalized venture that the great fiction writer allowed himself (outside, that is, the mordant prefaces to some of the novels, sarcastic treasures, pearls of scorn on Freudism and its followers which should be anthologized, chanted at self-help seminars, and on afternoons when Oprah is at her most windy).

Nabokov can be so clever that at times he is wearying, but *Speak, Memory* is Nabokov out of costume, less the acrobat of irony and cunning perspectives, less the technician. The aloof, mandarin persona and the multitude of narrative personas are set aside for once.

The cradle rocks above an abyss, and common sense tells us that our existence is but a brief crack of light between two eternities of darkness.

Although the two are identical twins, man, as a rule, views the prenatal abyss with more calm than the one he is heading for (at some forty-five hundred heartbeats an hour). . . .

Over and over again my mind has made colossal efforts to distinguish the faintest of glimmers in the impersonal darkness on both sides of my life.

This is *Speak, Memory*'s beginning, and it carries the tone and signature of the entire book. It is at once personal and philosophical, grave and funny.

Nabokov raged against time and its inexorable obliterations of memory, life, achievement, and love. His whole work is a protest against time, and *Speak, Memory* is virtually the artist's manual of how he built his defences and set his intelligence against the inexorable: "That this darkness is caused merely by the walls of time separating me and my bruised fists from the free world of timelessness is a belief I gladly share with the most gaudily painted savage."

It is also remarkable as a piece of unique social history. The Nabokovs were wealthy aristocrats in pre-revolutionary Russia, Nabokov senior, a social liberal and a statesman of considerable consequence. The nightmare of Leninism fell upon Russia and not only wiped out that class – pre-democratic, it is true, but not without pulses of enlightenment and human-ism. It also pushed that time, those people, the moment they lived in, almost to oblivion. The story of those days needed a memoirist, and a sturdy, unsentimental, gifted one at that. There is in *Speak, Memory* some-thing of that seriousness that derives from an act of moral redress, a debt repaid, a rescue. While *Speak, Memory* is far from being a summary of the age – Nabokov is an artist of the particular – it is an affectionate reawaken-ing of a period and a set of people almost lost to record. How he would have hated to hear it said this way, but *Speak, Memory* is an act of social justice.

Like all of Nabokov's books, *Speak, Memory* is dedicated without flourish of any kind "To Vera." Uninscribed, but almost certainly silently present, is an equal dedication here to his father and mother; the father he revered and emulated, and the mother, as passage after passage in this book tellingly and with piercing richness testifies, he loved with almost unbear-able focus. *Speak, Memory* is more, however, than a chronicle of family or marital love and respect. It is the chronicle of a gifted sensibility unfolding. The vivid, comic, often beautiful cameos of his childhood present, with great subtlety and pinpoint recall, the unfurling of the artistic disposition in Nabokov. *Speak, Memory* is as much a Portrait of the Artist as the cele-brated one to which James Joyce gave the title, and so to speak, took the patent. It is also its equal.

Speak, Memory is, then, all of these things. But for none of them, not for the picture of family life, the narrative of affection, the portrait of a unique caste of people in a unique time, is it to be urged upon a reader. It is to be urged for its art. *Speak, Memory* contains as much of the peculiar, charged, intense music of poetry as continuous prose can achieve.

It is also a book of deep, fundamental joy. In his life, he was twice beggared, unrooted as a young man, and again in Germany with the rise of Hitler, but he is absolutely unacquainted with even the echoes of complaint or self-pity:

> My old (since 1917) quarrel with the Soviet dictatorship is wholly unrelated to the question of property. My contempt for the emigré who "hates the Reds" because they "stole" his money and land is complete. The nostalgia I have been cherishing all these years is a hypertrophied sense of lost childhood, not sorrow for lost banknotes.

Speak, Memory is a gallant story told with brilliance and ardour, a work of "tenderness, talent and pride."

– *Ottawa Citizen*

The Memoir of a Casanova of the Mind

Errata: An Examined Life
by George Steiner, Weidenfeld & Nicolson, 1997

In the early part of the century, T.S. Eliot wrote a vigorous and quite famous essay on the poetry of John Donne. It may well be that Eliot writing on Donne was Eliot writing on Eliot, but all that is dust now.

Eliot was literary criticism's first and finest centrifuge. Typically, in that essay he sought to isolate those qualities of Donne's poetry (and those of his followers, the awkwardly named metaphysical poets) that marked its essence, accounted for its distinctive presence and force. And those qualities he located in a habit of mind Eliot saw as peculiar to a singular moment in the history of English poetry, mainly but not confined to the early seventeenth century. In brutal summary, it was characterized by the most lively interplay of intelligence and emotion, a moment when passion was intellect, and intellect was passion. The devouring wit of Donne and his disciples was remarkable for what Eliot called its "sensuous apprehension" of ideas.

In a formulation that teased criticism for at least two generations, he wrote: "A thought to Donne was an experience. It modified his sensibility." The touchstone Eliot lights upon is the peculiar, dramatic, and emotional force with which ideas, play of mind, sheer intellection, and the ardour of thought visited Donne and his nimble successors. Whatever the fertility of these terms for an understanding of Donne (or Eliot), they are surely the first items in any glossary of appreciation for the life and work of George Steiner. That life and work is now neatly and elegantly, not to say laconically

144

(186 pages, including index), available in a biographical memoir, modestly and yet not so modestly titled *Errata: An Examined Life*.

George Steiner is a literary critic (such as *After Babel: Aspects of Language and Translation* and *No Passion Spent*), a professor of comparative literature at Oxford, an essayist (hundreds of reviews and essays for such publications as *The New Yorker* and the *Times Literary Supplement*), a novelist (*The Portage to San Cristobal of A.H.*), and one of the very few active men of letters whose work and example vivifies and enhances the vocation of the intellectual.

As for the sensuous apprehension of ideas, *Errata* is the memoir of a Casanova of the mind. Thought, ideas, culture, literature, art – to continue with Eliot's parsing – in Steiner's case these are not just "an experience." They are life itself. As for "sensibility," so sovereign is Steiner's regard for human genius that he argues the achievements of intellect and imagination are not only the high reaches of the human condition, the consolations of our finite term – they may be (alas) our only passable justification for being in the first place.

He writes:

In the midst of the inhumanity and indifference of history, a handful of men and women have been creatively possessed by the compelling splendour of the useless (the Socratic daimonion). This constitutes the eminent dignity, the "princeliness" of our kind. It may be that together with the saints, religious or secular, this "pride" of mathematicians, composers, poets, painters, logicians or epistemologists (the inquirers into inquiry) in some manner ransom mankind. I am haunted by the possibility that out of our mammalian midst, a Plato, a Gauss or a Mozart, justifies, redeems, the species which devised and carried out Auschwitz.

It should be added that even under (because of) the weight of its ardent preoccupations, *Errata* is a first-class delight.

The delight begins with the sustained eloquence of the style. Steiner is one of the great rhetoricians of our age, and probably among the last to understand the full high-pedigreed glory of the term. He believes greatly, and because belief is a moral stance, he is obliged to persuade. Hence the great charge of his prose – rich, declamatory, full of high sentence, urgent – no one writes of high culture with the eloquence and mandarin force of George Steiner.

He is also in love – with thought and art. *Errata* is a testament to an urgent and lifelong courtship with high culture, what Steiner has viewed since the early days, when his father inducted him into the severities and ecstasies of *The Iliad*, as the monuments of Western culture. Hence the passionate assertions of value and alarm, as he seeks to bring others within the circle of that fierce and troubling embrace, and to warn against the abrasions of vulgarity and triviality that would exhaust it.

And yet. About the whole humanistic enterprise he is genuinely and painfully ambivalent. It is the hinge of his entire work that learning and art should "make a difference," should save us. Steiner wishes, desperately, that this should be so. But, with an even greater desperation, he glimpses that it may not be, that the pieties on which generations of artists, writers, and intellectuals have rested the case for art are a delusion and worse. An obliging fraud. A lie.

> The fundamental challenge I voiced – How are we to grasp psychologically, socially, the capacity of human beings to perform, to respond to, say, Bach or Schubert in the evening, and to torture other human beings the next morning? Are there not intimate congruities between the humanities and the inhumane?

For a mind such as the one portrayed here, with a character so founded, so anchored, in what Matthew Arnold calls "the best that has been thought and written" – Steiner's being is tethered to the humanities – merely to ask such questions is an act of great pathos and candour.

There is also great charm on display. My favourite chapter is one that offers five cameos of the teachers, the co-inquirers into inquiry, who have meant most to him. One is the Canadian Ernest Sirluck, then of the University of Chicago, "whose passwords were 'severity,' 'rigour' and 'scruple,' and whose commendations were terse and 'marmoreal.'" The story of Allan Tate challenging fellow poet and critic Karl Shapiro to a duel and consulting the young Steiner on the etiquette of such a challenge – given that Shapiro was Jewish, Tate was uncertain of the delicacies that might prevail and wished to be tactful before any armed encounter – is wonderful. The Oxford tutor and Greek scholar Humphrey House walks on, as well as the poet and critic R.P. Blackmur, both men generous, passionate, and somehow sad.

Gershom Scholem, however, student and scholar of Jewish mysticism and millennial expectations, a man curse-blessed with "an intimate clairvoyance into the fabric of language and symbolism," is a heroic presence. The introductory description says it all: "That Voltairian mien, the needling eyes, the bat's ears ever alert, the lips given to sardonic dismay, composed a mask of reason."

There is so much more to say about this book, about the thinking it offers on education, language, politics, war, the mass media, about its moments of personal revelation, bitter and joyful. But this is George Steiner. And it really will not do, for me at least, to "review" him. As soon review Niagara Falls.

It's a telling book about a special human being, a Midrash on a life of the mind, and I recommend it without reserve.

– Globe and Mail

TOWER OF BABEL

See Geri, See Geri Binge, Love Her Now

If Only
by Geri Halliwell, Doubleday, 1999

"Nothing human is alien to me," said the ancient philosophers. But their reach is beyond my feeble grasp. There are a lot of things human that are alien to me. Among those things beneath, above, or simply beyond my interest and ken is the British pop group the Spice Girls, curiously enough, along with the Three Tenors.

There's nothing emphatically distinctive about the Spice Girls. They are (maybe "were" is more precise at this stage) just one more in a great line of confected groups that stretches back earlier than the Monkees ("hey, hey") to the current pseudo-rage, the Backstreet Boys, groups that have achieved great pop stardom not because of brilliant talent and some marketing but brilliant marketing and some talent. They were the marketing equivalents of Cabbage Patch dolls or Go-Go Barbies, grrrowling winsome fatuities about grrrl power while throwing off lyrics ("all I really, really want") that would embarrass even a lyricist of such fortitude as Billy Ray Cyrus, author of the melancholy anthem "Achy Breaky Heart."

As all the world knows, or at least that part of it that pays attention to such fluff, the Spice Girls lost one of their founding members two years ago. Maybe a preteen heart went achy breaky when it was announced that Geri, a.k.a. Ginger Spice, the group's most mature member and by all accounts its brightest – and both these qualifiers should be seen as part of a rigidly limited continuum – was leaving.

151

The Spice Girls were truly a set. Despite marketers' efforts to give them a sheen of individuality, chiefly by the use of one-word monikers – Scary, Posh – they were a cluster of attitude aimed with a surgeon's finesse at the teen and preteen consumer, bubblegum in halter tops, who more or less have had their couple of days on the beach of faux fame.

Except for the smart one, Geri. She could have taken Melville's famous Jobean text as epigraph for this celeb bio: "And I only am alone escaped to tell thee."

What do we get from *If Only*? Well, it isn't Henry James or John Updike. We are in that peculiar modern territory where books are not at all necessarily concerned with the skill of the writing. Where style and organization, originality of thought or expression, descriptive artfulness or novelty of means, are nullities, *terra incognita*, extraneous and inutile. The celebrity biography sits on a thin, low column of purpose. That purpose is to glut the already infatuated. The celebrity is, by definition and etymology, already well known.

Also, by an equal logic, the celebrity is, for a portion of the population, liked and quite possibly adored. Adoration is as much an appetite as an attitude, and the appetite to "know" more about celebrities is one of the most depressing characteristics of our celebrity-swamped age.

Really serious fans – if that is not an unpardonable oxymoron – need more than the soup of fan magazines and MTV tour-promotion interviews, these latter such a cheerful mix of sycophancy, banality, and market guile that they are a dolorous art form in themselves.

Really serious fans want a book. And what kind of book? A mix of Cinderella and Moll Flanders, cosmetized for the age. Instead of brutish sisters and a hag stepmother, the fable of modern celebrity must surround herself with less-antique terrors.

I opened *If Only* with the deep certitude that I would not traverse its starlit pages for long without our heroine's encountering the twin dragons of modern martyrdom – low self-esteem and its excitable issue, bulimia. LSE and bulimia are the stigmata of any tried-and-true modern celebrity heroine. Princess Diana is of course the template, the ideal, the mould of fashion, in this as in so many other matters. Princess Di didn't just have bulimia, in the way that someone might have a bad bladder or suffer from migraines; the princess's oscillating relationship with the food she ate was more of a characteristic of her celebrity being.

I'm not denying that the binge-and-clearance routine was real, or that she did not cut a swath in the carpet running from dining room to loo. But it was part of the apparatus of her fame that she had such a *current* ailment to signal her connection in suffering to the adoring peasantry. All the original saints suffered, as it seems our plastic ones must also.

Suffering follows a curve of fashion, and the truly famous must be careful what they acknowledge to be the ills their pampered flesh is heir to. Geri suffered. And went, on her own, to a psychiatric hospital to be cured. The parable form demands redemptive moments of initiative.

They gave her Prozac and more or less told her to eat and get on with it. She knew then that this bulimia business had to be taken on by hers truly. And in a trice she was out and eating. Down, dragon, down.

It's worth quoting the moment of epiphany: "After 10 days I began to get restless in the psych ward. Perhaps the novelty had worn off. I didn't have any clearer picture of what had gone wrong but I felt as though I'd given my mind a [ministry of transportation] test or a grease-and-oil change. Everything was now in working order." And they say the unexamined life is not worth living.

I'll give Halliwell some credit. She declined an A-condition of "being abused as a child," which seems to be the option of choice for so many of her peers.

Otherwise the fable is everywhere true to form: early struggles, burning ambition, ruthless determination (early boyfriends and managers get dropped like socks), predatory agents and managers, aerobics classes, the big break, the high life, the rueful awakening to the thought that this isn't going to last. *If Only* is a custom tour through the unalterable patterns of the fable. Northrop Frye would have been pleased.

Like all fables, it must have an iron moral. Ginger is standing outside Mann's Chinese Theater following a brisk show-up at Planet Hollywood, the ultimate pit stop of hyped celebrity, on the day of the Spice Girls' movie premiere: "'This is my big Hollywood moment,' I thought. This is what I dreamed about as a little girl. But as I waved and smiled at the crowd, I came to a touching realization. . . . Suddenly, I understood that the reality would never match the scene in my imagination. . . . Each accomplished ambition is a dream that is dying." Not quite the death of Little Nell, but the celebrity-bio equivalent, the moment when it all comes together, wistful, neat, and simple.

The less-laundered message of *If Only* is truly wistful, if not so neat and simple. It's about the deep, neurotic desire to be a celebrity, which is comprehended by Geri Halliwell as ambition. Life is a surface phenomenon only, as slick and thin as cellophane. Life is real only when you are the one in front of the flashing cameras and the rest of the world (fandom) is tearing its throat out calling your name. Hustle, purge, and take no prisoners, so the moment finally comes when Oprah calls you for the interview, you get to stand on stage with George Michael, or rent a castle in Ireland with a butler for a Christmas break.

If Only is a bleak book. I don't think Halliwell and her fellow Barbies are any better or worse than the hundreds of other pop blossoms, from Madonna to Britney Spears. And I'm willing to concede that those who "succeed" in the pop business are, in most substantial matters, no better off than the legions that so fitfully support them.

The hollowness at the centre of celebrity culture, as we have come to call it, is – if fully encountered – searingly melancholy. If this book has one virtue, it is that it unwittingly (how else?) allows us to see that encounter. It is a window looking out upon our meretricious days.

– Ottawa Citizen

The Answer Is Blowin' in the Wind

My knowledge and appreciation of rap music is limited to what escapes from the open windows and thundering bass speakers of passing cars in downtown Toronto, and the occasional halt on one of the music channels, where the latest street poet delivers up the story of hard life in the 'hood in four basic rhymes, a knot of aggressive hand signals, and a lot of leaning into camera.

Between the bleeps and the high-volume override of the music, not many of the words seep through. Most rap lyrics, I am convinced – though this could be laziness on my part or the thought that the bullion is not worth the dive – could be in Sanskrit or ancient Coptic. I've tried to work through a few interviews with visiting rappers on one of the MuchMusic seminars, *Intimate and Inarticulate*, with no notable triumph. I gather, from the all-purpose mantra of these colloquia, they are "telling it like it is."

Blurring the words for the sake of the sound is nothing new. Bob Dylan, who is the very Homer of the mumble and the Shakespeare of strangled syllables, built himself a career that, for some, was very close to godhead, going on in a low whine that would challenge the acoustic skills of a nervous cat. The great Dylan anthem of all time, I suppose, and one of the most recklessly pretentious pop songs of all time – only Simon and Garfunkel's tumid "Bridge Over Troubled Water" and the great vaporous escapism of John Lennon's insufferably saccharine "Imagine" offer serious competition – contains the line: "The answer, my friend, is blowin' in the wind." And, if that wasn't clear enough, the next line offers the terse paraphrase: "The answer is blowin' in the wind."

155

I guessed the point Dylan was trying to make was that, as most will have gathered, the answer was blowin' in the wind.

Fatuous platitude and windy sentiment were a speciality of the boomer protest music. Anti-religious they may have been, but their unction was extreme. How some of them came to be regarded as poets might be put down to the pressure on a education system that not only tolerated hootenannies but actually, in some cases, encouraged them. The hootenanny was a horror of my youth, an ersatz festival of acoustic guitars wedded to mush so ripe it invited seizure.

The innocence of the protest generation, much like its high Eden moment at Woodstock, was always more indulgence than art. I don't know the medical payoffs of marijuana, and am indifferent to its legalization, but I do know that the cannabis haze of the boomers' radical period let many brains that were already impressively relaxed go limp altogether. The songwriters knew this. They were big on blur, and high on treacle. Cf. Peter, Paul, and Mary – "Puff the Magic Dragon."

All of it, despite the pieties of that time or the recall of those same pieties now as at the arsonist reunion of Woodstock 3, was commercial. Be it the Mamas and the Papas or the Rolling Stones or the Beach Boys, they may have been strumming peace, love, and rebellion, but their eye was on the charts and their real best friends were always the accountants.

It takes a pose. Then it was peace, today it's attitude. They are the same. The question ultimately, or solely, is: Does it move the record, the CD, or the video?

Hence the charming career of the latest wildperson of pop music, the delightful Eminem, a.k.a. the Real Slim Shady. Eminem has a turbulent domestic life. His wife very recently attempted suicide, his mother is suing him, and he himself is up on weapons charges. Should he falter as a rap hero, this is a one-man *Survivor* series. Eminem is notorious for the rage of his lyrics. I gather he slags just about everyone with great force and with, of course, the obligatory wild and unzipped language of rap, which is as stylized in its edge and raunch as the floral cooing of yesteryear's folkies or the hard blast of yesteryear's rock.

Trouble is, for many of the great pop consumers of the previous generation, it's *their* pieties that are being mocked or trod on this time. And so it has come to pass that the lyrics of the rapper, his homophobia, his disrespect of women, his hate language, are percolating a debate that calls to mind a hundred school-board meetings a generation ago when the "new culture" was waving its long hair and psychedelic posturing in the faces of its elders.

They shouldn't worry. He's just moving a product. Same old, same old. Anything for a buck.

The generation that cooked up liberation as an all-purpose philosophy for their gratification doesn't look cool trying to rein in a generation they trained. In the immortal words of a million forgotten sit-ins, let the circle be unbroken.

Rap on, Mr. Shady. Rap on. You the *real* Slim Shady.

– Globe and Mail

C-2 Much of C-3PO? I Have . . .

The *Globe*'s Rick Groen reviewed the latest *Star Wars* film, *Attack of the Clones*, Thursday. Remarkably, he seemed coherent.

I cannot imagine what it must be like to sit in a dark room watching another chunk of *Star Wars* sausage under the obligation to think and write about it afterward.

Mr. Groen must have an intellect of steel. The normal mind, if subjected to such torment, would fold, collapse, grind to painful paralysis. Perhaps Mr. Groen has a technique for "rebooting" his brain after such ordeals, for his column was notable for both its strength and lucidity. Either that, or there is a "stranger among us."

It's impossible to keep track of *Star Wars* any more. It can't keep track of itself. Allow me to demonstrate.

Star Wars: Episode II, Attack of the Clones is a prequel to *Star Wars* (the first to appear on screens), a sequel to *The Phantom Menace*, and a second prequel to the sequels *Star Wars: The Empire Strikes Back* and *Return of the Jedi*. It is then, simultaneously, a prequel, and a sequel to another prequel.

In other words, it is before some of the things it is after, after some of the things it is before, and is both before and after a whole lot of stuff that is before and after each other.

Vanna White will have worked out a neat two-line proof to Fermat's Last Theorem before anyone breaks the code on which *Star Wars* movie it is that is actually on the screen in front of them.

Fortunately, I have a shortcut to creating a diagram for the *Star Wars* timeline. Follow these steps:

a) open a tin of spaghetti;

b) dump it in a bucket of eels;

c) stir with a pointy stick;

d) tip that bucket.

You will then have what is called in logic a "messy convolution," or what George Lucas is pleased to call the plot structure of his *Star Wars* oeuvre.

The *Star Wars* schlockmobile has been with us now for almost thirty years. Three decades. Surely that is a long time to be sucking on the same jujube. Effectively, *Star Wars* is a fat comic book with lights. Now there's nothing wrong with comic books, or lights – if we just take them as they are and for what they are.

But from *Star Wars*'s first formidable launch, its promoters have been eager to sell the drones who make up its vast gullible following on the notion that it is more, much more. It is mythical, it carries vast cosmic themes, it is the epic of our technological days. Of course it is. And *Drabble* is *The Iliad*.

There are Britney Spears videos that carry more philosophical freight, and, for that matter, more interesting special effects, than the entire train wreck of *Star Wars* movies. I am thinking most particularly of "Oops! . . . I Did It Again," which features her hopping bountifully about on the moon, teasing some sad sack in a space suit. I think this must be Mr. Lucas's personal anthem. I'll bet he hums it all the way to the bank.

The Lucas franchise has an eerie pre-emptive hold on certain people. They say they have "grown up" on or with *Star Wars*. The intellectually homeless camp out on city streets for months for the extremely dubious distinction of being among the first to be exposed to the latest excrescence of Jar Jar Binks onto the big screen. The world, the real world, is busy, and rich and unfolding, but they are in a lineup outside some damn Cineplex.

It is deeply melancholy to witness such spectacles, part fetish, part narcosis. The dreadful *Star Trek* and all its interminable spinoffs, big screen and small, is another lotus pool of similar power. There are people "learned" in the lore of *Star Trek* and *Star Wars* who cram Web sites with their erudition, stockpile the paraphernalia of either series with the fever of medieval worshippers gathering relics, and waste their days learning Klingon or sorting out the genealogy of Darth Vader's cat.

Outside of Holy Water and a certain liturgy, I am not sure if there is a cure for this condition.

The real measure of *Star Wars* is the automatic comparison that is being made with its philosophical cousin *Spider-man*. Mr. Lucas declines the idea that *Attack of the Clones* is in any way in competition with *Spider-man*, but the Zeitgeist and its toothy messenger, Mary Hart, beg to differ.

Spider-man is a comic book with lights, too. And it's set to make about a trillion dollars. Comic books are the refuge and preoccupation of adolescents. They are teething rings for the yet unfinished mind, a confection of fluff, cheap thrills, and callow fantasies that distract them from the turbulence of approaching maturity.

There comes a moment, however, when comic books – if I may dip into the vernacular – no longer do it.

When the fables of Stan Lee and Marvel comics seem, you know, childish.

This is a moment that has been infinitely postponed – maybe it's been on hiatus – for George Lucas, and the millions lost in the banal drift of his light sabres and tin puppets, of his Yodas and Jabbas and Jedis, of all his confounded sequels and prequels.

It's called maturity.

– Globe and Mail

007: Licensed to Inhale

Thank God for the *Globe and Mail*'s brazen headline. I was about to see *Die Another Day*, starring Pierce Brosnan and Halle Berry. I grew up on Bond. It accounts for my furtiveness. The headline on Thursday tipped me to a minefield. The hyper-alert ninja of the anti-smoking brigades had spotted that this Bond film was about to wreck the social order. In it, the great assassin/hedonist smokes a cigar.

The serpent was back in the garden. Pavlov's dogs were loose again. I stayed home.

The lynx-eyed guardians of the anti-smoking movement of three countries were warning us of the consequences of the Bond release. We should not be surprised. They prowl the Zeitgeist with the subtlety of cat burglars and the radar of bats, keen to its every ominous tremor.

I don't know why universities bother to maintain psychology departments any more. The average on-line anti-smoking site, or any of their densely informative press releases, contain more truth about human nature – and, in particular, the impenetrable *terra incognita* of the teenaged mind – than all of Freud and Jung, or whole sackfuls of psychotherapists fresh from a debriefing with Dr. Phil himself. We owe them. Is it too late for a Nobel?

The spectacle of James Bond smoking a cigar, in Cuba, in a movie, will collapse in a trice the Maginot line of social control and legislative restriction that it has been the labour of two decades to construct. (The wily Castro has been getting a free ride on this one. Really Big Tobacco has never had a better friend, or billboard, than Marx's child in Havana. Was Mr. Brosnan suborned or seduced for this tidy bit of "Make Mine Cohibas" product placement?)

The cigar will lay waste an entire generation of North American teen-agers, leave them exposed and defenceless before the satanic machinations of the addiction merchants. The world's public-health industry, with its legions of missionary activists, will be swept away like a leaf in the wind, its exhortations forgotten, its work undone, when Pierce Brosnan (to think the man is Irish! Where is his mother?) reaches for the stogie onscreen, flicks his fatal and malodorous Bic, and shatters the social engineering of twenty years. Think it was an accident he played Grey Owl?

In the words of the head of the Non-Smokers' Rights Association ("The name's Mahood. Garfield Mahood"): "If icons like James Bond use cigars, it's not a long leap for young people to assume it's all right to smoke cigarettes."

No, Mr. Mahood, it's not a leap at all. They are but a puff away from perdition. Mr. Mahood, cautious as always, is soft-pedalling, doubtless to avert social panic. But all of us must pay attention when he says, "It's all very destructive in terms of role-modelling." We've been warned.

Now, one or two eccentric skeptics and, maybe, the odd Amish retiree might question whether James Bond is a role model. But all ludicrously handsome future assassins with a taste for high life, the appetites of a tomcat, a harem of supermodels, an arsenal the envy of Osama bin Laden, and the morals of a splinter, have held James Bond as the template of their lives. We're talking Everyman here.

And thanks to the gorgeous erosion of sexual difference in these enlightened times ("You've come a long way, baby"), every Jane can be a James, too.

The depravity of Hollywood is truly bottomless. But it's our fault: they've offered us everything – strippers and carnage, whores and gang-sters, death, mayhem and mutilation, Adam Sandler pissing against a wall, Madonna in the sand, Sylvester Stallone mumbling his way to mass slaugh-ters, exorcism, rap movies, Britney on a road trip, Eminem as the new Mickey Rooney, miles of Star Drek, serial-killing cannibals – every con-ceivable folly. They've offered us everything, including Steven Seagal and Michael Moore, and it wasn't enough.

We wanted that final titillation. And now we've got it. James Bond, onscreen, smoking for the first time in decades.

No need to concern ourselves about Kyoto or its protocols – they do not matter. North America will soon be cocooned in a cloud of Cohiba smoke so dense, ripe, and inescapable that we will long for the innocent days of mere global warming and climatic catastrophics. Life for the majority will be one long Humphrey Bogart movie, suck and puff, lighter and ashtray – "and all our yesterdays . . . [lighting] us the way to [smoky] death." We are pleased to welcome you to a total smoking environment.

Our only hope is the crack radar and precision sociology of the anti-smoking commandos. Maybe they could run off one of those powerful public-service messages they used to be so good at. *I Am Halle Berry's Lungs* might stay our Gadarene plunge off the Cliffs of Nicotine.

And she breathes brilliantly. Fighting fire with fire, so to speak.

– Globe and Mail

My Garret: The SkyDome

Vocabulary quiz: What's the technical term for renting Toronto's SkyDome to hold a reading? Circus.

And what a great day for the Republic of Letters it will be.

The world's première littérateuse, creator of the Harry Potter series, J.K. Rowling is going to give a reading at Toronto's SkyDome this fall as part of the city's International Festival of Authors.

The Potter is expected to draw a crowd at least equal to Tina Turner when she stopped over, and may surpass the most recent Monster Truck Rally and Wrestlemania IV combined. It's a great time to be a noun.

Opening acts will include Carlos Santana (*Supernatural*), Limp Bizkit, and (on the off chance some adults may attend) poet and singer (*Genie in a Bottle*) Christina Aguilera. It is not yet clear whether the Rolling Stones will drop by for a cameo, or whether Mick Jagger will just send a video of him and Keith Richards reading a few of the more gruesome stanzas from Coleridge's *Rime of the Ancient Mariner*.

Literature hasn't had such a good time since Jacqueline Susann figured out some odd uses for the semicolon.

I've exaggerated a bit. Santana isn't going to be there. Or those other celebrities. Keith and Mick aren't going to read; *The Ancient Mariner* cuts too close to the bone.

But J.K. herself, in all her Harry Potter-ness, is truly going to give a "reading" in the SkyDome. And further, it is true that the performance is part of Toronto's annual International Festival of Authors.

The stadium read. This is, pun fully intended, a novel concept.

A publicist for the festival indicates that it's novel for J.K. Rowling, too. In an elegant phrase from an article in yesterday's *Globe and Mail*, the publicist informs a hungry public that "the top she's done is 200 people." Which makes the SkyDome recitation truly a quantum leap for literature.

Greg Gatenby, artistic director of the festival, is also quoted: "It's a rare public outing for this normally reclusive author." Well, I dunno. Could be that J.K. Rowling is turning out to be the Darva Conger (*Who Wants to Marry a Multi-Millionaire, Playboy*) of long-form fiction. Darva had claims of being reclusive, too, but seems to be adjusting to the ogling just nicely.

"She's done [readings] in bookstores, but none ever this big before," Mr. Gatenby said. "In England, they just don't like readings like they do [in Toronto]."

Hush, Mr. Gatenby. What do the English know about reading – or literature for that matter? I suppose in England they "do" readings in tiny groups, and the book is the star. Why, man, that's not just old-fashioned, it's atavistic. So V.S. Pritchett.

Why, I hear there are parts of England where there are no readings at all, just individuals who take a book from a library, go home – brace yourself, clear the children from the room – and *read it themselves*. No one else in the room at all. No wonder poor Martin Amis had all those bad teeth. Grinding them for years in simple frustration over the essential loneliness of the literary transaction. In England, I'm told, some authors can easily be mistaken for hermits.

Not in Toronto. My garret, the SkyDome. Sixty thousand people are going to be there for readings from the Harry Potter oeuvre. I wonder if the festival organizers have thought of inviting Céline Dion to come out of her temporary seclusions and sing a few chapters from *Winnie-the-Pooh*, to kind of set the tone of the affair. I think such an addition could not fail to seal the night for literature. Céline and J.K. The *Titanic* and the Titanic.

"We'll have wizards and magicians working the crowd," we're told. Well, I surely hope so. It will be a sad thing if sixty thousand people show up for a reading and all they get – at an authors festival – is a reading.

Someone has very clearly cast a spell over the festival. Someone, somewhere, has waved a pointy stick, muttered abracadabra, and morphed the little symposium by the lake into a *Mad Max* movie for pseudo-intellectuals. Sixty thousand people at the SkyDome is not a literary event; it's a mass gawk. And let us, please, have none of the plastic platitudes that will wrap this travesty like an air bag: "Oh, if it gets just one child to read, it'll all be worth it." Carpet bombing children with hype and glutting them with spectacle is the sure way of numbing their imagination, and evacuating their sense of individuality, the very conditions literature and reading exist to repair.

There is enough and far more than enough high-octane celebrity fever corroding the sensibility of the world as it is and turning the minds of the young or the perpetually adolescent into little more than billboards for fad and trinket.

Reading may be the one last and tenuously held redoubt against the blizzard of fatuous enthusiasms and sterile recreations in a TV-Hollywood world.

We expected better of an authors festival. We did not expect them to rent the SkyDome and camp so triumphantly with the barbarians.

– Globe and Mail

The Ruckus Over Uncouth and Occult

It was a great week for merchandising. J.K. Rowling, the only begetter of the Harry Potter machine, roared through Toronto this week to give a reading at the SkyDome. I'm surprised that the Seattle crowd – those who roam the world casting spells to halt the plague of "globalization" – didn't mount a few pickets and give us a little street theatre in protest against what is quite clearly the Starbucks of literature.

I missed the reading myself and, partly as penance and partly to connect myself to literature as a mass activity, spent a few days rereading the works of Tom Clancy. I don't know if Tom Clancy will ever be invited to read at the SkyDome, but I'm sure at the peak of Clancymania he could pull a really good crowd on any aircraft carrier in the world. Aircraft carriers are big. Think SkyDome with guns.

As with so much of literature these days, reading is more a matter of venue and ambience, and that wonderful sense of losing yourself in the milling crowd, than sitting alone and antisocially chasing black dots on a white page in the hope of a quiet thrill over a turn of phrase.

The marketing of Harry Potter has had more than a little help from the forces of priggishness and sanctimony. A few of the truly dim have been protesting that Ms. Rowling's works "advocate" witchcraft and the dark arts. At a time when *Touched by an Angel*, *Buffy the Vampire Slayer*, *Charmed*, and even *Bewitched* crowd the TV schedule, without so much as a clucked tongue of outrage, it is difficult to take seriously any protest that we – those of us in the visible world – are being menaced by the forces of the invisible one, be they dark or light.

If we mean by witchcraft the power to cause unaccountable effects, usually by means of some verbal formula, then we shall quickly have to admit that witchcraft and literature are one. All good writing is an enchantment, and every good metaphor is a potent spell.

But to seek to put the Harry Potter phenomenon out of business by claiming it is in league with the devil can, I fear, only swell the progress of the young wizard's devotees. Nothing so infects the young with unbridled enthusiasm as the leering prissiness of their elders.

To which proposition I call in evidence the even greater numbers who thronged to the selfsame SkyDome to bathe in the sweet and rhyming cooings of the young minstrel Eminem, a.k.a. the Real Slim Shady. No less Mr. Bumbles of public virtue than Ontario's attorney-general and Toronto's Moose "R" Us mayor threatened coronaries of disgust that the young poet should even be let into the city or the country. There were public laments that the hate-crime laws were not elastic enough to constrict him. That's the trouble with so much criminal legislation – it's never vague enough.

I have a problem when representatives of the generation that loosed Peter, Paul, and Mary on the world, not to mention the unspeakable Donovan, and who still clatter with their arthritic potions and nitroglycerin tablets to the SkyDome whenever the Rolling Stones come by to parody their earlier selves, raise a ruckus over a stripling lyricist such as Eminem. It can't be a worry over the city. Toronto is strong. It survived *Cats*, *Phantom of the Opera*, Cher, and return engagements of Tony Bennett.

Can it be that overexposure in their youth to the yodellings of the Beach Boys and the demon thunders of too many electric guitars, or any portion of Pink Floyd, has fatally scorched the old brain cells? Is this not ye kettle calling ye potte blacke?

It could all be a ruse, of course. The anti-witchcraft lobby could be a creation of the global marketing conspiracy that is clearly fuelling the Harry Potter storm. Mel Lastman and his handmaiden, Ontario's attorney-general, might in the cunning way of these things have been executing a last-minute boost for attendance, ensuring Eminem there's not a head wearing a baseball cap backward that will stay at home. Is it too much to be hoped that Slim Shady will commemorate by way of one of his subtle anthems, perhaps in his next album, Toronto and its sales-wise mayor.

It's worth noting that a similarly crafty display of prudishness, way back in the early 1990s, banned Barenaked Ladies, thus ensuring their immortality. This was, I believe, during the world-class city's lap-dancing fever.

As Barbara Cartland says somewhere, all's well that ends well. J.K. survived and little wizards are cheering. And Eminem, bless his baggy pants, hip-hopped all over the SkyDome stage. Both mass convocations must be judged full artistic successes.

It's going to be a difficult week to top. I wonder how comfortable Britney Spears would be doing *Christabel.* Collagen and Coleridge. Uncouth and Occult. It couldn't lose.

– Globe and Mail

Céline's Child: At a Church Near You

It helps to understand the plot of *Titanic*, the movie, if we acknowledge that the great vessel's captain sought out the iceberg, and hoped for the collision, under pressure from passengers and crew.

It was the only way, finally, for all of them to escape the Céline Dion soundtrack. The submersion was a desperate cry for help against one facet of the omnipresence of the Céline Dion story.

That omnipresence is taking on theological, even mystical, tinges. On Wednesday, Ms. Dion and her husband, René Angélil, conducted the baptism of their son, René-Charles, at Montreal's majestic Notre-Dame Basilica. The event was described as a "private ceremony." For perfect drollery, this is hard to match.

An event that probably required greater logistical support than D-Day, beckoned more paparazzi than Diana's wedding, and sought to amplify the proceedings by inviting in the cameras of celebrity television may only be described as "private" because – as far as we know – it was restricted to a single planet.

A wonderful line in the *Globe*'s report runs, "He may be the first baby in Canada to have his baptism covered by *Entertainment Tonight*." It may be one of the few defects of that peerless court calendar of rich flesh and pointless renown that Mary Hart is a stranger to far too many of this country's baptismal fonts.

The Great Chipmunk has brocaded many an awards ceremony, many a first-night premiere. But we do not see her lurking in satin and stilettos outside this country's chapels and churches, following the inaugural rites of a great religion.

"Do you renounce Satan and all his works and pomps?" This is a question asked by proxy to the infant at baptism. And maybe it provides the clue to the drought of baptismal features – outside Céline's, of course – on *Entertainment Tonight*. The embrace of the "works and pomps" in question, indeed their manufacture, celebration, and distribution, is very much the work of *Entertainment Tonight*. And if we were to substitute Hollywood for Satan – and there can surely be no reasonable objection to doing so, given Hollywood's remorselessness in seeking the ruin of souls – then the presence of *Entertainment Tonight*, or any of its clones, may be seen as a quite fatal conflict of interest.

I fear the only sacrament that *Entertainment Tonight* might want to take to its sycophantic and always palpitating bosom, though in a quite different sense than any church intended, is extreme unction. The program that found time to bid adieu to Tom Green's departing testicle has a low liturgical threshold.

Another of the fascinating details of this private ceremony was that Ms. Dion and her husband held off on the baptism, in this country, for six months. Any earlier aspersion of the sacramental waters might have imperilled his U.S. citizenship. As against risking U.S. citizenship for the infant, an eternity in limbo – which among believers is the penalty for the unbaptized – is a trivial peril, and well worth the wait.

It may also have helped the decision that waiting a few months guaranteed – in the delightful lingo of Hollywood – that the baptism "opened wide." And that the caravan of limos and the unfurling of the "cobalt-blue carpet" for the VIPs attending the ceremony were not wasted on an unattentive world.

That such a moment could have been wasted, or sunk below the fold, is too piercing to contemplate. I remember the scene of Madonna's first wedding, the one to Sean Penn, during which the groom took to aiming a Howitzer at press helicopters as a strategy for subduing interest in the event. The supernovas of the celebrity world have a gift, maybe even a divine intuition, for guaranteeing that what they insist is most private achieves incandescent publicity.

The press agents of old had nothing on them. What could they offer? A star in the east, no room at the inn, a couple of snooping shepherds, three wise men, and swaddling clothes in a manger. Without Mary Hart. Try to get a script out of that.

What else could the Dions have done to keep matters even more private? They could have corralled Barbara Walters, I suppose, or Oprah, and re-enacted the Annunciation, or brought up some of the leftover camels from their second wedding ceremony earlier in Las Vegas, another Mecca for introverts. Only authentic second-wedding camels, please note. A stray desert humpback, smuggled in by a mischievous reporter to the precincts of Notre-Dame, was evicted by the police. Non–Las Vegas camels, heretic camels, were definitely not wanted.

Besides, it might have been surplus wattage. Céline has already "sat down" with Barbara on the conception, so maybe this was too sequelish. And importing the camels from the previous venue would not have been such a good idea. Camels tire in church.

And those camels are going to be needed for the next instalment. The Flight into Egypt.

– Globe and Mail

A Fine Moonwalker Whine

It was said that, after September 11, things would never be the same. I'm inclined to agree. Some people who were merely silly or annoying before that day have graduated to full obnoxiousness.

The Hollywood crowd – the pop stars, comics, movie and fashion icons – lost its balance for a couple of weeks, and experimented with novel notions of humility and withdrawal; the spotlight was on real heroes, such as firefighters and police officers, and no one really wanted to see the tinsel mimics. The Grammys were delayed – hardly anyone's idea of a sharp penance, but to this bunch a real burn on their very own Via Dolorosa.

Now they have come roaring back in all their trivial glory.

Exhibit A is this week's delirious preening of Michael Jackson, in attendance with Al Sharpton, beating a gong about racism in the recording industry. According to the Moonwalker, the industry has a grudge against him because he "passed" the Beatles and Elvis in record sales. And that he, being black (or at least having once been so – Mr. Jackson is not so much a person of colour as an experiment in sequential hues), the industry held this against him. According to His Gloveship, this explains his career's decline, the dwindling respect for him as an artist.

I don't know – travelling with a monkey, paying off the family of some young person alleging molestation, years of bleach therapy, living in a house called Neverland, playing mummy in a hyperbaric chamber a couple of times a day, in general conducting himself in a way that makes a solid case for Ozzy Osbourne as the Ward Cleaver of our day – these are factors that might also contribute to the public's satiety with the Jackson persona.

The bridge that connected Michael Jackson to his fans was long ago detonated by none other than Michael Jackson. It takes a sublime narcissism to drag racism into a discussion of a career that, in its early and middle years, was successful beyond measure. Grammys rained on him, the sponsorships were thick and rich, he was worshipped by millions.

In any event, he should be careful of comparisons to Elvis. Part of Presley's stranglehold on fame is that he, too, worked to explode a career also remarkable in its excess. By the time he died, he was a living caricature of himself. The one-time rockabilly rebel had morphed into a Las Vegas lounge act, sweating his way through Paul Anka's stake in the heart of music and modesty, "My Way."

Presley popped pills, ate with the discrimination of a garburator, aped the seclusion of Howard Hughes, and virtually threw away the most miraculous ascension in popular entertainment of a generation. He died at forty-two, at which point his career took off once again. Posthumous Presley is more ubiquitous and enduring than he ever was in his life, and he has surely been seen by a lot more people.

The weirdness that men do lives after them, and Presley is now a phenomenon, something between a populist saint and a plaster immortal. He has a commanding spot on the dashboard of eternity.

Michael Jackson, I think, has more musical talent than Presley. This is probably debatable. What is not debatable is Mr. Jackson's superior quota of weirdness. He has migrated from celebrity into some eerie, surreal region of self-worship.

He has leased his face as a hobby centre, a chop shop to itchy plastic surgeons. Compared to him, Cher is a dilettante in the epidermal arts of stretch, tuck, scrape, slice, import, and graft. He changes faces like some people do wallpaper.

So when he speaks of outpacing Elvis, is he talking of Elvis the performer or Elvis the desperate and self-destructive recluse? It is very likely he's haunted by Elvis, but that's hardly a monopoly: every supermarket in the world has made the same claim. Elvis is the poltergeist of choice in the food aisles of the world.

The king of rock 'n' roll, however, had one virtue that the self-designated king of pop will never own: Elvis didn't whine in public. For all his cravings, he had the one restraint that today's yuppie celebs have never contemplated. He never played the victim. For that, I'll give him a pass on "White Christmas" and (almost) forgive him for "My Way."

But Michael Jackson is just hungry for more attention, more money, and more meretricious fame. For him to invoke racism as a cause for his decline is a piece of monstrous egoism. For some people, September 11 just meant reconfiguring the schedule, some down time to chart a cheap comeback.

– Globe and Mail

Even Martha's Cooked

People have been predicting the end of the world since the world began. Apocalypse is very inviting to a certain type of gloomy mind.

Apocalyptics fall into two classes.

There is in every generation a bunch haunted by the dread thought that they are living in the End Times; these are the lads you occasionally see on street corners holding up for the attention of careless humankind crudely handwritten posters announcing The End Is Near (always a cheering thought on the way to work).

The other bunch don't live in dread of the end of time. They wish to precipitate it, to bring on the Apocalypse. Osamas and Adolfs belong in this black category. They'd like – it's a matter of ego – to see the world terminate coincidentally with their own termination. If they cannot own the world, or rule it, then the world is unworthy and should end. Call this class the activist apocalyptics. Fortunately, they are few, but what they lack in number they make up for in intensity.

The membership of both categories is nuts. No generation has been spared the loony warnings of an approach of the End of Days; prophets of doom are a dime a dozen and the world has learned to accommodate them. Every age has its litter of wars and disasters, and those on the receiving end of either or both can be forgiven for seeing, in the great fat diet of misery that was theirs to endure, some sign that God or Fate was about to abandon creation, or bring it to a close.

I'm not much of an apocalyptic kind of guy myself. I'm a pessimist. I think the world is going to go on forever. My faith, however, in the endurability of things is taking a fair beating these days. I'm not talking about the Enrons or the WorldComs, those great engines of hype and greed, the ravening maws of turbo-capitalism that have been such a scourge of late. There have always been pirates and con men; this bunch has merely upgraded the arts of depredation and deceit, and worked its ravages with the cellphone and the Pentium chip rather than the more honourable cutlass and shiv.

They've ravished the savings of hundreds of thousands, it is true, beggared some and ended the jobs of many more. But we've seen this stuff before, from the South Sea Bubble to that most florid of speculations, the tulip mania of a few centuries back. In this, there is truly nothing new under the sun.

No, cleaving my certainty is a more frightful portent: the (possible) Fall of Martha Stewart! The great Goddess of Yuppie pedantry, and Do-It-Yourselfer Empress of an entire class of people who never do anything themselves (they'd contract out breathing if it could be listed as a business expense), has been shadowed with allegations of insider trading.

True, it is for some piddling sum, about $43,000. In Martha's vineyard, $43,000 is spent on renovating the canary's perch ("a tube of alabaster surrounds this spindle of Brazilian redwood taken from the pith of the central column of an early Indian temple. Tweety will love it"). No, it's not the amount. It's the icon, stupid.

Brittle, fastidious, robotic, imperious, *perfect* Martha Stewart may have been – yikes! – careless. A splinter in the deep beams of Eternity, a fissure in the Rock of the Ages. I would rather contemplate the notion that Oprah isn't a true friend of Literature (this is an abyss we really don't want to stare into) – that maybe she skips the descriptive bits – than give oxygen to the consideration that Martha is sloppy.

The centre cannot hold. Things, untidily, fly apart. The blood-dimmed tide is loosed indeed, and who will mop up after? It may be, then, that we are on the brink of chaos, that the slavering guy on the corner with his cautionary graffiti is finally on to something. Afghanistan, the schism of the Liberal Party, Joe Clark musing about yet another go, the war on terror, the collapse of the markets, global warming – these are but the bric-a-brac, mere trinkets on the mantelpiece of our troubled times. We can shove these discomforts under the rug of our always-obliging complacency.

But we can truly hear the scroll of the heavens unwinding when Our Lady of Kmart, Madonna of the High Thread Counts (Egyptian cotton, please), proves to be frail and peccant like the rest of us. This is, emphatically, not a good thing. And as if to prove that Armageddon or a reasonable facsimile is on the horizon, and in John Crosbie's immortal rephrasing, "the Four Horsepersons" are burnishing their saddle gear, I've been four days in Newfoundland and experienced four days of *consecutive* sunshine. Sunshine in Newfoundland, and Martha mortal: surely the Second Coming is at hand.

– *Globe and Mail*

Buckingham Versus Bedlam

The Queen has delivered her annual message. It takes skill to tell one regal Christmas message from another. Are there patterns of inflection that vary from year to year? Does anyone remember any occasion when the second Elizabeth departed from her low-calorie script (even for the space of a parenthesis) to say something spontaneous to sully that patented liturgical monotone?

The Queen's message is more a duration than anything else. A buzz from the Monarch to the Commonwealth nations that assures by her presence, and its consistency over time, that she is still there and still the same: continuity, not content – that is its purpose. Its eloquence is purely gestural: she shows up.

I noticed this year that Her Majesty faced competition, an upstart rival, in the unlikely person of the wife of the child-adult rock star, Ozzy Osbourne. The Osbournes, all but hermits will know, are MTV's contribution to the sad "reality TV" genre of *The Bachelor*, *Survivor*, and other baits for the socially and intellectually anorexic.

MTV has woken from the slumber in which it dreamed that endlessly recycled teen awards shows and album-launch suck-up interviews constituted a perfect commercial universe. They gave us *The Osbournes*, a half-hour edit of a week in the life of Ozzy and his family, which turns out to be a weirdly charming piece of voyeurism.

Their conversation, the very bogland of scatology, would abash Tony Soprano. Take the f-word and its variant forms away from the Osbournes, and they could not say good morning to one another. But underneath the

continuous hailstorm of profanity, and separate from their strange relations with an ark-load of diarrhetic pets, something like affection raises its
cautious, perplexed, valiant, and unteachable head.

Sharon Osbourne is the normal one in this family – which I admit kind
of gives "normal" the day off. She is the closest thing to an adult in the
menagerie, and Ozzy clearly depends on her and loves her. This is exceptional only when it is recalled that, in 1989, in what most reports describe as
a "haze of drugs and drink," he tried to strangle her. An affection that survives attempted homicide, however brain-fried the aggressor, may not
claim the longevity of an oak, but is more than a match for its density.

Sharon Osbourne likes to cite the occasion in interviews (it surely beats
holiday pictures) and has been known to use it as a put-down on mewling
upstarts like the more demure Eminem: "I see that Eminem gets in trouble
for singing about killing his wife," she blandly related to one interviewer.
This was the set-up for the next line: "At least my husband actually tried to
do it." I hope that Eminem, the Real Slim Shady, was duly chastened.

On one level, Sharon Osbourne may be a genuine rival to the Queen. It
is reported that, in negotiations for a second year of *The Osbournes*, she
asked for a new house and "lifetime psychotherapy for her dogs." I'm not
suggesting Her Majesty endorses psychobabble for canines. Some slip of
sense remains at the palace. I'm merely pointing out that both seem to dote
on dogs.

The pre-press of the Osbourne alternative Christmas message made it
clear that it was intended as a real challenge to the House of Windsor. Press
releases stressed that Sharon would be "going head-to-head over the
nation's turkeys" with the Queen.

Just in case her own celebrity would not be a sufficient magnet to draw
viewers from the Monarch's address, Sharon generously confided in
advance of the talk that it would contain her compliments to Camilla
Parker-Bowles on the state of Ms. Parker-Bowles' cleavage.

"They're really solid," Sharon kindly remarked earlier in the year. This
news cannot have been cheerfully received by anyone, save Prince Charles
– who would have his own diagnosis at home in Buckingham Palace.

A while ago the monarchy was under siege for being out of touch. The madcap antics of some of the royal retainers, the feuds that buzzed during poor Diana's turbulent marriage, moved many commentators to suggest the royal family had to change its ways, and that the Queen herself become more accessible. No one was so daft as to suggest she go on *Oprah* – that would be a clash that would rend the Zeitgeist – but the prompts were that she go populist.

I wonder if the shrewdly mad Osbournes saw the wisdom of the same strategy – that the dysfunctional exhibitionists of the Hollywood Hills could extend their hold on the public by miming the protocols and traditions, at least one day of the year, of the longer-running family series.

Who is riding the coattails of whom? When monarchs collide – stay tuned.

– Globe and Mail

CANADIANA

Gretzky: The Great One

I know as much about professional sports as Madonna does about self-restraint, and have attended so few hockey games, I couldn't pick Eric Lindros out of a lineup if he was standing in full gear between Michael Jackson and Dolly Parton. That said, even I couldn't miss and be impressed with the wave of tears and tribute that swept the continent during Wayne Gretzky's farewell to the game he ruled and to the millions who loved and admired him for it. Some thought it was overdone. Well, finding fault with Wayne Gretzky last week was a little like carping about a sunset.

The farewell was a phenomenon: an ovation in Ottawa, where he played his last Canadian game, that lasted longer than some of the summers where I come from. And that was when people were only anticipating his retirement. And then in New York on Sunday, where it is said they are hard to impress and stony of heart, there was an outflow of public emotion and affection that would embarrass a hippie reunion hosted by James Taylor on Earth Day.

What was all this about? Well, it was surely about the legendary skills. Mr. Gretzky and hockey seemed to understand one another so well that anyone else on the ice at the time seemed to be dropping by for a visit – more to get a glance at the happy couple than to contribute anything to the relationship. He was so good at what he did that, when he was there, there was nowhere else to look. It was like trying to find if anything else was going on in a concert hall when Vladimir Horowitz was test-driving a Steinway.

We do like our virtuosi, and Gretzky was a one-man master class from the day he put on skates. But – and what a happiness it is to say it – his skill,

185

the sheer excellence of his play alone, didn't melt the hearts of millions and send a shiver of sweet anguish over North America when he said goodbye. In an age demented with celebrity and with celebrities so clearly demented, he stood aside. The tinsel trinity of most superstars in sports, politics, or entertainment are coin, ego, and exhibitionism. The rules are different for them in that, for so many, there aren't any rules.

Gretzky didn't choke his coach on a regular basis; he didn't use his office to fish for interns; he didn't explore his crotch, à la Roseanne, during a national anthem; he has yet, unlike James Cameron, to tell us he's king of the world. But he's one up there because, I suppose, unlike Mr. Cameron, that's what the world is telling him. All the hotel rooms he left untrashed; all the street language he left unsaid; no diva tantrums; no private escalator to the twelve-step programs; no entourage of thick-necked, under-brained bruisers to clear his path to the best seat in the house; no lingering to milk the last geriatric buck, like Mick Jagger or Rod Stewart. It's conceivable, now that we recite this list, that he wasn't a superstar at all.

Well, he was the real thing, and that's the point. He had a different trinity: decency, moderation, and dignity. He was the most illustrious example we have that vulgarity isn't the necessary twin of celebrity; that one can be great – and he was the Great One – without turning clown or monster. Even better, his career and the farewell to it were as sharp as a parable. Character enhances. Nice guys don't finish last after all. They have a queue of their very own. That wasn't a farewell last week: it was an endorsement, an endorsement of a decent human being. And of course, there was that grin.

– The National

The Loonie

The Canadian loon is not a happy bird. The bird has four separate calls, which are the tremolo, the wail, the yodel, and the hoot. According to the *Canadian Encyclopedia*, the tremolo sounds like a crazy laugh and is used for a variety of purposes, such as to signal alarm or worry or to denote annoyance.

The loon, which we informally called the loonie, is also the official Canadian one-dollar coin. It's not a happy bird either. It unfortunately does not wail or yodel or hoot. Considering its current value, it should. You might say it comes to our pockets without any preliminary warning. But it shares with its woodland namesake the ability to inspire melancholy and, for the holders of any great number of loonies, this same capacity for instigating great annoyance.

Another citation from the encyclopedia informs us, and I quote, "loons have difficulty taking flight." I don't know how much of a naturalist Paul Martin is, but I suspect he's familiar with this characteristic. Diving is what loons and loonies do. And at roughly sixty cents to the real dollar, our loonie is as good at going underwater as any of the great banshees of the northern lakes.

We should wonder at any sovereign state that names its fundamental currency after a crazy cheap bird. The Americans go for better birds when they name their coins. The eagle is a noble creature. It doesn't hoot or wail or yodel. The eagle flies. Their bird is an artist of flight. Ours, a fish with feathers.

And their coin is in the same category. The eagle is real money. It's ten imperial American dollars. The loonie, our loonie, is essentially a fat quarter, well on the way to being worth a thin dime. It's a ridiculous currency, embarrassing to ask for, embarrassing to receive. It's all weight and no value. All jingle and no juice.

People suspected the loonie was the wrong way to go from the beginning. A coin is always that, just change. When we dropped the one-dollar bill, it was really an admission that the Canadian dollar wasn't worth its own ink. Same thing with the deuce or the two-dollar bill which has an even more irritating name than the loonie. It's just a damn toonie. If we were to go by the names, *Romper Room* is in charge of the Canadian Mint.

In all this downward turbulence, Canadians have adjusted. Our pennies are useless. Our quarters are dimes, and I'm not sure what the nickel is for any more, except as a recurring disappointment at parking meters. The five-dollar bill is really our one dollar bill. We all know this. It's just not official. And we know too that the sad loonies and toonies are only a step away from the Monopoly board.

So when the loonie goes down in international markets, we have no one but ourselves to blame. You cannot name, I repeat, you cannot name your fundamental currency after a sad, tawdry, cheap bird with a reputation for craziness to boot and expect the international money markets to do anything but smirk and put it on the endangered list. The Canadian dollar is worth sixty cents. Is this a country or the world's biggest discount house?

– The National

Woodchuck Checkout: The Death of Wiarton Willie

There are signs that the little brush with winter may have unhinged some of the normally sober citizens of Ontario. Yesterday, I was much taken by television pictures of some people in white suits clearly – the suits, I mean – not medical. Although white coats may not be far behind, in the town of Wiarton, Ontario.

It looked like a New Orleans funeral, except that I didn't spot any jazz trumpets and, to the best of my knowledge, there wasn't a parade through town to the beat of "When the Saints Go Marching In." It was a funeral though, for a fluffy little fuzzball who, for twenty-one years, obviously touched the lives of the citizens of Wiarton a little more strongly than it may be comfortable to admit in public.

Wiarton Willie is mort; he has cast his last shadow. He has gone into that hibernation from which there is no wake-up call. His furry little snout has poked above the cold, cold ground for the last time. This dog is grounded. He will visit the daisies no more. He is fertilizing them. To those Canadians with lives, or who have embraced the idea that snow falls in winter, it probably has to be explained that Wiarton Willie is – well actually was – a groundhog. "Jeremiah was a bullfrog," but that's another ballad.

And for the good people of this province and beyond, he offered himself as a warm-blooded edition of the *Farmer's Almanac*, a weather vane with whiskers emerging from his underground bunker in the early short, chill days of February to tell them whether there was to be a spring or no.

Personally, I've always felt that the idea of consulting a sleepy underground rodent for information on weather cycles was rather impetuously unscientific. And standing over a midwinter hole in the ground waiting for a weasel's cousin to emerge into the light, or lack of it, well, you can see it as valid political research, but climate? I don't think so.

But there was something else about yesterday's funeral for the little shadow caster that was troubling. Wiarton Willie was sent off into whatever underworld or afterlife moles have to look forward to with a carrot for garnish and a group of pallbearers who look like they just escaped from a Tom Wolfe convention or an Elvis contest.

Was all this, so to speak, on the up and up above-ground? Or was there skulduggery involved in the demise of the skilled digger? Groundhogs are a motley crew: Wiarton Willie, Malverne Mel, Balzac Billie, Dunkirk Dave. And the grimmest little clairvoyant of the lot, Punxsutawney Phil. These are the kind of monikers we've come to expect when they list the consultants for Al Pacino epics or choirboys from the witness-protection program. I never met Wiarton Willie, and I've never received any invitations from Punxsutawney Phil either.

But something tells me, if you saw either one of them come at you out of a hole in the ground, yawning and blinking, you'd be thinking this is not the kind of gopher I want in my cabbage patch. There was something altogether a little too cheerful about yesterday's sendoff. Did it strike you that some of the mourners weren't really that sad? I think it all points to – and you'll pardon the expression, I'm sure – a turf battle. This spring forecasting was all a sham, a con. The little ratheads have always been in it for the publicity. Wiarton Willie was just getting too big for his burrow, and Punxsutawney Phil put the fix in.

Still, Willie had the last grunt. He made Leno last night. Too bad he couldn't have been around for the monologue. As with so much of Jay Leno lately, it was full of stuff that only a groundhog could appreciate. Willie, it won't be spring without you. As was said so elegantly and with such pathos at yesterday's woodchuck checkout, what a bummer.

– *The National*

Good Lord! The Barbarians Are Us

S hould Adrienne Clarkson be Governor General?
Not while Anne Murray has some spare time.

Now it should be clear I am not praising one to discount the other. Adrienne has a lot of things going for her. But Anne Murray – if I may invoke a phrase from a possibly forgotten Liberal leadership convention – Anne Murray is the Governor General of all our hearts.

I was inflamed to these considerations by last Sunday's Oscars broadcast.

Never one to bypass a free lobotomy when one is televised, I, along with a billion others, gave myself over to the four-hour narcosis. The generally agreed-on highlight of the show was a scamper by Robin Williams through the aria of the *South Park* movie, "Blame Canada."

Mr. Williams, surrounded by an RCMP (Baywatch detachment) chorus line, croaked out vilification and scorn on all we stand for up here, and everyone we care for.

This country hasn't taken such a beating, lyrically speaking, since "The Lumberjack Song" spiked our hardihood and manliness so many years back on Monty Python. The Mounties were more or less (Eric) idle props on that occasion, too.

"Blame Canada" was ever so much more thorough, vile, and mean. They slagged everyone. And called Anne Murray a "b*t*h," d*m* their Hollywood eyes! Earth felt the wound.

Or not. As the case may be. Over the next few days, a rustle of self-congratulation ran through this country over "how well we took it." No outrage.

191

This may have been a feat of Canadian masochism, perhaps unequalled since the reruns of *Jalna*, or the invention of the spectator at curling matches.

The Canadian chin, grateful for something to be taken on it. Or a slice of our celebrated self-deprecation, that is at times so robust it's flat-out creepy. Or a fit of paralyzing demureness in the face of those "vulgar" barbarians to the south.

Or was it? There was no tidal wave of Oscar-bashing hyperventilating chauvinist Maple Leaf fury because the damn song got it right.

Contrary to popular myth, and despite all our self-cherishing of the notion of our northern purity soiled by the Vandals of commerce and celebrity from down south, it's not the Americans polluting us – it's we, them.

Yes. The barbarians are at the gates. But they're not our gates. And we are the barbarians. Name the territory, we've fertilized it.

Game shows: Regis Philbin, damn the luck, is not a test-tube baby. He sprang full-blown out of Canadian Alex Trebek's *Jeopardy!*-raddled head. Was that your final answer, Alex? We've exported more TV quizmasters to the United States than hockey players. If *Who Wants to Be a Millionaire?* is now a blight on the planet, the preliminary spores were Canadian.

Lounge lizardry: Robert Goulet did not break the sod, but he surely deepened the furrow. Wayne Newton may be the last word in Las Vegas unhip and bone-vaporizing schmaltz, but I've heard Robert Goulet sing, actually sing, "They Call the Wind Mariah."

Divas: There's not an elevator in the world immune to Céline Dion. All of Canada, I am persuaded, is just one huge fertility clinic for the production of pop divas. How do I love thee? Let me count the brays.

Céline. Alanis of the jagged little pharmaceutical. And the reigning juggernaut of every top-forty pantheon – the Empress Shania. For every "Stand by Your Man" Tammy Wynette lobbed up here, remember we lobbed a "Whose Bed Have Your Boots Been Under?" with belly buttons, back tenfold.

Hollywood: Vancouver.

Slush and inflatables: The Americans may have invented jiggle TV. God made sand. Pamela Anderson effected the merger, and every adolescent

Y chromosome on the planet saw that both were good. (In the deep liturgy of pop culture, Suzanne Somers is not even a pimple on any part of sleek Pam's pelt.) The bosomization of American television may be laid, so to speak, squarely, so to speak, at Canada's feet, so to speak. All our best . . . never mind.

Tom Green: It may be said that the Canadian pillage of the American mind was complete when MTV offered the great suction artist (Tom is an udder man) and roadkill comic his own show.

I could add a wheat-train-load of names to this sparse sampling of Canadian cultural imperialism. And so could you. But this is not *Jeopardy!*, thank God.

So when Robin Williams and the hot-pants Mounties slung "Blame Canada" at us, it was merely tit for tat. The dark truth is, they've earned the right to slag even Anne Murray.

With some exceptions, those we have sent to infiltrate and dominate have altered the American temper. And when we, back on home soil through the mournful apparatus of the CRTC, or the even-more-grey guardians of cultural nationalism, summon the spectre of American domination, it really is a case of the Canadian blast furnace calling the homely American kettle black.

– Globe and Mail

Anne and the New Criticism

I saw from an article in Wednesday's *Globe* that an academic frontiers-person has figured out that Anne, of *Anne of Green Gables*, was a lesbian. Well, duh! Of course she was. The real question is, did she vote NDP?

Now, purists and sticklers are going to write in and point out that there wasn't even a New Democratic Party in the P.E.I. of Lucy Maud Montgomery's books, and very little attention at all, for that matter, paid to party politics of any kind.

Well, of course there wasn't. Which just shows how repressive P.E.I. politics was, and how fearful Lucy Maud was even of intimating "socialist desire" on the part of her heroine. So she cleverly "concocted" whole novels in which you couldn't find the NDP with a Geiger counter. Which proves she really was the hardest of hardcore social-activist, card-carrying New Democrats. I don't think you can get any more QED-ed than that.

This business of finding stuff in old novels that is clearly not in the old novels is very good for the mind, and a great way to spend the academic summer holidays. You get to go to Charlottetown, and it's liberating, and so sensitive.

Filmmaker Patricia Rozema recently turned Jane Austen's *Mansfield Park* into a lesbian-tinged exposé of a child-abusing, patriarchal slave trader. This was so current I was surprised the amateur theatricals in the book hadn't been updated into the making of a Gap commercial.

The only thing that wasn't in the film of *Mansfield Park*, outside of a rave party and a couple of deaths from ecstasy, was a condemnation of the war in Kosovo, an endorsement of Al Gore, and the best on-line site to order a pashmina shawl. The new criticism, like the new movies, is contemporary with a vengeance.

Back to Anne. We've established she was a lesbian and voted NDP. Here comes the kicker. She also dealt crack cocaine. Now there is absolutely no reference to crack in the Anne canon. But this is not a handicap to interpretive criticism.

In the language of the papers now frothing the academic waves, it goes like this: it is amazing how L.M. Montgomery "concocts a surprising array of creative alternatives" to the non-presence of crack cocaine in the *Anne* books. With this plethora of no references to crack, Anne *had* to be dealing.

By this logic, we have to face it, folks: Anne, the pigtailed, freckle-faced gamine of Green Gables, was a street-hustling drug pimp, with a habit longer than daylight in Colombia and more connections than the new Air Canada. I rest my case.

A little more study of what's not there, and is therefore clearly the only stuff that is there, and a truly randy appetite for relevance and controversy, and we will soon establish that Anne founded the Mount Cashel orphanage and was very likely the first mate on the Exxon Valdez.

They call it postmodernism – or at least they used to – and cultural studies, but these are clumsy terms for something that could be labelled much more clearly. It's the Bill Clinton school of literary studies.

It all depends on what "is" is. And isn't.

If lesbianism isn't there, it is. And if it is there, it isn't. It's quite simple once you get the hang of it. And they will give you a Ph.D. once you do. It's fun to play.

The woman in the attic in Charlotte Brontë's *Jane Eyre*? Easy. That was no woman. That was Jimmy Hoffa.

It doesn't even have to be a one-way street, gender speaking. Take Oscar Wilde...please. Those plays and essays of his, filled with young men named Algernon, Basil, Gilbert, and Cyril. Remorseless heterosexuals every one of them. A riot of repressed heterosexuality – that's the oeuvre of Oscar Wilde. But in the "gay nineties" to "come out" as hetero, well, Oscar, like Lucy

Maud, had to write in code, and wait for the lynx-eyed witness of cultural studies to come along and demystify the old charlatan: Toulouse-Lautrec, by the way, was a beach bunny.

Did you know that Iago was a florist? *Othello* is not a play about jealousy; it's an eco-critique of the flower business disguised as a tragedy of jealousy.

Uncle Tom's Cabin wasn't a cabin; it was a frontier bathhouse. Anne probably paid a visit. Lucy Maud, Harriet Beecher – the two first names are a giveaway.

Who Has Seen the Wind is W.O. Mitchell's cunning portrait of seaside S&M. It's "set" on the Prairies and has absolutely no S&M whatsoever on any page. Cunning? Hell, it's diabolical.

As I said, anyone can play. Ignore the words. Traduce the author. Skip the poetry. And above all, be trendy.

– Globe and Mail

Snowstorm

It's January, it's Canada, it's been snowing; we're in the territory of the desperately self-evident here. Propositions that need no argument: trees are green; water is wet; the APEC inquiry is a mess; Brian Tobin is ambitious. You get the idea.

However, it snowed in Ontario recently, and some of it fell on Toronto – a fair bit. And judging from the reaction, this is not only unusual, astonishing, and a great blathering horror; it's downright unnatural. Even as I speak, the trauma teams are assembling and snow counsellors are on twenty-four-hour call and the St. Bernards are being given Evian barrels and sensitivity training.

Unfortunately, I wasn't around when the ancient Egyptians had the ten plagues unloaded on them. But I readily surmise their reaction was very much like to that of the great city of Toronto over the last four or five days. Why us, O Lord? Why us? The Egyptians got boils and locusts; Torontonians have Pearson Airport and tow trucks. Very clearly it is not supposed to snow on Toronto; and in the unnatural and inexplicable event that it does snow – sometimes it's allowed to snow for a film shoot – then quite clearly it's not supposed to stay. This is elementary Toronto physics. In this city, the snow evaporates before it reaches the ground. Now, this is incontestably the idea that governs the management of Pearson Airport, the nation's great monument to meteorology for dummies.

Pearson in January isn't really an airport in the conventional sense. It's a great hostel with tarmacs, where snow removal is evidently under the supervision of a consulting team from Fiji. Rule one for clearing the runways: whistle till spring.

Part two of this wonderful equation clearly states that, if snow does fall on a busy downtown Toronto street, it is immediately classified as heritage-protected. Snow may be allowed to drift, but it must not be pushed; the snowbank is a delicate ecosystem and ploughing is crystal ecocide.

Another wonderful thing about winter in Canada's only megalopolis: every snowfall is a record. We are told that this most recent one is the worst in fifteen years. This is great for yuppie psychology, and makes tripping off to Canadian Tire for prefab fire logs, the starter toboggan, and Prada ice picks their own first-hand taste of the Franklin expedition. Not to mention the opportunity to try out the four-wheel-drive Jeep Cherokee, just like the real pioneers did. And it makes for great newscasts. This is the only Canadian city where film of cars sliding on ice or cars stuck in snow in winter is news. I go back to where I began: Brian Tobin is ambitious; the GST is here to stay; snow falls in January. If what happened here in the last few days had happened in Winnipeg or Bonavista, it would not have been called a storm; they would have declared spring break. Toronto isn't in the grip of angry winter. It's having a self-regarding yuppie fit.

– *The National*

FIVE BOOKS AND A THONG

Monica's Story: Andrew Morton Flashes His Thong
. . . but Close Your Eyes and Just Keep Walking

Monica's Story
by Andrew Morton, McClelland & Stewart, 1999

I t is a new Monica. There she is on the cover, hair sleeked back, bright button little nose, staring out on us with those wide and now-familiar Betty Boop eyes, eyes that have stared down Barbara Walters, across the witness room at grand jurors, and up – look way up – at Bill Clinton, like innocence on a holiday, all on a delightful, dazzling white background. It took me back to Newfoundland to see this. She could be a seal on an ice pan. What we call a harp, for, as even Andrew Morton, the genteel pimp who wrote *Monica's Story* – and he is a delicate little priss, with far too little, many will be disappointed to learn, of Ken Starr's lush appetite for the physical close-mapping of the Clinton and Lewinsky clinches and hooverings – she is no whitecoat.

Morton, it must be pointed out for the few who are not up on the artfulness of celebrity biography, was the late Princess of Wales's favourite ventriloquist. He shares one quality with Monica which must have made their collaboration far more a marriage of true minds than she ever found with Clinton, and that is an aversion to straight speaking. It's right there on the back of the jacket. Morton writes his own blurbs:

"This book exists because the Monica I came to know has no relation to the image projected to the Starr Report and the mass media."

Balderdash, Andy. She needed cash, wanted an injection of fresh celebrity. You wanted cash, and didn't mind a dash of celebrity. This book exists because you both think it'll sell. She has no shame for what's she's done. You have no shame for how you write. I think you're commercial soulmates. *Monica's Story* is the love child.

And it is Monica's story. The stress here must be on story, not "story" as in true accounts but "story" as in soap opera, as in she's dreamy, sensuous, needy, and sad (if you hear a grinding noise while "reading" this book, it's poor late Diana rotating in her plot to see her story welded on, as it were, to the White House tartlet) and this is a fairy tale gone wrong. If I may leave the ice floes for the rest of this piece, Mr. Morton wishes us to see Monica as Bambi, an ambitious overweight little doe with a zeal for oral sex who simply fell in love with the First Buck and then was set upon by hounds from the Special Prosecutor and the press. Not even Morton believes this. He doesn't believe a word of it. There's a rain of sweat on every page as he hauls this grotesque and cumbrous tabulation to its dreary preshaped end.

One thing is worth noting purely as a literary consideration. Monica talks as well as Morton writes. Example: Monica says early on, "I told him once that he was like rays of sunshine, but sunshine that made plants grow faster and colours more vibrant." As opposed to that other sunshine we must presume, the stuff that stunts the plants and washes the colour out of everything. You know, non-sunshine sunshine. Morton, desperately seeking some horsepower, at one point goes for the poetic gold: "like blood seeping from under a closed door, the truth began to dawn." You know it's Sunrise for Truth in an Andrew Morton book when red stuff seeps under a door.

Not that Morton is a great narrative shaper. As literary architecture, *Monica's Story* is a mud hut. A door, a roof, and something, anything to stick together for the walls. In fact, and this is rare in literature, the index is at times more coherent, as a story, than the book.

She says she contemplated suicide. "Contemplated" is the wrong word there. A couple of brave and lonely neurons may have tried to forklift something that resembled a thought across the dizzy open spaces of that head, but I don't think the circuit board in question is really up to "contemplation." It's like her use of the word "subtle" in the Barbara Walters interview to describe her flashing the thong underwear at the president. For

Monica, anything short of lap dancing Bill in front of Hillary or posting a hourly rate on the Lincoln bedroom is, like, you know, a signal. "Subtle" is not so much a word for Monica as a sound she's heard somewhere and that her "capacious memory" (Andrew Morton's awestruck assessment) tucked away under "thong" and "flashing." As for suicide, assuming she really, like really, knows what it means, and that it's not just something she's watched on *As the World Turns* and you come back after in an even better role with a new slim body and everything, or that it's more than closing your eyes and holding your breath for a really long time and that when you open them again Tom Selleck (this is her world remember) is bending over proposing marriage and Ken Starr is being eaten by wild dogs, and, oh yes, they've fired Oprah and given her show to you – well, suicide is just another way of making sure you're the centre of attention. And besides you've got to juice up the book. Given Andrew Morton's prose – it is Sominex alphabetized – it's good she "contemplated" suicide.

Actually, she contemplated suicide twice. We know the first time was when the inquisitors had her in the Plaza Hotel, described in the chapter that bears the winged inspiration "Terror in Room 1012." Sounds like an old Farrah Fawcett movie. The "terror" included a walk around the mall, a phone call to cancel a date, pizza with the agents at Mozzarella's American Grill, a look and walk through Macy's, and, finally, watching *There's No Business Like Show Business*, starring Ethel Merman and Marilyn Monroe, on TV with the G-men in the hotel room while waiting for her mother to show up.

It has to be mentioned also that Morton/Monica (which is the air? which is the head?) likens Starr and his men to Stalin of the show trials. When you think of the mass famines, the gulags, tortures, and executions, it occurs that, even as a bad joke, he's carrying the special pleading for his besotted fellatrix just too damn far. A million dollars for this "book" and two hours with the Gaia of therapy TV, Barbara Walters, is not breaking rocks in 1930s Siberia. Much like Monica telling Babs that her name for the day Bill dumped her was D-Day. Someone should tell her Normandy was a courageous invasion, not a cowardly pullout, and that some beaches are emphatically not *Baywatch*. But what's history when, in the immortal words of Sheryl Crow's hymn to the boulevard that bears Monica's name, "all [you] wanna do is have some fun."

But did you know she also contemplated suicide when she heard about Jane Doe No. 7. In her own unimprovable and elegant account, "If there was a Jane Doe No. 7 it meant that everything he had ever said to me was bullshit that I meant nothing to him and that the whole two-year relationship was a farce." Morton (the Homer of stress-management narrative) continues, and the telling can't be bettered: "When she got back to her apartment she debated whether to take an overdose of pills or slit her wrists. She weighed up her options and decided to call up her therapist, Dr. Susan." This is the quickie version of the Dark Night of the Soul. She talks to Dr. Susan – I think it must be a law of California acquaintance that nobody has a last name – and goes to bed. I quote the book again: "When she woke up the next morning she found she had a fresh perspective on life." I think she should go to bed more often.

The winding down of the suicide "crisis" continues: "Moreover the whole incident had a more or less happy ending . . . *there was in fact no Jane Doe No. 7*" (my italics).

Well, you can see again that contemplation really isn't her long suit. I think this is Morton flashing his thong. Morton does the best he can with the little he's got, and the best he can is not very good, and the little he's got is hardly anything at all. In the middle of all this – this is a busy little intern/Pentagon employee – she has another affair with another married older man, gets pregnant, and has an abortion. I do hope she called Dr. Susan again. Or at the very least had another good sleep.

What else is there? Well, nothing else new. Starr gets the boot. Tripp gets the boot. And fine. People with double consonants at the end of their name are invariably a bad lot. But Clinton only gets a partial boot. I think this is strategic on both Morton's and Monica's part. It wouldn't do to make him the total manipulator. He's got to remain something of a prince or Monica can't be a part-time Diana-Cinderella.

If you read all this, and *read* really is too strong a word, is there anything to learn? Sadly, maybe. The tabloids haven't invaded American politics.

American politics has invaded the tabloids. Monica is a brazen, reckless, scheming airhead, but she is also woefully immature and, in the wrong hands, desperately easy pickings. Leave aside all morality and partisanship, what Clinton did was mean, brutish, and nasty. The whole affair, impeachment, and romance, was a slush storm. The most remarkable thing about the entire business is that there is no one person, not one – from the press, the law, the politicians, the pundits, or from Monica and her tribe – that hasn't in some way demeaned the currency of public behaviour and public discourse.

Monica's Story is a malign exorcism. It's the casting out of all dignity from American public life. Don't buy it. Sprinkle it with Evian water and walk on by.

– *Ottawa Citizen*

His Master's (Surprisingly Clear) Voice

The Right Man: The Surprise Presidency of George W. Bush
(An Inside Account)
by David Frum, Random House, 2003

Céline Dion, Shania Twain, Avril Lavigne, even Pamela Anderson. The export of high-calibre Canadian female celebrities, divas, and doxies to the United States has become so unexceptional that it hardly qualifies as news any more. Avril Lavigne, summoned to hyperstellar status as the anti–Britney Spears – it's a contest between street-corner girl and harem-queen stripper, authenticity versus anatomy – is the latest avatar of this happy swirl of the Zeitgeist.

David Frum, though, is an anomaly. He doesn't sing and, as far as I know, doesn't make public appearances in stylized lingerie for a living, either. But he is, albeit in a more rarefied ether than either Shania or Pamela, a superstar too. He has earned a place at the high tables of the American conservative movement. He sits regularly on TV panels that have featured such incandescences as William Kristol and Pat Buchanan, and has toiled in the very chambers of its modern incubation, such as the *Weekly Standard* and the *National Review*. Indeed, he has scaled to the summit of the op-ed pages of the *Wall Street Journal*, the court circular of muscular Republicanism, its very own *Osservatore Romano*. This is a real accomplishment and it is singular.

It is nothing, however, to the singularity of serving as a speech writer for the forty-third president of the United States of America. It is not to be thought that, in this twenty-first century, simply anyone, and a foreign national to boot, walks into an appointment at the White House. Not many are called, and fewer are chosen. The presidency retains, even in an age gone sour on politics, immense status, and direct association with the White House, even in an ancillary capacity, is a signature of great accomplishment and rare honour.

David Frum may share the charisma-averse exterior of, say, Preston Manning, but it is quite clear that he has a talent for getting on. Writing speeches for other people is a spectral and may even be a demeaning occupation. Whatever its torments, when the notepad holding your imperishable jottings for another's lips is headed 1600 Pennsylvania Avenue, The White House, mollification is at hand.

Now, a president doesn't have just one speech writer. They are legion and, in the case of George Bush, whatever their number, no one will argue a surplus. Bush and the English language are not agreeable companions. This is especially true in formal encounters between the two. He mauls individual words, has a precocious instinct for malapropisms and mispronunciation, the syntactical register of a not very bright Valley girl, and an alarming tendency to view the predicate of any given sentence as an opportunity to launch an attack upon its subject. Every sentence is its very own little Baghdad for George Bush. So Frum's help was necessary and welcome, but, as he laudably underscores, he was merely one of many, an auxiliary in the Bush speech camp, not a chieftain.

But still, quite an accomplishment. He was Jewish, Canadian, and intellectual in an emphatically Christian (prayers before the morning meeting), superpatriotic, less-than-academic White House. I can see why he took the job. The Fates must have been working overtime to arrange so fastidiously errant an appointment. Who but a churl would spurn their handiwork? And Frum has a journalist's curiosity. Inside the White House, however tangential his role, he would still own a cat's-eye view of the day-to-day operation of the greatest power centre the world has ever seen, and have meaningful contact with the master personalities of an empire. Frum repeatedly asserts it was the honour of serving at the White House that attracted him; I'm sure it was, right after vanity and curiosity.

The irruption of the events of September 11 have eclipsed the bizarre motions of George Bush's accession to the presidency. We have to strain to bring to full recall the astonishing equivalence of the 2000 election, and the lunatic strivings of the Florida recount. Who now but desperate late-night comedians recalls the saga of the hanging chads, the manual recounts, the Chinese checkers of court challenges and decisions, the tempest of votes counted, lost, contested and recontested, the raging fires of partisanship that for a while threatened to consume the legitimacy of the electoral process itself?

It was within this tumult of electoral equivalence and partisan zealotry that the Bush presidency took first air. Frum joined the White House to help a president who had been but half-elected, had very little moral prestige, was scorned by millions as a mere frat boy, silver-spoon-in-the-mouth, Texas-patrician incompetent, one whom luck, the intercession of the Supreme Court, and the brassiness of privilege had tossed into the highest office in the world. Bush's getting into the White House may, now that I think of it, have been more astonishing than David Frum's being hired by it.

Frum very usefully summons the atmosphere of those early days. And it's essential to the record that he's offering here. *The Right Man: The Surprise Presidency of George W. Bush* is essentially an extended essay by way of memoir of how, in Frum's view, this most unlikely of presidents has (at least to now) become one of America's best-liked and most successful.

It offers a portrait of the evolution of Bush under the impact of September 11, and makes both a strong emotional and argumentative case that Bush, despite his intellectual shortcomings, his near-defiant incurios-ity about the world beyond America, and his sheer ignorance of foreign affairs, has become something very close to a great president.

One draw of the book is that Frum was not initially, and is not tem-peramentally, a great fan of Bush. The folksiness of the Texan is very plainly not Frum's natural idiom. (I suspect he would love to serve William F. Buckley as president.) Nor, one guesses, is the penchant for nicknaming; on one occasion Frum is the receiver of a playful tap on the midriff and a pres-idential "Nice to see you, Davey me lad." It is too much to hope that Frum responded with an equally matey reply.

He argues that one or two "large ideas" can inhabit the soul of a man who superficially might not be said to offer any residence whatsoever to ideas, big or small. That being smart is not the same thing as being wise, and being good is greater than being either. Essentially the case that Frum presents is a portrait of character.

Bush's disinclination to bend the truth in small things, his instinctive respect for the traditions and dignity of the White House, his belief – emphatic after September 11 – that he is on a mission, all of these, for Frum, speak to aspects of character. I think what Frum is doing, and this is somewhat surprising, is painting a picture of a temperament and a personality in very many ways the opposite of his own. Bush is instinctive, a-intellectual, very much a man seeking an intuitional accord with the times he finds himself in, which, once found, he embraces with great and possibly frightening confidence as the right way. This accord supplies a bedrock certitude, and fortifies an already strong will.

For those who had doubts on one cardinal matter, Frum offers unqualified assurance: Bush is the boss. He is not in thrall to the greater minds and powerful personalities surrounding him, either Donald Rumsfeld or Colin Powell or Dick Cheney. *The Right Man*, again surprising from such a source, is a hymn for heart over mind. I am not sure this portrait will comfort anybody who has watched the unfurling of the war on terror, the innovations in foreign policy, not least the doctrine of pre-emptive attack, as developments fraught with peril and anxiety for the world. The anti-Bush zealots might actually take more comfort from their caricature of the simpleton-puppet. Under that view, there is always the hope the White House Darth Vaders, Rumsfeld and Cheney, or the obvious adults, Powell and Condoleezza Rice, might rein the child in. The thought that Bush is in real control, that he is the principal in these deep-ranging and potentially earth-shattering policies, offers them less of a mattress for hope.

What reads like an argument is actually more of an assertion, more of a statement of faith. Supporters of Bush are asked to take very much on faith. That he is good. That he, however mysteriously, has acquired a vision for America. That his innate, personal decency is somehow a warrant for the virtue of his administration's policies. That this man who arrived at a contested presidency with less obvious preparation for the position than anyone in at least a generation, a man not notably "serious" for a good part of his adult life, has nonetheless, by processes we are unable to divine, been "scripted" for the particular "mission" that the brave and strange new world of post–September 11 presents. This kind of faith is much like taste: it cannot be disputed. And like taste (as very much in Frum's own case), it's acquired.

Intelligence, we like to feel, is always a virtue of leadership. No one wants a pet rock, a geological sample, as president or prime minister. But intelligence is never sufficient, it can be perverse, and it has besides its own limitations, not least of which is cocksureness and arrogance.

Character, whatever we mean by that wide term, is a more copious and less tractable concept. Let us read Frum again, after Iraq, and, God forbid, after North Korea. I do think Frum has a case when he argues character: Bush is far more of a leader than those who despise him dream; whether he even comes close to being the exemplar Frum and other acolytes already believe him to be is something I am willing to hope for but unable yet to tell.

Frum's tenure with the White House has earned him the kind of satisfaction dreamed of by the minor poets: he will live forever in the quotation books. There have been a few more eloquent phrases in some Bush speeches than "axis of evil," but none so memorable, and certainly none so active or consequential. "Axis of evil" wasn't the formulation that Frum came up with. He had been asked to find some summary phrase, some concise tag, to designate the threats posed to the United States following September 11, some string of words that would hint at both the philosophy and menace of those "enemies" of America, a phrase that would be part of Bush's address to the joint session of Congress.

He looked at North Korea, Iraq, and Iran, and, borrowing from the parallels he saw with the Second World War and its Axis powers, and perhaps hoping to draw some rhetorical substance from that period of incontestable moral clarity, came up with "axis of hatred." His superiors in the speech-writing machine liked "axis," but (rightly in my judgement) plumped for "evil" over "hatred." It conformed to Bush's fundamentalist vision of terrorism. Since September 11, "evil" and "the evildoers" had been the leitmotif of all Bush's formal and informal addresses on the subject of terrorism.

Subsequently, some carelessness with the personal e-mails of Frum's wife alerted the world that the only begetter of this phrase, pre-revision, was the Canadian speech writer. "Axis of evil" was problematic from its first utterance. To Bush critics it was illogical – why was North Korea linked with Iran and Iraq? – and simplistic. Even for those not genetically hostile to Bush and his presidency, it smacked of rhetorical overreach. Frum was talked about on the TV panel shows and mentioned in the high columns of conservative pundit Bob Novak. And when Frum announced that he was leaving the White House, it became a conventional assumption that his departure was punishment for violating the first code of the wordsmith-for-hire. Standing out. Taking credit (even when due) for the boss's words.

Frum argues staunchly that this was not the case. I don't know whether to accept his assertions or not. Aside from his getting hired at the White House in the first place, nothing is more perplexing to me than his choosing – if it was a choice – to leave it so quickly. Whatever the reality, and despite the brevity of his tenure, David Frum, Canadian, had the peculiar satisfaction of being part-progenitor of a three-word description that, even as I write, is inflecting the conduct of world affairs. North Korea has boiled over into belligerence and crisis, and some people at least are saying that not the least reason its manic dictator is doing a nuclear jig is the stored resentment of being called evil in a speech by an American president almost a year ago.

The Right Man is also very smoothly written. Frum is a very able essayist. It's worth the price of admission to read of the moment when Frum is being urged by his wife, on September 11 just moments after the attacks, to get out of the building.

Frum is having a personal "frontier" moment. He's not going to leave: "I felt a surge of what . . . battle fever? . . . 'No,' I said fiercely. *No!* I am not leaving. I clicked off the phone, ready to . . . well I don't know what I was ready to do – whatever it is that speechwriters do in a time of war. Type, I suppose, but type with renewed patriotism and zeal." He's also very good on the atmosphere of the White House, the sense of those within that they are a very select tribe indeed. He has a keen eye and a dry mind.

But the value of the memoir is that it opens the door and I think honestly lets the reader in on the day-to-day dynamics of the Bush White House, gives measured access to the play of personalities within, and therefore offers grounds for judgement based on a portion of reality. Frum is not a tell-all kind of guy. This book is framed by discretion and loyalty. There's enough to let us see what goes on; nothing that might trespass, fundamentally, on the confidence being invited to the White House in the first place bestows.

It's a partly open window and, considering the times we live in, this nervous, high-anxiety, potentially calamitous period, any view of where and how the big decisions are being made is something a little more than just useful: we are owed it.

– Globe and Mail

Communism's "Useful Idiots" Scorned

Reflections on a Ravaged Century
by Robert Conquest, Norton, 1999

Robert Conquest is pre-eminently the historian of the second blinding horror of the twentieth century, the great terror inaugurated by the revolutionaries of Russia in the name of building a classless society. The realization that Lenin and Stalin are, with Hitler, the great criminals of the century owes much to the work of Conquest, in particular to his monumental indictment of Soviet totalitarianism, *The Great Terror*.

The Great Terror was an attempt to see communism as it really was. It argued, and documented, that the totalitarianism of Soviet Russia was a deeply purposeful engineering of misery and cruelty that lost little in comparison with its Hitlerian twin. The book banished the idea that, because communism professed an ideal end, a millenarian classless society, it had somehow earned a moral pass on the ravages wrought in its name.

Conquest's new book, *Reflections on a Ravaged Century*, is a compendium of how intelligent minds, in the Soviet Union and the West, bent themselves into pretzels denying the obvious and rationalizing the unjustifiable. It is an inquiry into the nature of intellectual allegiance, particularly when that allegiance is to an ideology. How did some people retain their belief and continue their support of communism after the facts – terror, butcheries, gulags, famines, and unendurable repression – became available?

Conquest's question, the theme of his inquiry, is, why has the century just past exercised such timidity in facing up to the bankruptcy and evil of communist ideology, when moral horror is the common response of all sane people to Nazism? Wilful blindness may explain people's readiness to overlook lesser matters, but it cannot begin to explain the obstinacy and cowardice of those who excused, bypassed, or rationalized the murder of millions, a regime of terror, and the tyrannical reign of a man who trumpeted his despotism as the path to socialist utopia.

Maybe big lies are the best ones. But the grim maxim fails when even the big lies are known to be lies. Why did *New York Times* reporter Walter Duranty cover for Stalin, deny the famines he knew to exist? Why did the fatuous Sidney and Beatrice Webb, H.G. Wells, George Bernard Shaw, a whole parade of intellectual celebrities, extend such tolerance and understanding to this horror, when it was so indisputably there? People whose moral sensitivity and outrage operated at laser intensity and unqualified clarity when they saw injustice or inequity closer to home, went blind and mute when they toured an entire system of injustice and cruelty.

As Conquest reads the phenomenon of selective outrage, it springs from many sources. I think he goes so far as to say that ideology, the lure of the big idea, for some amounts to a morbid condition. Communism had many baits. It was, however, riddled with inconsistencies and non sequiturs. Subscribing to the ideology meant subscribing to the so-called progressive wing of mankind. It flattered its (particularly Western) adherents and offered a meretricious moral superiority.

Conquest sees a distinction to be made between the gods of communism – Lenin, Stalin, and Trotsky – and its intellectual cheerleaders abroad. Lenin would have subscribed to Rosicrucianism if it gave him power, if he could be leader. The role of ideology for the revolutionary is that it offers a cover program, a convenient tool with which to attack those the revolutionary wishes to displace. All revolutionaries are moralists before they sit at the top of the wheel. They preach the evils of a system or a government, call the idealists to their side, and flatter them with the notion that they have subscribed to a noble crusade. The allure is strong. Those who heed the call are a self-appointed vanguard, the moral superiors of those who have not rallied against the tyranny of the present. They are also, in the dismissive words of Lenin himself, "useful idiots."

What is truly astonishing, and what Conquest illustrates with almost painful detail in the case of Soviet communism, is that long after the great change – long after the new system was in place, and the old and all its injustices stripped from the earth, and the new leaders and the new system were obviously infinitely more regressive and tyrannical than the ones they replaced – followers and worshippers remained immune to the toxic hypocrisies in which they had invested their faith and their lives.

Maybe, as Conquest argues, it is the idea of utopia itself that is dangerous. The idea of a perfect future, cleansed of injustice, inhabits the mind of the idealist with such force that it deadens all other capacity for reflection. A great idea, a perfect future, can be the pretext for every sort of horror exercised upon the present: institutions, societies, individuals. It inverts the normal operation of human conscience. The goal is so great, the idea so sublime, that it excuses the abolition of conscience, if conscience is seen as an impediment to the victory of the idea. Marxism is the casebook example. Marxism licensed a gamut of depravities, injustices, intolerances, butcheries, and insane cruelties under the "liberating" idea that it was building a better future.

There is more than a touch of homage to George Orwell in *Reflections on a Ravaged Century*. Orwell's career, in part, was dedicated to a similar anatomy of the contagions of ideology: what big ideas do to the people who adopt them, and to language when it is corrupted in the service of big ideas. "All men are equal, but some men are more equal than others," to paraphrase *Animal Farm*, is the classic text of this process. Orwell gave us the parable of the phenomenon. Conquest has written the handbook.

The focus of *Reflections* is the great dark example of Soviet communism, but Conquest has written this book with something more in mind. The period of the great "isms" may well be past, but there is a whole pack of little "isms" wandering in the space they've vacated. Human beings like to package their likes and dislikes into systems, to see the world through the aggressive simplicities of single ideas, fashionable causes, or one-dimensional theories.

Every ism, right or left, is incomplete; every ism is a refusal, finally, to think honestly.

Reflections on a Ravaged Century is a powerful meditation on a perennially necessary theme.

Nasty, Mean, and Sly:
Paul Theroux a Foul "Friend" to V.S. Naipaul

Sir Vidia's Shadow
by Paul Theroux, McClelland & Stewart, 1998

Linda Tripp is the appalling woman who taped "her friend," Monica Lewinsky. By common consent, the revulsion for Tripp's act far exceeds the scorn now directed towards whatever acts, confessed or denied, Lewinsky or Clinton engaged in. Monica Lewinsky got off easy. She could have been friends with Paul Theroux.

Paul Theroux is a highly successful travel writer and novelist. Sir Vidia S. Naipaul is the same. These men were, by Theroux's telling, friends for over thirty years. Something happened and they were friends no more. Theroux has written an account of that "friendship," *Sir Vidia's Shadow*, which is like no other account of friendship you will ever read. By comparison with his book, the Tripp tapes are the work of a half-hearted amateur. *Shadow* is professional to the greatest degree.

It's a nasty, mean, sly little work. Theroux's ratted out his friend. The minutiae of thirty years' worth of acquaintance, conversation, and correspondence are here unloaded. Not, of course, in their raw state, but as Theroux has chosen to remember them, as he has chosen to select them and process them. And quite a theroux little bastard he has been. This is the *Iliad* of a petty heart.

The reader of *Sir Vidia's Shadow* will learn much that is charmless and some that is sad about its subject. Sir V.S. Naipaul has no redeeming qualities. He's smug, cheap, élitist, vain, precious, obsessive, and a snob.

Furthermore, he makes a fetish of punctuality, is a corrosive influence on his younger brother, treats his first wife like a servant, is sexually repressed, despises most other writers alive or dead, and talks funny. But he was Paul Theroux's friend. And under that charter, very obviously, much may be forgiven; but on the evidence of this book, very little, if anything at all, has been. In fact, as one comes to the close of its three-hundred-plus whinging, crafty, and acidic pages, a question that had whispered its presence way back in the second chapter screams at full throttle: If, Mr. Theroux, he's such a total creep as you manifestly and with such relishing rigour declare and demonstrate him to be, then what in God's name have you been doing toadying around in his miserly and pernicious company for over thirty years? As his friend? I see this as something of a logical dilemma, if not a psychological mystery.

But human relations are rife with perplexities, so we may, for the nonce, set this question aside. V.S. Naipaul may be all that Paul Theroux has written he is, and Theroux may still have found his company for almost thirty years an ointment and a balm. We are often puzzled why some people, whom we like, like certain other people, whom we detest. *De gustibus non disputandum* applies as much to people as to fashion.

However, there is a problem that precedes the perplexity. Before, in words that Johnnie Cochran has done so much to make forever golden, we "rush to judgement," it must be asked, how do we know that this merciless portrait is a faithful execution of the original? For make no mistake about this, *Sir Vidia's Shadow* is an indictment, masquerading as a memoir of disappointed love. "M'luds, you will hear that, on the fateful day of luncheon at the Connaught, the wretched Naipaul stuck our client, the impecunious Mr. Theroux, with the cheque. Seventeen pounds, M'luds! And thereby forced him to take the bus – the bus, M'luds – back to his home. [Cries of 'Shame! Shame!' from the court.]"

Well, we know it's true, mainly I suppose because Paul Theroux says it is. And because he announces, in full italics, in the book's very first chapter, and its very first paragraph: "*I remember everything.*" God, Paul Theroux, and slighted elephants. I am not sure that everyone will grant Mr. Theroux quite the retrospective omniscience he is so comfortable claiming for himself. However. We will all agree, certainly by the end of this book, that there are some things he is clearly quite unwilling to forget. Naipaul's not picking up the cheque for that lunch at the Connaught being clearly a scar that will never scab.

This very first chapter is interesting. It is the only chapter in the book in which V.S. Naipaul is not V.S. Naipaul. He's introduced here as Urvash Vishnu Pradesh, "a saliva-making name like a cough drop that forced you to suck your cheeks and rinse your tongue with sudsy syllables." (A cough drop and a soap powder?) And Paul is Julian. Now, why this little memoir starts out with such a vain transparency is puzzling. The fiction will be dropped for the rest of the book. We will know most emphatically, and in their proper persons, who is writing whom. The claim that he remembers everything, it must be underscored, will not be dropped. But I suppose kicking in to full-recollection mode, remembering everything, is a little like Scottish pipe music. You've got to wrestle around a bit with the apparatus and get the air into the bag first. Hence this first chapter. And hence "Urvash Vishnu Pradesh" with all those saliva-coaxing sibilants. It was probably just too good to let go. Let the hissing begin.

From the second chapter on, however, it's all Vidia and me. How young Paul, brash, sexy, nonconformist and fired with a writer's ambition, met the older (only slightly – nine years separate the two) equally ambitious, disciplined, confident V.S. Naipaul. Theroux was a lecturer in Uganda. He wrote poetry and had started a novel. Naipaul had come to Africa, financed by a grant from something called the Fairfield Foundation. Theroux's department head captured the visiting writer for a visit and this is how, to borrow the book's subtitle, the "friendship that crossed five continents" began.

Theroux chums him up. He swots up on Naipaul's writing (the First Rule of Author Cultivation is ready acquaintance with the work). He professes admiration (the Second Rule; there are only two Rules). The rest is readily told. He shows Naipaul his stuff. V.S. makes appropriate noises. They are friends for life. Damon and Pythias with typewriters.

Both writers hop around a lot. The exigencies of travel writing and building a reputation demand it. And naturally, they correspond. Naipaul is troubled because, though a darling of some critics, his readership is small, his worth not fully acknowledged. Theroux is building his career and takes Naipaul as his model. Others will say mentor, but there is little in *Sir Vidia's Shadow* from Naipaul's mouth to indicate that Naipaul assumed that now-trendy mantle. He was encouraging. He did give advice. He accepted Theroux's quite voluntary homage. Mentor he was not.

Theroux undertook to do an introduction to V.S.'s work. Naipaul was delighted and wrote to Theroux – what author would not? – of his pleasure in the idea. From that 1970 letter Theroux mines one of the epigraphs to *Shadow*:

> You must give me the pleasure of seeing what I look like. It would be like hearing one's voice, seeing oneself walk down the street – if I know for instance that I was once young; and that I have changed; lost and gained and sometimes strayed, as I have grown older. Show me.

It's terribly unfair, and mean, to use these words, penned in the days of mutual reassurance and amiability, in kindly response to a projected act of tribute and gratitude, as the opening motto for this grim salvo of retribution and attack. A thank-you note is not a licence to maul.

It's worth paying a little attention to Naipaul's words here, and how he marshals them. How clear they are for one thing. Simple. Direct. Plain and bare. No showboating. How trusting they are! And how charged with wide self-consciousness: "that I was once young; and that I have changed; lost and gained and sometimes strayed, as I have grown older." I don't know if Sir V.S. Naipaul is nice. But I do know that he can write. The cadence and simplicity of address is masterly.

So when Theroux is picking over the bones of their "relationship," mocking Vidia's inconsistencies – accepting the knighthood, for example, when in conversations so long before he had scorned honours – or cataloguing his quirks and idioms, razing him for his "superiority" and miming his manner, I wonder: is it the writer he (now) so resents, or the writing? Is that what all this is really about?

It's a better explanation than any that appears in the book. For all

Theroux has to tell us is that he received a strange fax from Naipaul's second wife, and that Naipaul "cut" him one day – that antique act of dismissal once the weapon of the upper orders. That would wound. But it would not call a response of the magnitude and bitterness of *Sir Vidia's Shadow*.

Theroux's book is a treasure house of stored and nursed resentments. And therein lies its essential duplicity. Far from being the story of a "friend-ship that crossed five continents," it's more like the cashing of a postdated cheque, one Theroux issued himself sometime at the beginning of this long transaction. Probably inscribed, "I'll put up with this man – for now." Friendship it has never been. And once it is realized the book is a lie, is not the memoir of a friendship, then it loses its force.

For whatever reason it was written, it is not worth reading. Theroux has thoroughly indulged himself. There's no reason in the world that I can think of why, by buying and reading *Sir Vidia's Shadow*, we should season his self-satisfaction.

– Ottawa Citizen

Saul Slays His Thousands, but Strictly in Straw

Reflections of a Siamese Twin: Canada at the End of the Twentieth Century
by John Ralston Saul, Viking, 1997

I would argue that the hero of *The Hound of the Baskervilles* is neither the phosphorescent apparition, so startling to men's wits, that gives the tale its title, nor that other great Hound, the detective Holmes himself. Rather, it is the great brooding moorland on which, and against which, the drama is played. At the centre of that "desolate, lifeless moor" lies the Grimpen Mire, a horrible sucking bog that claims the unwary and the artful alike. *The Hound of the Baskervilles*, in other words, is much more atmospherics than plot. On certain days (minus, of course, the Gothic colouring), I think the same of Canada. We have a Grimpen Mire too: the quest to determine the Canadian soul. The latest detective to set up house upon the moors is John Ralston Saul. *Reflections of a Siamese Twin: Canada at the End of the Twentieth Century* is an extended – one is tempted to say heroic – meditation on the nature of Canada and Canadians. It's a brood on how we see ourselves and how we wish others to see us – in Saul's idiom, our "mythologies."

Let's get right at it. Very early on, Saul declares in the accents of aggressive certitude that we normally associate with the ardent cockiness of election manifestos: "We are overcome by a desperate desire to present ourselves as a natural and completed experiment, monolithic, normal, just another one of the standard nation-states." Who's the "we"? Where's the desperation? Why are "we" so "desperate" to present ourselves as "a natural and completed experiment"? And why is the desperate craving's compulsive target that of being another "normal, monolithic, standard nation-state"?

It's not on my Christmas list. And try decently as one might to pair the brassy assertion with an answering reality in Canadian opinion or Canadian politics – something to justify the trumpets – the match just isn't there. Canadians desperate for a monolithic normalcy? We may have wish-fantasies in this country, *un*desperate the pack of them, but the lust to present ourselves as a monolithic, standard nation-state is a "light that never was, on sea or land."

The sentence is like a lot of other sentences in *Reflections of a Siamese Twin*. It summons no echo, sparks no flash of recognition, of any reasonable configuration of Canadian sentiment, aspiration or temper. It's a rhetorical sound bite. John Ralston Saul is as good in his domain with sound bites as some of the politicians and corporate interests he clearly despises are in theirs.

Then we come to the governing trope of the book, a little parable that deals with Siamese twins: "The heroes are Siamese twins, they have only one body, two heads and two separate but interrelated personalities. Together they are very interesting. Most people want them to be separated – to be normalized. Banalized. To become like other people. To give up their real non-conformity for perhaps a mere self-indulgent, less demanding sort. Gradually they lose track of their sense that to be different is a positive. In the end, they agree to be separated and so conform to the norm." Hans Christian John A. Macdonald Diefenbaker Grimm.

Let's look closer at this. Together they are "very interesting." I'm not sure, to begin with, how important it is, for people or countries, never mind Siamese twins, to be interesting. Moreover, it is more than simply discon-certing, under the terms of this analogy, that we are only interesting "together." In less-sensitive days, there were whole sections of carnivals where, for a nickel down, people gathered to ogle this kind of "interesting." And then, is our being interesting, because "others" find us interesting, quite the kind of interesting Saul wants us to endorse? I would have hoped that whatever interesting qualities Canada has came with some endowment of self-estimation and self-regard. I couldn't give a fig what Finland and France, or whatever "others" Saul wants to line up, think.

But the legerdemain of the story comes in the next sentences. "Most people want them to be separated – to be normalized. Banalized. To become like other people." Who are these "most people"? Other nations! Whoever they are, apart from everything else, they're a crowd of rude busybodies, but let that pass. On the poetic logic of the passage, the entire pressure for cleavage, for severance, is external. It's outside opinion. Well, this simply won't do. The clamour for surgery, in the Canadian case, last time anyone checked the charts, is purely an internal combustion. It's one of the twins. It's French-Canadian nationalists in Quebec. The theory that Canada will fracture out of obliging conformity and a fear of being different from other standard nation-states is awesomely original.

Canada's permanent separation crisis is many things – tedious, exasperating, tragic, and unending. But it is not a script for *The Elephant Man*. It's not, in other words, a result of our desire for some factitious normalcy in the face of a chorus of outside nations, staring at a twin-headed constitutional calf, chanting, "Get normal. Be banal."

Saul is inimical to the declared spirit of his book here. He is resisting the complications of our reality, the actual situation, denying its complexity, and serving up something of a feel-good therapeutic fable in its place. This is not fair practice in a book that bristles with exhortations to respect and engage complexity, identifies the acceptance of complexity as the cardinal virtue of Canadian public being, and thunders with contempt for those, mainly politicians and corporations, who would deny it.

It also displays a failure of touch. *Reflections of a Siamese Twin* doesn't try to be a conventional argument – all analysis, logic, and accounting. Saul calls upon a considerable resource of poetry to present and buttress his portrait of Canada. Further, he's the most vivid evangelist this side of George Orwell in calling for discretion and finesse in the use of language, a respect for the quality of civil discourse – keeping the instruments clean – central to mature democratic exercise. Yet here, in the book's paradigmatic example, the poetry is off-centre, the logic slippery, and some of the language almost certainly (it's difficult to tell in these cases) on undercover assignment.

Too often the myths to which Saul offers countermyths aren't, in any real sense, myths to begin with. There's a problem with terms here as well. "Myths" and "mythologies" are expansive shells of words. A myth may be simply a pervasive fiction, a genuine world view expressed in high archetype, or a thematic tale, such as Faust. The word means many things, from the profound conception to the casual error. But in *Reflections*, I get the impression it keeps running up and down the scale of its various meanings, and is sometimes ascribed to what would be better accounted for as a passing mood.

The residue of colonial nostalgia for the "mother countries" of England and France is a desperately attenuated passion. The yearning for "world-class status" on the parts of Toronto and Montreal, which he excoriates as immature and debasing, is (a) not nearly as intense, even in those it possesses, as he makes it out to be, and (b) as much a self-deprecatory Canadian joke, a piece of northern irony, as anything else. Hero-worship is the least-practised form of reverence in this country. Saul needs to discriminate heroes from celebrities. Madonna may be famous – well, she used to be – but outside Camille Paglia and a few teenyboppers, she was never a hero.

More tendentious than any other of these (purported) myths is his conviction that we Canadians have, regionally and nationally, bought into the victimhood cult, the myth of the victim. We are a fractious bunch. That's true. Were there space I could, like Saul, catalogue the master list of gripes and whinings, frictions and factions. But there are two observations, in the interest of owning up to the complexity of things, to be made. To complain is not, per se, to claim victim status. There are times we complain, individually and collectively, because there's something happening to us that merits complaint, and complaint is the first polite route to remedy. Second, politics is very largely society's chosen mechanism for dealing with complaints. Democratic politics can be viewed, if I may reach for a cant phrase, as a form of conflict resolution.

Take a snapshot of the nation's politics and complaints will, of necessity, fill the picture. We call these complaints issues. From megacity to the salmon wars, the Free Trade Agreement to land claims, separatism to deficit reduction, the air is filled with competing voices, and the sum of this grand

cacophony – part passion, part posture – is the messy business we call
Canada. Even in the one case where Saul's categorization might prevail, the
Who-has-humiliated-us-today? school of Quebec separatism, I'm really
not sure how much of that is pure pose and public-relations martyrology.

The Quebec question brings him to a meditation of referenda, which
he despises on principle. Referenda "emasculate language," are "anti-
democratic," and "install an atmosphere of rigorous anti-intellectualism."
Which referenda: the one held in Toronto recently on the subject of the
megacity, and so cheered by Citizens for Local Democracy? He objects to referenda because they impose a strict Yes or No formula on complex realities.
They speciously simplify, insist on one-dimensional responses to multi-
dimensional problems.

Actually, the one truly consequential referendum of recent times, in
Quebec, was wrong or imperfect or repugnant for precisely the opposite
reasons. The question was so (deliberately) muddy that it didn't call for a
ruinously simplistic Yes or No, In or Out. It was a piece of artful miasma, a
swamp of calculated ambiguity, a Grimpen Mire of a question that allowed
a Yes vote to mean anything from total rejection of Canada to continuing to
elect federal MPs in a post-separation Quebec.

There are several good things in the book. The discussion of Quebec,
the vivid assertion of the civic powers of education, the centrality accorded
the imagination as the primary resource of a living politics, and, of
course, the continued emphasis on reform and reconciliation as the vital
reflexes of a genuine Canadian sensibility. On the ground, so to speak, it
works very well. But there's a tincture of Icarus, a variant of the myth if
you will, about *Reflections of a Siamese Twin*. The higher it rises, the more
it obscures.

– Globe and Mail

Orwell and Hitchens: Enemies of Compromise

Why Orwell Matters
by Christopher Hitchens, Basic Books, 2002

"All animals are equal but some animals are more equal than others."
I thought that line was brilliant when I first read it many years ago, and I think that still. A mere bit of cleverness, some might say. On the contrary. To be that clever, in so short a space, to make so vast a point with so few words, is the gift of a very few. There's a lifetime of experience in the message of that bitter aphorism, and a lifetime of learning how to work a sentence to say so much in so little.

The line is George Orwell's, as all have recognized, from his one book that is a true classic, the pathos-rich, satirical masterpiece, which put paid to the lie of communism before people ever dreamed of the Wall coming down: *Animal Farm*. In that single line, the grotesque lie of the "dictatorship of the proletariat" was spiked mortally as the mere cloud of lying words it always was.

Communism was always the manipulation of the credulous by the ambitious. Its egalitarian theoretics were never anything more than bait, an elaborate articulation of the miseries of the masses as a species of persuasion. The intelligentsia dissected to deceive; they cried "justice" and plotted overthrow. Communism was always a mode of rhetoric, or concealment through language, of an unappeasable need for a few to dominate the many.

Orwell "saw through" communism because of the acuteness of his linguistic gifts. He knew when language was being bloodied, syntax corrupted, meaning crushed – made to do the opposite of what, morally, it is supposed to do – to lie, to screen, to confuse and anger and hypnotize. He knew when language was an instrument of power or the sly means to get power. It is one of Orwell's legacies that he has made it easier for many others, not as instinctive as he in catching the lie on the wind, to sense its toxic approach. Orwell, in a basic sense, helps people as citizens.

Orwell has an illustrious and very capable admirer in Christopher Hitchens, who has written this slim but fervent volume, *Why Orwell Matters*. Hitchens, columnist of *Vanity Fair* and recently of *The Nation* (with which he split over the war against terrorism), is a real and able polemicist in an age of talk-show shouters.

He's a former Trotskyite and a self-described contrarian. I think he is far more a contrarian than he ever was or fancied himself a Trotskyite and, for both of our sakes, I hope I'm right.

The main qualification, however, that Hitchens brings to this tight hymn to Orwell is that he is himself extremely keen on the proper business of words and sentences. He has an ear *and* a head, a combination that places him at least one sentient faculty in front of the majority in either journalism or politics.

To appreciate Orwell is to appreciate before anything else the fidelity of language to experience. The fidelity was a passion. It charges the bleak landscape of *1984*, where words say the very opposite of what they mean. It is the passion of his journalism.

Watch how language is used, pay attention to what is being said, and how it is being said: distilled, that is the core of Orwell's entire imaginative and journalistic enterprise. Hitchens is, unsurprisingly, a great fan of Orwell and a worthy scholar. Orwell may not vibrate as largely now as perhaps he did a generation ago. A glossier age, and one so greatly fevered by the journalism of images, may have lost the appreciation for him. He belongs to a more reading time, a more patient audience.

But Hitchens does some very good work. And as a handbook of Orwell's practice, a highlighting of what the man stood for, *Why Orwell Matters* deserves its title.

Hitchens gets the central message right: Orwell's pointing out of the discrepancy between the slogan and the intent, the gap between the gooey formulation and the messy deed, the manipulation always present in politics – but in much besides – by those who use language to achieve power, leverage, consent, or domination.

"Politics and the English Language" is the classic locus of Orwell's attention on this fertile, dismal field. It is in that one stringent, angry essay that Orwell laid down the tricks and traps by which party, bureaucracy, or state "corrupts" language, makes of it an instrument of guile, distortion, evasion, or seduction. The essay can be seen as the program notes for his massive and compelling indictments in *1984* and *Animal Farm*.

This is where Orwell matters – in crystallizing, rendering with imaginative charge, the insight that language is the first clue when things go wrong. It is our common "distant early warning" system.

So successful was Orwell in this that the very process whereby meaning is twisted by power into its own contradiction, where words are nullified or morphed into their opposites, now bears – as warning – his name. "Orwellian" is a word I have met with at least a dozen times in the week or so since I've read this book. Two writers have given their names, in adjectival extension, to the mean and bitter twists of politics in the twentieth century. Kafka came to name the nightmare of politics, the meaningless and enigmatic horror of bureaucratic power. Orwell gave his to the process by which this nightmare begins in language.

Why Orwell Matters is partly a rescue operation, fully a celebration. I hadn't realized how much Orwell had been targeted for obloquy from both the right and the left. He was one of the early ones who "deserted" the communist cause, and that leave-taking in the atmosphere of the 1930s and 1940s and, sadly, a number of decades since, was enough to earn him the opprobrium and active hostility of the ideologues and fellow-travellers who lacked both his stomach and his eyesight.

The left always privileges its instinct for heretics over a commitment to "seeing the thing itself." And the left, even more conventional than pietists, has a long memory and no reflex for forgiveness. Orwell wasn't forgiven for being right and saying so. Thus Hitchens's reminders of the cost for Orwell in saying what he said, when he said it – diminished work, social scorn, frequent calumny – is useful as well as noble. The truth will set you free; but saying the truth, among the ideologues, is bitterly costly.

That Orwell was not a god of the right, or that he should be less than a hero to the privileged and powerful, is no surprise. I don't quite see the point of rescuing him from the carping or contumely of that quarter. It's what one would have expected, and criticism from the enemy camp already comes with a generous discount.

I'm not convinced that Orwell needs to be rescued. The attacks on him are known only to the dedicated, or to the coteries who follow the disputations and rivalries of a politics now past. Orwell, the Orwell still active in politics, is a presence. His foresight into totalitarianism entered the ethos. The rigorous skepticism and testing of language which were his hallmarks had both admirers and students. His suspicion of ideology, his diagnosis of how ideology can be made to twist both thought and words, was an invaluable gift to his time and ours.

I think he inhabits a very great deal of the energetic and powerful skepticism of Christopher Hitchens. Hitchens on Orwell is a fine salute from one very lively writer to another formidably clear-eyed one.

– *Globe and Mail*

VAGRANT OPINIONS

Pope John Paul II

This is the Pope's third visit to Canada. Either he likes us or he's not sure we're getting the message. I don't think there can be any skepticism however that the vast crowd at yesterday's World Youth Day event got the message.

The Pope is one of – if not the – most galvanic, magnetic leaders on the planet today. It is not less than astonishing when we consider his age, his condition, and in particular his message, that this frail old religious man can so electrify his followers and, to a fair extent, even neutral spectators. He has great personal force.

On the 1984 trip, it was easy to ascribe his force to his superb vigour, the crowd skills of a former actor, and the natural enchantment of the great office he held. What a contrast between then and now. On the 1984 visit, we had a man who had great physical confidence. He might have called on Trudeau had there been a trampoline nearby.

On this visit, the ravages of Parkinson's and simple old age, in addition we must assume to the mighty stresses of a great office, see him shrunken, tired, moving always with difficulty, and speaking only with the greatest effort. There has to be a monumental will power at work in John Paul II and a sense of duty so profound that it actually overrules his physical decline. Determination and conviction at this level of exercise are not often seen, but when they are on display, as they were yesterday on the shores of Lake Ontario, they steal admiration, even from the most skeptical observers.

But in tandem with that ferocious willpower is another quality that comes partway to explaining the greater lure of his presence. We saw it in the embrace of a ten-year-old girl, Georgia Ray Giddings of Ontario, in the first hour of his visit. It is the Pope's immense delight in personal contact with individuals – and, in particular, the young. And we heard with great charm from the young girl herself what that contact means for those who have experienced it.

Some people like to confuse or explain the Pope's power of presence with celebrity, which raises great horrors in my mind. I think of Regis Philbin exchanging encyclicals with Bono, or Cher doing plainchant with Madonna, and the mind goes into a terrible dark. Celebrity is all surface, no depth, all sail, no boat, all gloss, no teeth. It's gospel is gossip, the sacred writings of the Church of *Entertainment Tonight*. Celebrity hates anything older than yesterday. This aged Pope, as he's called himself, is the anti-type of celebrity. Far from tacking to the fashionable, he offered the young of 170 nations a two-thousand-year-old sermon and, in an age consumed by consumption, insisted that being is always more important than having.

Finally, I think John Paul II's appeal is something very simple: that leadership is a submission to duties, not an elevation to office, and that example was always more powerful than exhortation, in politics as well as religion. The young cheered and teared because he showed up to be with them. He was frail. He could barely get about. Speaking is an effort and travel must be a torment. But he shows up anyway. Duty and example. It's so rare, it's chilling. And that's chilling.

– *The National*

Clinton: Pinocchio Priapus on the Potomac

The distinguished ethicist and moral philosopher Geraldo Rivera – friend of Marcia Clark and Johnnie Cochran, *National Enquirer* epistemologist (let's get this over with), the Ludwig Wittgenstein of trash TV – has been one of the most frantic pack mules of presidential prevarication for more than seven months. *Rivera Live*, the professor's nightly symposium on CNBC, has really been little more than an extended course (complete with live demonstrations) on when lies are not lies and when sex is not sex and when lying about sex is neither sex nor lying.

Geraldo, the truth seeker, has spent not a little of his vigour during this period roundly denouncing the hypocrites and puritans who took offence, or otherwise thought it wrong, when Bill Clinton lied, and lied under oath, on the subject of the serial gratifications he suborned from the enchanted and enchanting Monica Lewinsky. It's difficult to reduce anything Geraldo Rivera says to its essence but, as best we can, it's this: lying about sex isn't lying.

If you take out the small qualification in there – about sex – you'll note that it reads: lying isn't lying (*cogito ergo dumb*). I guess you can only host so many panels with Johnnie Cochran and Barry Scheck as guests before the old brainpan is good for nothing more than catching lugnuts.

It will also be noted that "lying about sex isn't lying" is a Second Stage refinement. The First Stage was "the president isn't lying." This was the "I believe the president when he tells the American people he isn't lying" stage.

So, Stage 1: he's not lying. Stage 2: he's lying (but it's about sex), so he's not lying.

But then there was that pesky business that the Great Equivocator had gone under oath to lie and not lie. Remember oaths? Oaths occur when people sacredly swear to God that they're not lying. We're in Third Stage forked-tongue surgery here. This is the "lying under oath, about sex, if it's in a civil disposition, isn't lying" lie.

An eel couldn't crawl through this logic and have any hope for its spine.

Geraldo Rivera, of course, is only the pilot fish, or pilot snake, for a vast zoo of spinmeisters, truth doctors, flacks, hacks, legalists, and weasels who have spent the same period of time trying to convert raunch into right-eousness, and to pummel a disobliging and disgusted public into accepting that oral sex is not sex, that the Oval Office is a private place, and that slag-ging a vaporous on-the-job intern for eighteen months should be taken as nothing more than a sagacious exercise in stress management by the Frat House King. They have also been trying to tell us that lying isn't lying, and that the only time you want to foul your hands or mouth with the truth is when it becomes absolutely unavoidable to tell it.

People have lied before, sure. Politicians have lied, sure. And there have been moral cold spells in Washington before too. But with the arrival of Bill Clinton, Pinocchio Priapus on the Potomac, this is the Ice Age of Mendacity. Miles deep and glacially thick, the place is rigid with duplicity.

They lie so much, they lie so often, they lie so vigorously – I (furrow the brow) did not have (grit teeth, don't bite lip) sexual relations (is this going to work?) with that woman (oops!) Ms. Lewinsky – and they lie so fully and so well that you are sometimes brought to wonder, truly and anxiously wonder, did we get it all wrong when we were young, or have we been so wrong ever since, that lying in itself, just plain lying, is hardly ever right? And were we also wrong to hold that public men and women, lying in public, to the public, were practising the most corrosive kind of lying?

Can't a president have some privacy? they ask. Bill Clinton's sex life is private, they say. Yes it is. Bill Clinton's private sex life is with his wife. It's that other one, going on in the Oval Office with the one-woman reception line, that isn't and never was private. That bonk was public property from day one and every month thereafter. So even the defence (sic) that it's okay to lie about sex, because sex is private, is a lie.

But whence came the dispensation in the first place (was there a Vatican Council we all missed, or did *Cosmo* have an issue that never made it to the doorstep?) that lying about sex, public or private, wasn't lying, that deceit about sexual deceit wasn't deceit?

The principle is really very simple: in the Clinton catechism, lying about the one thing you do get caught at isn't lying. If he'd been nailed on Whitewater, rather than nailed on nailing Monica, we'd have heard, "Who in the real-estate business doesn't lie? You can't buy or sell land in Arkansas without lying. The president lied – yes. But it was a lie about real estate. A land deal, for God's sake."

The mystery is where these guys and gals got the notion that lying itself had lost all sanction, where they got the courage or the effrontery to start lecturing and hectoring an entire nation about which lies weren't lies, which were non-lie lies, or lies that didn't count, or lies that were right. That by some grand and invisible executive flourish, when it suited the First Philanderer and his gypsy lust, they could de facto cancel, at the snap of a finger and the rev of the spin machine, the great ancient code of simple truth-telling.

And so it came, like John the Baptist after feasting on locusts – the times will find the man, the ethos its braying emblem – that there emerged as chop-logician to His Randiness, the low priest of Monicaspeak: Geraldo Rivera.

Tricky Dick. Slick Willie. Why has it taken so long to see that these are exact synonyms? With no apologies to James Carville: it's the lies, stupid.

– Globe and Mail

Sorry, Jean, the Career Is Your Legacy.
What's Left Is Footnotes

I caught a few snatches of Bill Clinton with Larry King this week. I didn't watch the entire fawning-fest because I'm convinced that watching Larry King is not risk-free. It chews up the brain cells and is almost certainly narcoleptic.

Bill was allowing that he probably wouldn't, after all, take up that much-rumoured job as a talk-show host. I fancied I could hear America grieving. Not right now, anyway, but if he did, he'd surely like to have Larry as a guest. There was *so* much he wanted to ask Larry. And Larry appeared to believe him, which marks an entirely new mine shaft in the Land of Desperate and Vain Gullibility.

There was no Monica on the set, of course. That would have been too perfect, though I predict the day will come when the awesome duo who brought on the great Impeachment Follies will be shopping themselves to the talk circuit as a team. Larry won't get them. Something that tender sobs for Oprah.

Nonetheless, seeing Bill again induced a tepid fit of nostalgia. Things were simpler when he was in the White House. There was no war on terror then, and America's biggest nightmare was what was crawling around under the president's desk.

Hiding Monica when she was on the property, and trying to keep her out after his ardour had cooled, was the highest priority of the finest brain to occupy the White House since John Kennedy was smuggling and snuggling Marilyn Monroe.

It's widely agreed by American historians – Montel Williams, Connie

Chung, Regis Philbin, Aaron Brown – that Mr. Clinton squandered his chances to build a legacy because of the dalliance with poor, smitten Miss L. The last two years of a second-term American president have come to be understood as the time that those presidents who are lucky enough to get two terms use to build their legacy.

They know they can't run again, and so turn to measures and policies that they couldn't "afford" if they had to play politics as usual. They can afford to be unpopular, is the theory, so they are free to do what is right as opposed to what is merely expedient. It's a strange view of politics, this: the idea that leaders only start to do what they think they really should be doing when they no longer have any responsibility to take the electors into consideration. It reduces their entire careers before this "liberation" into something not much better than a continuous deceit.

Something of the same is now infecting Canadian politics. The most dramatic evidence is our prime minister's astonishing performance at the great babblement in Johannesburg. It was there that he announced to the world that Canada was signing on to Kyoto. This is not something he would have done last year or, for that matter, at the beginning of the summer now departing.

What's the best way to put this? Until very recently, Jean Chrétien had not unshackled us from the fright, or himself from the dream, of a fourth term. He was having too much fun playing cat and mouse with the Liberal Party's Prince Hal, Paul Martin, to give any clear signal about his future plans. But the few months of summer were enough to tell him that a showdown with Mr. Martin at the February leadership review was going to be a disaster.

Mr. Martin had a lock on the party machinery, and there was nothing Mr. Chrétien could do about that, except acknowledge it by the back door of his own promised resignation in 2004. Which, of course, he's done.

And now, curiously, all the talk is about Mr. Chrétien's legacy. He has many months to do all those things that, for nearly forty years in politics, he was kept, by politics, from doing. Now that he knows he will not be running again, a greatly emboldened prime minister is free to do what he would never have dared to do if he were a prime minister planning to stay.

Hence the startling pronouncements on Kyoto. Hence, too, the much-anticipated Throne Speech that Canadians will get at the end of September. Legacy-building is a great release.

This is absurd. The career, not its coda, is the legacy. The legacy, for good or ill, is built already. Mr. Chrétien has been active and significant in the exercise of Canada's public life for almost four decades. His personality has been a part of the texture of that life, as his leadership and policies have worked to frame and define it. He has shown rare endurance, significant guile (this is not always a bad thing), considerable passion, and commendable commitment.

He has also, on occasion, been petty, imperious, careless of parliament, needlessly partisan, and ethically cute. These are the deep grooves and contours of his tenure in politics – and no recess from "politics" for eighteen months before he leaves will alter them a jot.

And, by the way, the legacy will never be Kyoto. It's Quebec.

– Globe and Mail

The Only Thing Worse Than Being Irish Is Not Being Irish

The Irish are a very busy crowd. They would have to be. According to author Thomas Cahill, they have saved civilization.

I think Mr. Cahill, in his otherwise laudable enthusiasm for a wild, mostly lovable people, has gotten ahead of himself. We're not so sure, in this corner, that that game, i.e., civilization, is saved. But what parts of it there are, and may be said to be functioning, owe as much to the Irish as any other clan you could care to nominate.

The Irish, for one thing, may be one of the few broods that are left of which it is safe to speak in this manner. One has to be so careful offering generalities these days, clustering people under what are so fashionably disdained as "stereotypes." The Irish, Cape Bretonners, Newfoundlanders, and (some) Scots are (thank God) impervious to mingy fashionableness, and about these sturdy strains it is still possible to offer slivers of characterization without fear of exile, mortification, or the furies of those curious oxymorons, Human Rights Commissions.

The Irish spice things up. St. Patrick's Day itself is an example. It is not easy to think of other saintly commemorations that have leaped from the liturgical calendar of one people or country as an occasion for licence, liquor, and jolliment the world around. Christmas we will exempt from the comparison, because Christmas has become so fat a feast, so unmoored from its shivering and holy origins, as to be featureless.

St. Paddy's Day, on the other hand, is a lend-all bacchanal for whoever wants to join in. We Canadians are particular beneficiaries of this arrangement. Trust the Irish to found a respite from the lingering sadisms of eternal

winter, and offer the world one last fling before the unfolding of the mani-
fold disappointments of spring. As we crawl through March with its sly
flatteries and grim revocations – so fine one day, a raging arctic howl the
next – St. Paddy's Day is a little tent the Irish have pitched for the boon and
spiritual shelter of all of us who weary our days in a northern climate.

It comes, I suppose, from the Irish gift of invention. They invent where
others repine, and with the excess, hyperbole, and zest that denotes the Irish
imagination, they simply out-manufacture reality.

Irish celebration is always tuned to the imagination, and tuned by it. It
is this faculty that has given them lordship over English, even as through
their mixed, tumultuous, and painful history, the English have had lordship
over them.

For Irish invention is primarily verbal. The pathway to an Irish imagination is through a good ear and a heavy dictionary. When Oscar Wilde
went romping in the high drawing rooms of London, he drew them with his
crafty tongue, a mechanism, that tongue, for the production of epigrams
which, for finish and ruthlessness, the world has yet to offer an equal. It is a
curious thing, for some, that wit, which is quintessentially an English thing
– it has a hardness and brittleness and aggression that belongs to "superiors" – found its champion in an Irishman. But under Wilde, wit became
more than weapon; it lost some of its aggressiveness and took on charm.
A typically Irish appropriation.

And if the past century was anything, in literary terms, was it not the
century of the novel? We can allow the Russians some standing in this
roomy house, but the mansion is essentially English. But it was an Irish
giant and patient wordsmith, James Joyce, who virtually emptied the entire
English language into his two mammoths, *Ulysses* and *Finnegans Wake*, and
left almost every other novelist who followed seem pale and loitering over
an exhausted landscape.

The thought is not new and the examples could easily be multiplied.
But mainly we remark on the exuberance of Irish performance. Be it
Wilde or Joyce, or for that matter Yeats or Shaw, how fully, how completely
they trace one genius of language to its finish. They like to make things up.
And this extravagance of invention is characteristic of a stance towards

reality. Reality, as we non-Irish know it, is reality. For the Irish it is merely raw material.

The Irish have a way of turning life merely by telling it. And while there is in the Irish way of telling things always a temptation towards the sentimental, there is also a more central and irrepressible element of celebration and fun. What else is to account for an otherwise plain tale, such as *Angela's Ashes*, which has hung like Everest over bestseller lists for what seems like a decade, but that, for all its "hard times," the life that it recounts has been seen by Frank McCourt as material for a good story.

The Irish attitude to life, to politics and history, is that it is malleable, that the facts of life are its least interesting component, that the best resistance to what Sir Thomas Browne in a typically English concession called "our few and evil days," is to retell and celebrate them as we go. That spirit of the Irish has been a benign contagion unto the world, and St. Patrick's Day is its flag.

– Ottawa Citizen

Babble from Genocide's Bystanders

It's hard to know what to make of that grand festival, the U.N. World Conference Against Racism, Racial Discrimination, Xenophobia, and Related Intolerance, being held in Durban, South Africa.

Just judging from its official title, it's obvious they went after the synonyms with a front-end loader, but having made it to Xenophobia (not, it should be pointed out, hatred of the busty television show, though that is a dread all too easy to share), they decided to go scattershot and reached for Related Intolerance as a quick end to the catalogue, and to avoid stressing the letterhead.

The U.N. is always at its best when it goes broad-gauge and fuzzy. It's like Oprah, on one of the afternoons when she lights her studio with candles and orders out for extra wind-chimes.

There are six thousand people invited to South Africa for a steam bath of pieties and platitudes to deplore what is already, by all civilized people, universally deplored; this is less a conference, a venue of exploration or dissent, than a jamboree for true believers. The U.N. – tattered, ineffectual, rife with hypocrisies – probably feels it scores some valuable public relations when it hosts such a jubilee, much like decaying rock stars who "hook up" after a famine to do a "We Are the World."

The U.N. has more need than the rock stars. It is, after all, not many years (only seven, to be precise) since the horrors of genocide in Rwanda, a cataclysm of butchery and slaughter to which only Pol Pot's murderous exertions and Hitler's inexhaustible bloodthirst offer serious competition.

The Rwandan genocide was a classic "ethnic" tragedy, surely deserving

244

of classification under one of the present conference's rubrics – Xeno-phobia (fear of strangers or foreigners) – and hardly having to pause for breath to earn a standing under Related Intolerances.

By gross estimate, a million people went under the earth in that racial extermination. A greater exploration than I can offer is given in September's issue of *Atlantic Monthly* magazine by Samantha Power. Her article "Bystanders to Genocide" should be read out loud at least once an hour for the duration of the Durban conference.

One of the article's unfailing, remorseless themes is the artful impo-tence of the U.N. when faced with genocide as reality, rather than as con-ference theme. It is almost impossible to read again the by-now-familiar story of Roméo Dallaire and his sadistically compromised mission as a peacekeeper. Impossible to read of the warnings ignored, the posturing, the epidemic of buck-passing, evasion, and compromise, which consti-tuted the U.N.'s and the "world community's" response to an epic outburst of racial hatred.

I cannot forgo the quotation from the article itself of General Dallaire's own words:

My force was standing knee-deep in mutilated bodies, surrounded by the guttural moans of dying people, looking into the eyes of chil-dren bleeding to death with their wounds burning in the sun and being invaded by maggots and flies. I found myself walking through villages where the only sign of life was a goat or a chicken, or a song-bird, as all of the people were dead, their bodies being eaten by vora-cious packs of wild dogs.

This was the scene from which he issued the great stream of cries for help to his masters at the U.N. and elsewhere. The perverse beauty of that quotation is almost a weird indictment.

There was no beauty in the non-response he got. The moral crucifixion of General Dallaire is a bitter parable of our age. Shout "genocide" when its presence is a phantom, or as pure rhetoric; it's a good conference word. Suffocate its expression when a *real* genocide is in progress.

The other important lesson from Rwanda – and it bears directly on this mad talkfest in Durban – is how little it impaired the moral functioning of countries and leaders who had not acted during the event. Four years after, U.S. President Bill Clinton, who must hold a copyright on the Act of Contrition, said in his best teary voice that he was sorry. Stagy apologies might do for frolics with the office staff, but late tears for a genocide are chilling.

The U.N., which was explicitly designed to halt genocide, has blithely ignored the mortal wound it suffered. Its moral energies were birthed in the Holocaust. That is where the determination that racism would "never again" so infect the world as to trigger another genocide has its roots.

This is the U.N.'s mission statement. All its other activities are mere brocade. There is more than a good argument (as Ms. Power's article makes clear) that the U.N. declined a full response in Rwanda because it feared what failure would mean for the U.N. more than any other consequence.

It can't hold conferences on this stuff any more. It has forfeited the moral capacity to do so.

– Globe and Mail

Let's Try Zundel-Denial

If Ernst Zundel is a refugee, Daffy Duck is Albert Einstein. I don't think we'd hold hearings to test the latter. Some propositions are so ludicrous that they are a betrayal of common sense and human dignity if allowed a moment's oxygen.

What some are pleased to call the refugee process of this country may be porous and contorted to a fault. An impulse of laudable charity may lie at the heart of its manifest confusions, delays, and inefficiencies: better a cloud of pretenders earn this country's protection than a single genuine case of human persecution be rejected. But however wide its faults, and however deep its charity, the refugee process was not set up – and cannot be allowed – to serve as a legalistic trampoline for the recreation of a repugnant and proven anti-Semite.

We can suffer ambiguity or ambivalence on many subjects. The great question of whether a homicidal despot such as Saddam Hussein should be deposed by the force of another nation illustrates how wide legitimate debate can be. A move to rid the earth of even one of its tyrannies and charnel houses would seem to offer little room for a second opinion. Why Saddam Hussein should not be deposed is a fairly barren theme. But even on this slender ground, sane argument can flourish.

The case of the wretched Ernst Zundel is mercifully more particular. Of all the bigotries in this bigotry-infested world, the bigotry of anti-Semitism is the most perverse and stupid. The shades of six million people who went in torment and degradation to their death still haunt some living memories. Because one man hated Jews. Hated Jews because they were Jews. The sheer monumentality of the Holocaust sets it down literally as human-kind's best effort to date to install hell on Earth.

We need not do the precious dance on whether or not real evil exists when we speak of the twentieth century and the fate of Europe's Jews. Evil exists and, for a while, it ran the shop.

And now the boy-toy of anti-Semitism, kicked out of the United States, deliciously "stateless" (as the *Globe* editorial noted yesterday), fearing "persecution" in Germany, wants to claim refugee status in Canada. This is too rich. The Holocaust denier is scared to go to Germany. Well, cry me several rivers. "Anywhere but Germany."

This is a *Saturday Night Live* skit written by Dante. He fears he will run afoul of Germany's hate laws. Not to worry. Maybe some kind fellow anti-Semite in a country Ernst Zundel says never had a Holocaust can hide him in an attic for a couple of years. He could keep a diary.

What should be done? The idea that Canada should declare him a security threat is wrong. Why should we construct a fiction in law to get rid of someone whose own fictions have made him a pariah? That smacks of unintentional tribute. He's not a security threat. He's an embarrassment.

Of this I am certain: if we in any degree take this "claim" of his seriously, and throw it into the maw of procedure and process and thereby extend the publicity lifespan of an indisputable hate-monger, then the last thread of credibility that attaches to our real refugee system is snapped forever. Ernst Zundel is a burden it cannot bear.

And if we get too artful in devising the means to deny his attempt to play with that system, we contribute a dignity to his claim at the same time as we derogate from the dignity of all genuine refugees. This creature, by his own works, has put himself beyond the pale. We don't have to ostracize him. He has ostracized himself. And if there is no other justice but the poetic, let him please return to Germany, where (by his own argument), with no Holocaust having happened, there can be no hate laws that have grown out of it. It's his own petard. Let him be hoisted by it.

We cannot go through the transparent folly of taking his claim to be a refugee seriously, of letting our addiction to process suffocate the claims of common sense. He left Canada in 2001 and headed for the more cosmopolitan ozone of Tennessee, but not before offering the immortal witticism that he was now "in Canada-denial." Fine by me. We should return the gesture.

I suggest this country put itself in Zundel-denial. "Never heard of him. Wasn't here. Ernst who? You say you were in Canada for forty years? Never happened." I never thought I'd find myself making a case for repressed memory, but if there was ever a moment for trundling out the sad baggage of the talk-show therapists, this is it.

Ernst Zundel never happened. He wasn't here. We never heard of him. We can't give him a hearing, because he never existed.

– Globe and Mail

Tampering with the Tree of Knowledge

It doesn't get much more basic than the human gene. Scientists tell us that, in most human beings, including Liberals, genetic structure precedes even partisan political affiliation. That's pretty deep. If life is a mystery, then genes are the key to it. Which is why the project to map all that stuff that makes us what we are is both so frightening and so fascinating. We, meaning scientists mainly, have been playing around with life a good bit lately. They cloned a sheep a few years back – an innocuous enough enterprise – and called it Dolly, probably out of mistaken homage to Dolly Parton's reassuring twins. We're not afraid of sheep, and cloning one of them gave more amusement than anxiety. Recently they managed a whole batch of identical piglets from the same process. Multiplying the planet's supply of pigs, all under the good intention of eventually providing a resource for organ transplants, doesn't distress too many people either.

But some of us do feel an itch of discomfort that things are coming into the world not by the old-fashioned way – a little courtship, a glass of wine, and a romp or two around Club Med for swine – but at the prod of a microscope and a twitch of biogenetics. From what I have read, all sorts of little bacteria have been interfered with in the name of scientific inquiry, and we humans take some comfort from the consideration that, as with the sheep and the hogs, well, that's them. But the boundaries between what is human and what is not are not as stringent and distinct as human vanity would like to have them.

The Human Genome Project, as it is grandly called, takes this probing and coding to its absolute conclusion. It is a grand-scale effort to draw the map and name all the places of our fundamental being. Now science has been threatening to draw back the last veil on life since it, science, has been around. But this time, apparently, they mean it. Hello, Dolly, indeed! This is worrisome as such. It is precisely the kind of project that cries out for the disinterest of true science, something that should proceed only under the ancient rule of knowledge for knowledge's sake. They're not researching a new design for winter tires here or a better way to crowd the Backstreet Boys onto a smaller CD. If there were ever a case for public enterprise, with public goals and public intent, then the Human Genome Project is it. Unfortunately, inevitably in our commerce-maddened world, things are rarely so pure and never so simple.

We see and hear daily of patents taken out on genes by private researchers. And there is a competing enterprise, Celera Genomics Corporation, which is entirely private. Celera has already amassed six thousand – *six thousand* – applications for gene patents. I don't know how you feel about it, but the thought that our cellular bits are awaiting patent by either some drug company or some high-powered franchise greatly distresses me. Bill Clinton and Tony Blair's joint announcement that the results of all such researches should be available to all scientists everywhere is entirely the right idea. We do not want corporations even thinking they can own what makes us, or how we are made. Life is not some intellectual property or some dreadful stock-market issue, nor do we want it marketed on-line. The last time someone tampered with the tree of knowledge there was all hell to pay. Well, there's no difference now, except hell has gotten hotter.

– The National

Selling Something, Dr. Suzuki?

The campaign for Kyoto is in high gear. This week David Suzuki headed a press conference, put on by some Canadian doctors, to tell us that "Kyoto is about saving lives" – sixteen thousand people dying each year in Canada. They're dying mainly from the effects of global warming, we must presume.

Questions occur. The most salient are about the number of "Canadians dying every year." How rigorously is this connected to global warming? Is the number "scientific" – backed by evidence, tested by observation, obedient to objective laws, insusceptible to massage or spin?

One thing I have no question about is that we were meant to take the number as scientific. That was the point of its precision, its emphatic particularity. We weren't told that a vague "lot" of Canadians have medical problems that are aggravated by smog and pollution, which are themselves aggravated, it is thought, by global warming. We were offered, instead, a shiny, hard, round number.

It was also the point of having Canada's most ardent environmentalist flanked by physicians to deliver the message. Herd a crowd of doctors into a room, *and* David Suzuki – all you need is to throw in a few beakers and a chart of the periodic table (wall mural of Isaac Newton massaging his head and frowning at the apple) and you've got yourself a state-of-the-press-conference lab.

That sixteen thousand Canadians die every year is a very *particular* claim. It *must* be scientific. And if it is a piece of proven science that sixteen thousand of us die every year because of global warming, then only those people who don't care about the deaths of a horrifying number of fellow citizens would oppose ratifying Kyoto.

I don't buy the "science" of the press conference for a minute. These are "advocacy" numbers. They have as much science, in the strict sense of that term, as the phrase "more dentists recommend . . . ," which used to pop up so unpersuasively in ancient toothpaste commercials. The point of advocacy numbers is to pump a cause, not make a finding. Advocacy numbers are the rhetoric of an age that can't write perorations; they are argumentative quickies, meant to sidestep the preliminaries, finesse the intermediate niceties, and get the meeting over with.

There was yet another point to Mr. Suzuki's brandishing of sixteen thousand Canadians heading early to their plots should Kyoto not be signed. The number was meant to put paid to another, more awkward number. That number was two hundred thousand, and it was a number Canadians almost didn't get to hear about at all.

It's the number of jobs that Kyoto may cost; it was apparently deleted from a briefing paper prepared by federal officials for the cabinet. Unemployment is not a trivial misery: it comes attended with all sorts of stress, anxiety, depression. Not to mention that the absence of a paycheque on a regular basis can play havoc with the mortgage and the diet. Unemployment, would you believe, is a major health problem. Poor people die sooner – would "prematurely" be the right word here? – than those who are not poor.

But death trumps unemployment, even in Canada, and if sixteen thousand are going to die every year if Kyoto is not ratified, then I guess two hundred thousand lost jobs is a small, though uncomfortable, price to pay. Better the pink slip than the waybill from the undertaker.

I point all this out mainly to remove from the minds of the few people who still hold it the idea that the debate over Kyoto is a scientific debate. It's a public-relations war. Further, I do it to highlight that the much-touted consensus over Kyoto is not a "scientific" consensus.

A lot of scientists agreeing on something is not the same thing as a scientific consensus. Any sentence that begins "A majority of the world's scientists agree . . ." is not reporting a scientific finding; it's announcing a preference. It's a poll. Real science doesn't do polls. E = mc² wasn't arrived at by a show of hands; the equations that spell out the workings of the universe were not put to a vote.

When we hear of a consensus on global warming, we are being told – covertly, but told nonetheless – that it isn't a scientific *fact*. And when we're told that it "contributes" to the death of sixteen thousand Canadians, even when we're being told by David Suzuki, we're being hectored, as opposed to informed.

The other side is hectoring, too. But at least they don't wear lab coats and drag in the actuarial tables. Ratifying the Kyoto Protocol is a real debate, has real costs, is a mix of guesses, best estimates, and conflicting claims, with real consequences – whichever way it's decided. For the sake of the debate, let's lay off the science unless it is science.

– *Globe and Mail*

SEPTEMBER 11 AND AFTER

No Room on This Planet for Us Both

September 11 was meant to produce two kinds of explosion: the physical one that caused such havoc, and the psychological one that would continue echoing through the resolve of America and its citizens.

The actions of that day were choreographed. They were designed to produce maximum impact. Not just on the Twin Towers and the Pentagon, but on the minds of all whom the terrorists knew, via television, would see them.

The buildings and planes were meant to explode, literally. And the images, which would inundate the United States and the world in this visual and wired aged, were meant to carry a further psychological blast. And they did.

There was a depth of sinister imagination in the planning that was chillingly awesome. The terrorists who conceived this lethal theatre placed imagination in tandem with hatred. The small cluster of minds that originated last week's horrors included the consideration of spectacle in their planning. They possessed the grisly insight that spectacle on this scale is itself a force – in a different way as mighty as the explosions of jet fuel and the impact of airliners on targeted buildings.

September 11 was a marriage of physics and psychology. The terrorists knew the force of the spectacle would multiply the impact of the physical deeds. Their tactics included not just all those particular actions that would lead to the destruction of the Twin Towers and the obliteration of one wing of the Pentagon, but that the image of the destruction would be an explosion, of another kind, in itself.

This is not some dreadfully artsy point. September 11 has obliterated so many of our routine dispositions, altered the psychological landscape of so many people, continues to work its damage on the stock market and the economy, precisely because it was so vivid as a scene, and carried such a symbolic overlay. Scene and symbol were the cluster bomb directed at all the rest of us off-site.

That secondary explosion is even now far from spent.

This was a horrible act of deliberate carnage. It was conceived by perverted, but gifted, imaginations – imaginations more ripe than those of Hollywood, more fertile than those of most novelists, and more cunning than those in the world's intelligence agencies whose dire business it is to dream up "scenarios," to project an inventory of potential terrorist actions.

Terror is primarily psychological. Its purpose is never just explosion and death, the destruction of this building, the killing of those people – on whatever scale. Destruction and death are the means to trigger the greater, more diffuse, aftershock. The purpose of terror is to breed fear and to sap the nerve of people and governments. At the most basic level, terrorism is a contest of wills.

Given how meticulous the planning for September 11 must have been, and the malign grandiosity of its conception, it is safe to conclude that these terrorists were not unwilling to go the whole way. All the talk that followed of biological and chemical and nuclear threats to the West were clearly and rightly based on the assumption that the people willing to cause death in the heart of America were not going to hesitate if greater means of devastation and heartbreak came within their grasp.

The Americans – as the world's superpower and as the citizenry most directly attacked – were presented with a challenge. Did they have the nerve to respond? Here is another aspect of terrorism. It is a form of silent extortion. The deed screams, "Don't respond or we will do more." No response, or a timid or factitious one (convening a meeting at the U.N., say), is an announcement: "Yes, you have scared us. Come again."

September 11, on this understanding, cannot go unanswered. George W. Bush (or the people around him) has divined that the only reply to terrorism on this scale is a controlled and directed fury, a reply without finesse or nuance. All the cowboy talk of dead or alive and smokin' 'em out of their hidin' places may have sounded naive to those unfamiliar with the idiom. But it placed the contest with terrorism on its proper terrain. It is either yielded to, or it is vanquished, utterly.

The president's address to Congress on Thursday night was a little more ornamental and generous than the limited text of a wanted poster. But its message at heart was just as terse and equally ominous. It declared his nation's nerve was not only intact but strengthened. It was not going to buy off the extortionists with inaction. It also declared that George W. Bush understood the terms of the game.

The security of its citizens is a nation's first virtue. The response to those who appropriate the "right" to mass slaughter had to be unequivocal.

George W. Bush had it right. As between terrorism and democracy, there's no room on this planet for both of us.

– Globe and Mail

The Prince of Darkness Visible

> ... But many shapes
> Of Death, and many are the ways that lead
> To his grim cave, all dismal.
> – Milton, *Paradise Lost*, XI

Terrorism is the politics of death. Death is its means. Death is its goal. On all other politics, it doesn't want to turn back the clock. Terrorism wants to blow up the clock altogether.

Not even terrorism, however, wants to go naked. Nobody wants to look upon death – not even its purveyors. So terrorism is always reaching for a garment of exterior purpose.

For those who incinerated more than five thousand people on September 11, the cloak *du jour* is "the Palestinian problem." I used quotation marks to indicate, in the context of September 11, that, while the concerns embodied in the phrase are real, raising those concerns after the blast, by those who caused the blast, is spurious.

The problem itself is not spurious. But tapes from Osama bin Laden or his al-Qaeda network giving a post-mass-murder exposure of the problem are items of grisly opportunism. The terrorists do not wish their deed to be seen unadorned, in all its horror, simply as it is, and for what it is. We may presume they hijack an agenda with even less reluctance than they hijack a plane. If Palestine will not do, then throw in the suffering of the Iraqi children. Or U.S. bases in Saudi Arabia. Or U.S. foreign policy.

None of these is a root cause. All are after-the-slaughter Post-it notes –

mass murder seeking the expedient of an alien moral prism, the unnecessary murder seeking the necessary excuse. The mind that conceives and executes the murder of thousands of people is not a mind that will hesitate before a little duplicity. After you kill five thousand, it's no great exertion to offer a lie or two. The agenda of terrorism is terrorism.

The world is full – always has been – of problems of varying degrees of tractability. People in different regions of the globe go about trying to solve these problems – with all the frustrations, pain, and simple misery that the majority of them involve – by all the different methods (discussion, elections, rallies, publicity, pressure, diplomacy) that stop short of killing the other side.

Trying to solve problems without resorting to death as a tactic or a goal is what we call politics. Politics is the agreement that the other side should be allowed to live, while the problem – however imperfectly – is being dealt with. This meaning of politics is one measurement of the human race's long march from our bestial origins.

Terrorism, however, doesn't recognize politics, and despises its practitioners, be they Palestinian or American. The terrorist is beyond, or above, the ardent imperfections of politics, of how human beings, finally, have settled on settling their differences. The Parliament of terror is the graveyard.

The mind of the terrorist, to itself, is perfect. It has the range of divinity. So, too, is his will – it executes whatever others will dare to do for it. Neither that will nor that mind discriminate. The nineteen simpletons who stole the planes were as much detritus in the mind of the one who sent them as the innocents those nineteen assassinated.

Death to his instruments; death to his "targets." And whether or not it be the same "he" who is mailing the anthrax dust, that mind is equally pleased that the threat of anonymous death, the rumour of death, which now covers our continent, is alive and roaring through the minds and sleep of millions. Death is his message. Death is his medium. Death is his method.

So please let us not coat with noble fictions the why of this miserable enterprise, nor offer the clothing of a reasonable cause for an action that despises reason, that is in itself a notice of irrevocable contempt for the idea of reason as a human, living, property.

The terrorists have leveraged mass death into the present world, as a mechanism they hope will become domesticated and familiar, by hoop-fastening it to the dilemmas and cruxes of some of the world's most exhausting issues.

They wish to associate their abandonment of civilized means with the civilized hopes of those who have not chosen that abandonment. There can be no discussion with those who have chosen death as their way of introducing a topic.

The message of September 11 is primal. I kill you first; now agree with me. In that order, it must be emphasized. First, I blow up the buildings and kill all the people. Then, let us talk.

At the core, terrorists pose a bare question. Fortunately, it was phrased more than four hundred years ago, with a point and simplicity that defies rearrangement: To be or not to be. That, as the man said, is the question.

– Globe and Mail

Osama, Try Reading Gibbon

The great poet of imperialism in all its guises – in its might, in its decadence – is Edward Gibbon. Gibbon didn't rhyme, and *The Decline and Fall of the Roman Empire* (thank God) isn't ladled out in couplets. Yet the superb sonority of his elegy to Roman power is second in the majesty of its art only to Milton's. The "sound" of poetry is the means of its ability to charm or enchant.

Milton is the very wizard (need I say we're not talking Hogwarts here) of poetic "sound effects." Of the passage in Milton's *Lycidas* that ends "Look homeward Angel now, and melt with ruth," T.S. Eliot wrote that "for the single effect of grandeur of sound, there is nothing finer in English poetry."

To rank Gibbon as second only to Milton is then the highest praise. The reliance of both writers on the sound of words, sound almost for its own sake, is why they are frequently referred to as musical. What is more lyrical – more musical – than those lines, perhaps the most familiar of all of Gibbon, when he bids farewell to the mighty task that has consumed him for more than two decades: "It was at Rome, on the fifteenth of October 1764, as I sat musing amidst the ruins of the Capitol, while the barefoot friars were singing vespers in the Temple of Jupiter, that the idea of writing the decline and fall of the city first started in my mind."

Ah! those barefoot friars singing vespers, they will break your heart every time. That quotation is from his autobiography, but for the full cannon-effect of Gibbon one must go to the mighty *Decline and Fall* itself. It was the contemplation of great power and empire that called forth the full Gibbonian orchestration.

The extent of the fallen empire, the catalogue of its provinces, the roll call of its satraps and minions, all under the inescapable sway of the Emperor, seemed both to alarm and awe him. Roman power ran uninterrupted over the then-civilized world, and even outside its orbit, "barbarian" kings and lords were willing or eager to bend a trembling knee in the direction of that power.

Roman power was ubiquitous. It offered no shelter from its reach. Its contemplation moved Gibbon to his most gorgeous speculations. He pictured a fugitive seeking to avoid the eye and touch of Roman power, as invested in the Emperor. Where would such a person go?

"But the empire of the Romans filled the world, and when that empire fell into the hands of a single person, the world became a safe and dreary prison for his enemies. The slave of imperial despotism, whether he was condemned to drag his gilded chain in Rome and the senate, or to wear out a life of exile on the barren rock of Seriphus or the frozen banks of the Danube, expected his fate in silent despair."

If we were to tinker with names, and instead of the "barren rock of Seriphus" speak of the "caves outside Kandahar," the passage takes on a contemporary ring. And if we conjure the figures of Osama and the Taliban in the place of the "slave of Imperial despotism," it turns positively prescient. As Mr. Gibbon, long before the voice-overs of the war correspondents, puts it: "To resist was fatal, and it was impossible to fly. On every side he was encompassed with a vast extent of sea and land, which he could never hope to traverse without being discovered, seized, and restored to his irritated master."

American power differs from Roman in that, in addition to its ubiquity, there is the marvel of its terrifying technologies. The Americans, when they want to, can see and hear *everything*.

Osama's in his cave, but the eyes and ears of American power are, alas for him, everywhere. And when I read of the "irritated master," I found a prophetically succinct sketch of Donald Rumsfeld.

In less than two months, the world has seen an exercise of power that is *aweful* – the older spelling reminds of the word's scope. It may be that the great consequence of September 11 is that America has been shocked into an understanding of its true, simple might. Gibbon, in the same passage, speaks of the remaining dimension of imperial power. Those not under its dominion wish to have its favour or its rewards.

This is Osama's biggest worry, that of "dependent kings who would gladly purchase the Emperor's protection, by the sacrifice of an obnoxious fugitive."

I wonder if the *Decline and Fall* is on Osama's night table. There are abridged versions, in paperback, suitable for the traveller. On the other hand, the full – some have complained, near-interminable – text ("Another dammed, thick, square book! Always scribble, scribble, scribble! Eh! Mr. Gibbon?") is ideal for long and anxious solitudes.

– Globe and Mail

The Dogs of War v. the Dogs of Law

... lawyers find out still
Litigious men, which quarrels move.
   – John Donne

The families of the 9/11 victims have decided to let loose the lawyers. They are going to sue all sorts of folks – some banks, some "charities," members of the Saudi royal family, part of the bin Laden family's construction firm.

The family members have been joined by some of the firefighters and rescue workers of 9/11. Calling themselves the 9/11 Families United to Bankrupt Terrorism, they are seeking the money "to force the sponsors of terror into the light and subject them to the rule of law."

They are suing for one trillion dollars. Welcome to *Bleak House*, the twenty-first-century version. That grim classic was the story, most will remember, of a great endless Court of Chancery suit, *Jarndyce v. Jarndyce*, which spread its miseries to the generations caught up in its dark web. The book was Charles Dickens's prescient scream of warning that it is best to keep some things away from the law.

The families of the 9/11 victims might want to read it before they leap into this astonishing litigation.

This age, as opposed to the one in which Dickens wrote his lethal satire, has added television and news coverage to the grinding miseries of vast lawsuits. The right kind of trial is now the content of the twenty-four-hour cable news channels, and fodder as well for all sorts of talk marathons. Fox talk-show host Greta Van Susteren will train her surgically widened eyes on this epic. *Hardball*, *Larry King Live*, *TalkBack Live*, and a legion of lesser chatter factories will spin this interminably.

So there are two treadmills that they are about to mount: endless litigation and non-stop television and news coverage. This is a combination that not even the athletic imagination of Dickens could have spanned.

We're going to hear a lot that "it's not about the money." This is a difficult bait for even the most gullible to swallow. When you set one trillion dollars as the goal of a lawsuit and then insist that it's not about the money, you've dug a fairly large and conspicuous trench between what is being said and what is being done. Not a canal, a gulf.

Furthermore, when some of the lead lawyers in this case are the same public-spirited knights who were successful against the tobacco companies – which resulted in awards in the billions, and in some of the richest fees in the history of lawsuits, the protest that "it's not about the money" is not just feeble, it's risible.

The other claim that some spokespersons are putting forward is that they intend the lawsuits to do damage "to the terrorists." Well, there is a more direct route to that laudable ambition and, surprisingly, it is remarkably uncluttered with trial lawyers and dreams of a trillion-dollar bonanza.

Any damage being done, or to be done, to the terrorists is being done, and will be done, by the armies of the states pursuing them. There are young men and women even now, eleven months after the attacks, in harm's way in Afghanistan and other parts of the world, doing "damage to the terrorists." And if Osama bin Laden or any of his homicidal henchmen are quaking in their caves at this minute, it isn't because a few lawyers or family spokespersons are due for a guest slot with Greta or Larry.

It's because aircraft carriers and jets and special forces and ordinary soldiers are still in pursuit of those who dreamed and executed the butchery of innocents less than a year ago.

None of the victims' families, in the U.S. at any rate, have any right to claim that their suffering has been ignored. September 11 was the occasion of an almost epic display of sympathy and regard for those caught up directly in its misery. As it should have been. The families have been cited innumerably; the firefighters and police officers who acted so courageously have become icons; and governments all over the world have joined the U.S. in the hunt for those responsible.

There is a war being conducted because of what happened last September. And there is nothing more serious than war. This lawsuit is a vulgarization of the events of 9/11. It is an attempt to transmute a tragedy into a tort with a very large price tag.

It is, all spokespersons to the contrary, bringing money into a territory in which money does not belong, and a kind of law that should govern products and contracts into an area much more profound than either.

Endless and histrionic litigation is both wearisome and, ultimately, empty. It also corrupts the sentiments of those who engage in it.

This is what Dickens chronicled so mercilessly and prophetically in *Bleak House*. That's why he called it "bleak."

– Globe and Mail

A Wake-up More Than a Nightmare

Everything hasn't changed. There are unalterables, pleasant and unpleasant. The splendour of sunsets. A good book, a soft chair, and a cold beer. The hypermonotony of film-festival panels – the star, the director, and their damn "chemistry." (The star and the director should be thrown into a burlap bag until all that chemistry dissipates.) Connie Chung, the sigh-master. The unchallengeable sovereignty of arctic char "chased" with bakeapples (the exquisite Newfoundland marsh berry that is God's own master gift to the human palate).

Our repertoire of pleasure or annoyance is the same as it's always been. When people portended after last year's cataclysm that "everything has changed," they weren't thinking of the "common stock of harmless human pleasures." Or, for that matter, the equally large common stock of human pains. September 11 did not alter our nature, or the things our nature, with its mixed receptors, responds to.

Everything never changes. The instant motto in the aftermath of 9/11 was a leap to stamp that day's horrors with some meaning, to provide rhetorical purchase while people gathered the resources of spirit and intelligence necessary to read its final import. It was never meant to say the whole truth about that day, or to be taken at any time in full literalness.

In a curious way, the "everything has changed" message actually carried quite the opposite meaning. Since the close of the Second World War, the West has been, in comparison with most parts of the globe, on something of a holiday. We had begun to think the holiday was "normal." Great wealth,

longer lives, technology, the absence of conflict – this side of the globe was
saturated with the hubris of its own exceptionality.

We had forgotten the common lot of our kind, which is, sadly, that the
world, for all its wonders and beauty, is also and inevitably a place of pain
and sorrow and, all too commonly, blood. Uninterrupted peace is always
more rare than war. Harmony is the contingent experience, conflict and
tragedy the rule.

The "everything" that had changed was a wealth-cocooned dream, the
fantasy that the West was past tasting the horrors of history, that on this side
of the water history, in its cruelty and madness, was something we caught
up with watching those other places on TV.

That certainly changed. I think New York last year, and Washington and
Pennsylvania, shocked us out of a comforting illusion: that we were exempt
from the turbulence of the world, that history had two faces – one grim, one
meek – and reserved the soft one for us.

The deeper seriousness that was said to follow September 11 was just
the old seriousness returned, the realization of every generation that the
comfort and shape of everyday life is something most generations must
consciously construct and defend.

That it doesn't just happen. That everyday life is built on hard-won
habits, structures of tolerance and civility, on forms of self-governance
achieved only after much experiment and determination, on values nursed
over generations and often articulated at the price of great sacrifice.

Every previous generation has also understood, or learned the hard
way, that the world harbours much menace, that violence is more common
than its absence, and that evil men are at least as busy, and considerably
more energetic, than good ones. This great line of Yeats has much poetry,
more truth: "The best lack all conviction, while the worst / Are full of passionate intensity."

Hitler, unchecked, would have placed the planet in an eclipse of pain
and tyranny. Stalin yoked the lives of millions to the nightmare of police-
state communism. Starvation, prison, torture, and execution were "normal"
in all the despotisms of the twentieth century, from Idi Amin, who still
crawls the globe, to Tito, who no longer cumbers it. There are always giant

egos seeking to corral humankind, and a few outsized madmen dreaming of enslaving it.

We had forgotten that bitter lesson until last year. Osama bin Laden may turn out to be a cartoon pygmy of a villain who got "lucky" with one big strike. Saddam Hussein may just be a monstrous buffoon who collapses with the next exhale of determination. Or these men may be signals of even greater portent.

September 11, in all its vicious suddenness, was a return to business as usual. The world is more hostile than tranquil, and being always on guard is the necessary condition of every state that takes the safety of its citizens as its first virtue.

All those pleasant, ordinary experiences that make up our everyday lives are ours to spontaneously enjoy only because we have built and maintained the systems to house and protect them. The everyday doesn't just happen. It is an achievement.

So everything hasn't changed after all. We're back, alas, to normal.

– Globe and Mail

"The Poetry Is in the Pity"

There was to have been, this past Wednesday, a gathering at the White House to celebrate poetry. It was Laura Bush's idea. She dropped it because one of those invited had called on some others also invited to protest against a war with Iraq. There were the usual cries of suppression and censorship, and the hardly surprising charge that the postponement showed "how little they [the Bush White House] understand poetry and poets."

I don't think it's that neat. I'm not sure that any of us understand either poetry or poets. And the opinion of those who see poetry as intimately involved with the politics of the moment and, in particular, as a form of protest or social commentary is at least as benighted and parochial as that of the least-lettered aide in a Texan White House.

There is a presumption built into the idea that poets who oppose war are doing what poets are supposed to do, and a further presumption built into the idea that poets who challenge power are answering the truth of their vocation.

But there is absolutely no reason why a poem deploring war – or a given president – will be any more worthy, any more a poem, than one support-ing one.

Has there been a greater "political" poem yet than the nineteenth-century anthem "When Lilacs Last in the Door-yard Bloom'd," Whitman's piercing lament over the death of Abraham Lincoln? Lincoln, the Great Emancipator, presided over the greatest carnage America has known – the Civil War. If true poetry is inimical to war and violence, then surely

Whitman betrayed his muse when he sang of the man of power by whom "the war came."

The truth is, poetry is neither anti-war nor pro-war, and whether it scourges power or celebrates it matters not a whit to its success or, to be precise, to its being as poetry. Poetry can equally proceed out of great reverence as great rage. But when poetry links up with a cause, it almost always resigns its citizenship and becomes propaganda. Very good propaganda it may be – but poetry it is not.

Should not poets voice their opinions? Of course. Unless they have a poem waiting, in which case they should do the really important thing first, write the poem, and march later. Poets have as much right as electricians, CEOs, or journalists to speak their minds, and at least an equal purchase on the issues of the day.

But they are not, despite the romance that invests their practice, "the antennae of the race," nor are they, in any degree, shamans or seers. There have been poets as wise as wisdom will allow, and versifying fools as deep as folly itself. And some, maybe most, have been a mix of both.

I think of Ezra Pound, a man of wonderful generosity and a poet of luminous gifts, who was – alas – at times so squalid and hateful that it hurts to read him.

Pound choked his own muse with a mess of anti-Semitism and strange politics. He worshipped Mussolini (dear God) for a while. He also wrote lyrics of imperishable beauty and (after imprisonment forced a reckoning with himself and knocked the "politics" out of him) some lines that are the honour of the twentieth century: "What thou lov'st well shall not be reft from thee." The *Pisan Cantos* are a masterwork.

Western poetry began with a war on the fields of "windy Troy." Virgil, looking back to that example, begins his epic "Of arms and the man I sing." Milton calls out all the brass in his formidable orchestra for the war in Heaven in *Paradise Lost*.

It is not a consideration whether either of these artists were "for" war. Poetry doesn't reside in the attitude towards its subject. It resides in the art of the language with which the subject is invested.

Wilfred Owen comes close to my idea of a genuine anti-war poet. He has enough respect for his anger over war's brutalities to house it in art. Much of what passes for anti-war poetry in the last while is mere attitudinizing in poorly camouflaged prose. I wish there was more space to quote from Owen, because his lines, which are now almost a hundred years old, are as fresh and as poignant as if they were written yesterday. That's because they are poetry. "News that stays news," to bring Ezra Pound back into it.

The quote I can offer is the one most familiar to those who know his work and is its epigraph: "My subject is War. And the Pity of War. The poetry is in the pity." As for pity, consider that the armistice bells were tolling the war's end on November 11, 1918, when, at his parents' home, the doorbell rang and a telegram arrived, to tell them their poet-son was dead. "And each slow dusk a drawing-down of blinds."

– Globe and Mail

What Joey Could Teach Saddam When It Comes to Elections

I am away in a far country as I write this.

Actually, I am only in the United States, which is, of course, about as Canadian-near as it is possible to be, but the wistfulness of "away in a far country" has a charm for me almost impossible to decline. I could plead I am far from Newfoundland and Labrador, but it's a worthless finesse and I know it.

The *Globe and Mail* has a fearsome rigour and its scrutiny is ruthless; I am, then, away in a near country. In New York City – to be particular. And find myself, curiously, revolving thoughts of Joey Smallwood.

Joey Smallwood, the great first premier of Newfoundland, is not some tutelary spirit of mine. I know I present him occasionally in conversation or print, but that is not because he can be said to "haunt" me. He was an exceptionally vivid personality, a politician of intensity and passion, whose remarkable theatricality was not always calculated or spurious. I think he shows up a lot in my chatter because he is an emphatic contrast to, sadly, a great desert of present-day political tedium.

I know that Mr. Smallwood spent some time in this city in his early manhood, dallied with the labour movement of a now far-off time, and practised what he was ever after amused to call journalism. But it is not his association with New York then, and my being here now, that summons him. There's nothing of New York in it.

I remember him rather as a great vote-getting machine. He was a natural harvester of ballots; gathering votes lured him as lust does more narrowly hungry seekers. He was very good at it.

Six times, he solicited the voters of Newfoundland and six times they said, very significantly, "Joey is our man." In his second-last race as premier, he won thirty-nine out of forty-two seats. There was a seventh time, but that's another story, for a longer day.

There are some people in Ottawa, now, who are very full of themselves for winning a picayune *three* times. Mr. Smallwood would dismiss such a performance as being, so to speak, still under warranty – a mere tryout, just practice.

I know, too, that not long ago there was a premier who won every seat. Frank McKenna ran the table in New Brunswick. But this doesn't count. It is generally acknowledged that Frank McKenna is so nice, and New Brunswickers so drastically civil, that Mr. McKenna's unanimous sweep belongs more to the history of etiquette than politics.

Joey wasn't nice. He could be – but he rationed the effect. And for an abrasive, polarizing politician to sweep the polls as many times as he did is beyond doubt a triumph of the arts and wiles, and outright neediness, that we properly assign to the real and high calling of persuasion politics.

Actually, I think what summoned Joey to mind was Saddam Hussein. I read today in the *Wall Street Journal* – not my normal choice to greet the fresh world of morning – that Mr. Hussein held a plebiscite on whether he should have another seven years as imperial autocrat, or illustrious dictator, or whatever it is he calls himself. And that, in this plebiscite, as opposed to a previous one, when he scored a mere 99.96 per cent, he got 'em all.

I mean every one of them. One hundred per cent of Iraqis want all Saddam, all the time. I fear poor Joe, so long my hero in this department, was something of a slacker after all. Compared to Saddam, Joe's landslides were agonies of ambivalence.

Now, it must be said in Joey's defence that his elections were sometimes untidy. Other people ran in them, and against him. Mr. Hussein is more fastidious. So we should factor in voter distraction.

And if Joey talked of some issues as being of life and death to Newfoundland, it was mostly platform exuberance and all metaphor. Mr. Hussein doesn't do metaphor.

He's a sad little guy, far too easy with death, for those in his own country and those in countries nearby. A voting machine in Iraq has too much in common with the hangman's trap door, and a tick in the wrong box – if there is another box – is braiding one's own hemp.

One hundred per cent is a unanimity that only fear can account for, and power produce. Which makes me wonder why Mr. Hussein, or his kind, have plebiscites at all. They know how grotesque is this parody of choice.

I think it's envy. Envy of other men (they would not think of women) who really ask voters for their approval and really win it – again and again. Without the sword or the cell, the rack or the whip, to assist their persuasions.

Envy of their pleasure, too: envy of the sweet rush that Mr. Smallwood sought and found so often in little Newfoundland when he asked people to vote for him and they did. It's the asking that buys the pleasure. A despot's plebiscite is a worthless finesse to both parties of the desperate exchange.

Mr. Hussein's 100 per cent elections are not worth a fraction of one of Mr. Smallwood's six. Saddam doesn't deserve, though I've let him loose, to be in the same train of thought.

– Globe and Mail

Saddam Is a Stand-in Osama

Where is Osama? Time was, the archfiend of September 11 was in heavy rotation. Before and after his homicidal irruption into history, the fall of the towers and the assault on the Pentagon, the one-time playboy, construction engineer, and now terrorist and mastermind was wont to float his visage in neat little home videos.

A parley outside a cave, a chortle over supper after the deed, a fatwa here, a call to strike the infidel Jews and Americans there – these were the themes and settings of his modestly frequent releases.

But since September 11, 2001, beyond the home video that we suspect was never meant for air, there has been very little. Has Osama bin Laden gone sour on terrorist stardom, or, more worrisomely, has he (by perverted analogy to certain rock artists) taken time off "to work on another album"? We can but hope it is not the latter. Those who, in the days after September 11, were promising to "smoke him out" and were after him "dead or alive" must very much hope the same.

A few months ago, an audio tape was released, poor in quality but said to be authentic. The original response to the tape was that the voice belonged to Osama. Presumably the best audio laboratories of the world were harnessed to its analysis, and the most acute ears of the keenest agents of the world's greatest intelligence organizations gave the tape an audition that even J.Lo can't buy.

Originally they pronounced in the fiend's favour, that, yes, it was the great shadowy McCavity's own voiceprint. True, the voice was not as strong, the cadence was muffled and occasionally halting: it lacked the panache of the unquestioned originals. But yes, so the consensus had it, it was Osama, al-Qaeda's master's voice.

Those tepid certainties melted with time, and word then came from some Swiss laboratories (and they are very meticulous in Swiss laboratories) that maybe, just maybe, it was not the voice of the gaunt and pale one himself. That doubt was in addition to another consideration: Osama had up until then been strictly a man for video. The gratifications of vanity, on-air presence, beckoned perhaps more keenly than was wise for one in his circumstances. I'd guess that the one invention of the decadent West that he finds most congenial is the cable network.

It became an argument. Osama on audio tape alone could not be the real Osama. To retreat to a previous medium, one that offered so much less of himself, was not in keeping with the stridency of his earlier visitations upon the world's attention. So, a little after the audio tape was accepted to be his – remember, it was the one in which our own pacific and compromising country made his vendetta list – the conventional wisdom, as conventional wisdom is frequently pleased to do, reversed itself.

It wasn't Osama. And furthermore, because it wasn't a video, we should never have thought it was him in the first place.

So where is he? Or, more fundamentally, *is* he? Whether he's in hiding, or in dissolution, the absence of Osama is more than a perplexity. The failure to find him is, with almost exquisite fastidiousness, off-topic these days. The discount of his significance, which spokespeople from the president down offer almost daily in their catechism with the press, is merely a finesse on his not being found, the utter inconclusiveness of his status, alive or dead.

Were he to be found, either above the earth or mixed with its dust, it would be a Fourth of July day. But in the absence of success against September 11's perverted architect, new goals, goals of some equivalency, have had to be set.

One of these, the default target, is Saddam Hussein – the great consequence of which is a very likely full war against Iraq. The war on terror, which is both the oxymoronic abstraction that its critics charge it to be, and the very real and necessary search-and-destroy mission against terrorists everywhere that its advocates understand, must have a central and sub-stantive goal.

Absent the prime mega-villain, Mr. bin Laden, it moved to the next and most plausible facsimile. There are arguments independent of the fate of Osama for the removal of Saddam Hussein. It's not *all* about Osama. But the intrinsic nebulousness of a war on terror, the play of abstraction over an enterprise of combat, demands a palpable focus.

Mr. bin Laden hasn't been caught, and it is not known if he's brilliantly hiding or stolidly dead. That consideration has grooved the determination of the Americans towards Iraq and the much more (if I may put it this way) tangible Saddam. If Saddam Hussein is toppled in the next few months, he'll have Osama bin Laden to thank for his misery at least as much as George W. Bush.

– Globe and Mail

The Phony War's About to Get Real

We move closer and closer to what seems to be an inevitable war with Iraq. Monday will be a telling day: January 27 is fixed as the day the inspectors report to the United Nations. On Tuesday, President George W. Bush makes his annual State of the Union address.

The odds that the inspectors' report will give a clean bill of disarmament to Saddam Hussein are those of a lottery. But the Americans are in no mood for temporizing. So it's as near to certainty as politics and diplomacy allow that the State of the Union will be Mr. Bush's last statement of the case for the removal of Saddam Hussein from power and the beginning of conflict.

These are momentous times. For once, that piece of boilerplate is more than a cliché. Any war is momentous. War in a time of terror is also full of diffuse and incalculable consequences. And the motions of North Korea, and its strange despot, add the shadow of the ultimate menace – a nuclear exchange – to the fearsome permutations that open conflict may bring into play.

The "phony war" was the phrase, since licensed by historians, for the strange lull that descended over Europe after the Germans had overrun Poland at the start of the Second World War. War had been declared and total war had been expected. Instead, there was a period of some six or seven months, between October 1939 and May 1940, during which France and England sat waiting for the horror that did not come.

It was a strange time, as is evident from the rich literature and memoirs of that period – a time of frail hopes that war, real war, would not occur, and a time of strained nerves and continual apprehension, leavened only by those hopes that proved so vain.

We read that, after a while, many people came to believe seriously that war was not on, that it was all a matter of atmospherics, part of the deceitful game that politicians and generals have always played with one another at the expense, and to the torment, of ordinary citizens. Hence, the "phony" in phony war.

One would have to have lived in England or France to know how people felt then. But it occurs to me that some features of the phony war have re-presented themselves six decades later in the aftermath of the Twin Towers' destruction and the attack on the Pentagon.

Newtonian law says every action has an equal and opposite reaction. Alas, the symmetry and precision of Newton's formulation abides only in the clarity and rigour of classical physics. In what we so winsomely refer to as "the real world," the perfect balance of action and reaction is a phantom never glimpsed.

The incursion into Afghanistan, the overthrow of the Taliban, the capture of some and the scattering of many of al-Qaeda's grim executives, felt in its early days like the "equal and opposite" reaction to September 11.

But unless you were in Afghanistan, it did not seem like a real war. We, meaning the citizens of North America, consumed it on television. And television, despite all of its intensity of image and immediacy of report, remains a film of – and puts a film over – reality.

From a North American point of view, Afghanistan was a soldier's war. Here, aside from interminable lineups at airports and a slightly more energetic interest in "foreign" news, there was not too much to distinguish ordinary life pre-9/11 from life post-9/11.

And yet, the scale, surprise, and malign success of the September 11 attacks were a massive breach of the assumed invulnerability of this continent. North Americans have felt differently since that day. The scale of the attack was what constituted it as an act of war.

And however much some people would like to contain September 11 by some statement of the "reasons" behind it, to contain it in a framework whereby it is explained as a "rational" outcome of some of America's foreign policies (the familiar "root causes" delusion), it is not so containable.

September 11 was wild in the way that all war is wild, in that it unleashes consequences that defy the mightiest foresight. We have known, at some depth of consciousness, that the campaign in Afghanistan was not the full response to September 11.

We have known that an act of its stunning power would have more reaction – and, because of what it said about our vulnerability, that it must. So we have been living in the twilight of half-certainty, in a suspense half created by our hope that nothing more has to happen, and half by our deeper intuition that something very grim will. It is the state of mind of the phony war.

Monday and Tuesday will very likely end this anxious period. And maybe introduce us to more substantial anxieties.

– Globe and Mail

September 11 Was the Smoking Gun

Secretary of State Colin Powell went before the United Nations Security Council this week to make the case that Saddam Hussein is not in compliance with the most recent resolution demanding that he disarm, and demonstrate that he has disarmed.

I think Mr. Powell made the case and then some: that the dictator is engaged in evasion and deceit, that there is an arsenal of concealed chemical and biological weaponry, and that the world should not be too comfortable on how eagerly he is pursuing the acquisition of nuclear weapons, or how close to getting them he may be.

I have only one difficulty with Mr. Powell's presentation: it should never have been made.

The wrong person, from the wrong country, stood in the U.N. making a case about Iraq's weapons and Iraq's compliance. If there is any persuading to be done here, it surely has to be done by Iraq. And if there are any U.N. member states that insist on demonstrations of proof about the honesty of Iraq's compliance with Resolution 1441, then surely it is Iraq, not the United States, that bears the primary burden of response.

I will go one step further. The resolution in question came into being (it is the fifteenth of its kind on Iraq) as a compromise. The U.S. was prepared to go to war with Iraq when the idea was offered, by means of Resolution 1441, to give Saddam Hussein one last chance. He was to restore the weapons inspectors he had kicked out, commit to disarming, and supply the proof that he was so doing. It was on that basis that the U.S. decided, for the moment, to give the U.N. its last chance to enforce its own resolutions on Iraq and the matter of weapons of mass destruction.

So there should have been a second presentation at the U.N. this week, and this one should not have been made by Colin Powell, either. Rather, it should have been Kofi Annan making a presentation to the world body, and the U.S. in particular, on whether the fifteenth resolution was all the U.N. promised the world and the United States it would be. A presentation that demonstrated, to the satisfaction of Washington, that Iraq was in compliance, that it was disarming, that it was ridding itself of all weapons of mass destruction.

Resolution 1441 was crafted by its supporters as a device to achieve by peaceful means what the U.S. is determined to achieve by peaceful means or by outright war. If the threat that the U.S. perceives still remains – and certainly Mr. Powell, the least war-inclined member of the Bush administration, perceives it as still remaining – then it is surely Iraq first, and then the U.N., that should be making the case to Washington as to why it should forgo the military confrontation.

I wonder what the Security Council would have done had Mr. Powell gone before it in February 2001 and argued that the Taliban regime in Afghanistan was harbouring and aiding terrorists and that, without a pre-emptive attack, those terrorists would very likely launch some mighty assault on American lives and territory. If he had shown photos of training camps, argued a link with Osama bin Laden, and suggested that, if action were delayed, there would be great loss of civilian lives some day on U.S. soil, what would the U.N. response have been then?

I wonder whether the U.N. would have even called for weapons inspectors. Or would the response have been that the U.S. was being belligerent for its own sake, or that it wanted control of Afghanistan to secure oil reserves? Very probably. Very probably, too, there would have been tremendous calls for more proof and a smoking gun.

Well, four smoking guns – or, more precisely, hijacked planes – did show up, on September 11, compliments of Osama bin Laden and al-Qaeda. Mr. Powell didn't make a case then. No one did, because no one could conceive, other than the terrorists themselves, the kind of murderous horror they were willing to – and sadly did – perpetrate.

This point is worth underscoring: for the Americans, September 11 is the only smoking gun that counts. It was the demonstration that terrorists are willing to kill as many as they can, whenever they can. Mr. Powell's case is predicated on the horrible example of that day.

That case may be crudely summarized thus: the U.S. is not willing to allow the really bad guys to get all their bombs and chemicals lined up, and not willing to allow one heinous dictator to make a useful alliance with another heinous terrorist, so as to obliterate as many U.S. citizens as possible whenever an opportunity is afforded them.

It's up to the U.N. to prove to Colin Powell that, at the very least, Iraq is out of the game.

Not the reverse.

– Globe and Mail

To War or Not to War: Canada Faces a Morality Test

It is not a light thing to contemplate a war, to declare one, or to decide – if another nation is going to war – that our nation will join it. However much these endless debates, at the U.N. or in the streets and assemblies of the nations, about whether or not there is to be a war, and the arguments for or against a war – however much time and passion these debates consume, we should be grateful that they're being held. It's a question of war. And we should be grateful that war, the decision to go to war, to shed the blood of soldiers and civilians, is a question being considered.

We know the two nations – or with greater precision the two leaders – who have settled the question of whether war with Iraq is necessary and who have also decided – and it's not the same question – whether war with Iraq is right. They are George W. Bush and Tony Blair. There are other countries that have decided to join these two, but the United States and United Kingdom are the principals. And of these two, it is somewhat ironically Mr. Blair – the willing ally – rather than Mr. Bush – the originating protagonist – who has made the clearest, widest, and most articulate argument why war with Iraq is both necessary and right.

I do not think the citizens of the United Kingdom, even the many who disagree with their prime minister, have grounds for feeling that Mr. Blair has acted in any way inconsistent with honour or his role as a leader in how he has faced the issue of war.

He has sought a moral basis on which to ground his decision and, despite all the risks to his very standing as prime minister, has made his case openly, repeatedly, urgently, and reluctantly. Mr. Blair is not eager for war.

It is only because he sees it as necessary and right that he has taken the course he has.

George W. Bush is not gifted with Tony Blair's powers of presentation, but of all the criticisms that are levelled at the American president, the two that seem most unfair are that he has decided to rush to war, and that he has decided to go to war other than for reasons that he sees as right and necessary.

If war against Saddam Hussein is right and if it is necessary, it is so regardless of what the United Nations will decide. And if a war with Saddam Hussein is wrong and unnecessary, it is likewise wrong and unnecessary regardless of what the United Nations will decide. The U.N., after all, is but the collective utterance of the individual decisions of leaders and nations on these very questions. Well, we are now at the very end of the discussion and debate and, one way or another, it looks as if there is to be a war.

What Canada owes to its dignity as a nation, and the prime minister owes to the country, because he is its leader, is to declare whether the idea of going to war against Saddam Hussein on those grounds championed by Mr. Bush and Mr. Blair, or on other grounds, is the right thing to do and the necessary thing to do. To say we will join the war if the U.N. passes a resolution approving it is to sidestep a moral and political decision that we don't have the right to sidestep.

If the war is right and necessary, we must join it. If it is neither right nor necessary, we must stay out. This is not a decision to put out to franchise. We must make it, and the prime minister must explain it. Is war with Iraq right or wrong? The question is plain, profound, and inescapable. And it deserves the very clearest of answers.

– The National

In Search of Past Glories

It was the philosopher George Santayana who gave us the axiom, "Those who cannot remember the past are condemned to repeat it." Like most axioms, it offers a truth too neat for real applicability. As the nations of the globe contort themselves on the when, if, and why of war with Saddam Hussein, and as the most determined of this generation's "allied leaders" gather this weekend in the Azores, the past is being mined with some severity for the lessons it has to offer, either by way of analogous circumstances or personalities.

The difficulty for the miners, of course, is that the past, or history, despite the certitude of Santayana, doesn't *repeat* itself. The frame of one set of events will never fit exactly the set that follows.

History does have consistent themes – war, despotism, conquest, even progress – but when history is in a mood to set a theme in play, it is always with variations. History, like the devil, is in the details.

The shadow of history is playing over the present imminent conflict. Conjuring the menacing example of Adolf Hitler to add rhetorical pressure to the case for removing Saddam Hussein is both easy and, in my judgement anyway, not entirely inaccurate. Mr. Hussein does have reservoirs, both of practice and temperament, that save the comparison from being ludicrous. He has an easy way with the death of others, and a very obliging acquaintance with brutality, both master attributes of his grisly prototype. There may be a personality match.

The comparison fails, however, on historical scale.

289

Saddam Hussein lording it over Iraq in 2003 is not Hitler with his massed army and titanic hatreds presiding over the industrialized Germany of 1939. Nor is the United States of 2003 the militarily unready, and soon to be isolated, Britain on the eve of the Second World War. Even the argument that stopping Saddam Hussein now would be equivalent to stopping Hitler before, say, the occupation of the Rhineland in 1936 fails, I think. It does not fit.

The menace from Saddam Hussein comes not with the annexation of other territories. It lies in a smaller region, in the intersection of his malice towards the West with elusive and scattered agents of world terrorism. It lies in his potential ability to supply chemical or biological toxins to deadly "freelancers," such as al-Qaeda. His ambition is mass injury, not conquest. If left unmolested, he won't be seeking to impose a system, but to inflict a massive hurt.

The attempt to find in the dark occasion of the Second World War either guidance or example to assist in dealing with the present crisis has other difficulties. The nexus of terrorism and rogue states is by its very nature numbered with shadows. It is vague and imprecise. It has to be. The contest of the century past, even at its outset, was gifted with clarity. That Hitler was mean, mad, and megalomaniacal, that Nazism was a creed of deep perversion and fundamental malice, was a judgement everyone, save Hitler and the Nazis, could see as self-evident.

It was Winston Churchill, of course, who saw it before anyone else, saw it when Nazism was but a germ. But then clarity, as I am reminded by John Keegan's account of Churchill in the worthy Penguin Lives series, was the Churchillian virtue par excellence. His "clear-seeing" was a form of prescience. The categories of history, the story of England, the very notions of honour and courage – none of these, as Mr. Keegan reminds us, were shifting coin in Churchill's view of life or politics.

Clarity wedded to purpose is conviction, and out of conviction spins eloquence. Mr. Keegan's book is useful at this time, not as a prop to one side or other of the issue at hand, but because it points to how much has changed from Churchill's day to this. I've said that Saddam Hussein is smaller than Hitler. Equally, and somewhat sadly, the leadership on the other side is smaller, too.

This may not be just the fault of the particular leaders. The times are more murky, the threat more diffuse; politics has become a playground of cynics and, in many cases, mediocrities. The moral definition of an earlier, more stark, period is denied us. Mass media elevate instant and image above pattern and address.

I think that, aside from zealous partisans, most people are troubled and ambivalent over the current crisis. Partly, this is because there is no Churchill to tell the moment and, partly, because we have passed into an age that denies the kind of clarity a Churchill was capable of. The old great words that shone in his speeches – "honour," "courage," "will" – and which gave them their reach and suasion, are no longer trusted. Tony Blair is reading Churchill's example, but not even Mr. Blair – and he is the fullest leader in this affair – with the Yalta-like echo of that example, is capable of drawing the response that Churchill would. The best we can get from the past in this instance, from history, is a cue from a different play.

There may be as much mischief in remembering the past as in not knowing it. T.S. Eliot in "Gerontion" was closer to the nerve of the business than Santayana:

> History has many cunning passages, contrived corridors
> And issues, deceives with whispering ambitions,
> Guides us by vanities.

– Globe and Mail

The Removal of a Tyrant:
George W. Bush Got It Right

George W. Bush got it right. It's amazing that a born-again Texas pea-brain, as his more intense detractors like to designate him, got the really important thing right – that Saddam Hussein had turned Iraq into a house of power and pleasure for himself and a dungeon for everyone who wasn't one of his henchmen.

The street scenes in Baghdad – when the crowd, assisted by the U.S. Marines, toppled his iron effigy, kicked the bronze head and beat its face with their shoes – was the one demonstration after so many demonstrations in every capital except Baghdad that actually counted.

George Bush saw the obvious, and Tony Blair, a much more articulate man, had the courage when it counted to agree with him that Saddam was a monster, his regime a tyranny, and that the cause of removing him was a moral one. We can have no doubt, no one can have any doubt now, what a horror Iraq was – that its poverty was imposed on its people by a dictator who furnished himself with palaces and built chains of deluxe bunkers.

The great stop-the-war movement was always incomplete. The millions who marched in the streets of the capitals of the world had a hundred banners to ascribe motives to Bush and the Americans. Of all of those protests, there existed barely a stick or a sign to highlight the realities of Saddam Hussein. The projected motives of George W. Bush – oil, imperialism, and hegemony – always crowded out the real practices of Saddam Hussein – invasion, internal slaughter, and despotism.

Saddam's Iraq was a country frozen in fear: a realm of torture, amputation, murder, rape, and a jail for children. The question was always being asked: Is it right to go to war against Iraq? The American campaign, now that the world has seen three full weeks of it, has made it clear that George W. Bush said what was the truth: it was not a war against Iraq but a war against a regime.

Insofar as it can be said that war may be waged with care, this one was. That care will not diminish one iota the pain of those whose children have been killed or who have lost innocent lives. But if a calculus has to be brought to bear, those scenes of innocent dead and wounded have to be set against those who, as a result of this war, have now and in the future been spared rack and rape, execution and repression.

Maybe the real question should have been: In the case of a truly inequitable dictatorship, is it right – if the means exist – not to bring it down? The Second World War ended with one truth inscribed in the blood of six million people: Never again. That "Never again" is turned to a lie every time a Joseph Stalin (Saddam's "Godfather"), a Pol Pot, a Nicolae Ceauşescu, or a Saddam Hussein is left unmolested to work pain and death on his own people.

No one will argue now that both Saddam's spell and his rule are over. And after the bronze head was sent rolling down the centre street of Baghdad, kicked and scuffed by the freshly liberated, it is apparent.

That truth is most understood by the ones who waited so long for someone to deliver the means for them to embrace it – the Iraqi people themselves. Whatever else may be wound up in the fabric of this war, the fact that the world is minus one of its most miserable regimes is enough reason to offer thanks to the Americans and the British. It was a hard mercy they delivered, but on balance, it was a mercy nonetheless.

– *The National*